THE
LONDON
A D D R E S S   B O O K

Text:	Catherine Carpenter
Staff Editor:	Nora Hill
Production Coordinator:	Roland Bettex
Design:	Flavia Cocchi
Photography:	Jeremy Grayson
Cartography:	Falk-Verlag; Thames map: Max Thommen

We would like to express our thanks to the following for their invaluable help in the research and preparation of this guide: Ruth Baldwin, Lindsay Bareham, Ken Bernstein, Richard Ehrlich, Sarah Fleming, Mary Trewby, Ann Wilson and the London Tourist Board and Convention Bureau.

2

We have made every effort to ensure the accuracy of the information in this book. But London changes very quickly. A shop might close its doors, a museum undergo renovation, a nightclub lose its charm; prices, telephone numbers, addresses and circumstances in general are constantly subject to alteration. We cannot, therefore, take responsibility for any factual errors of this kind.

Your opinion matters, however. If you find a change or a new place we should know about, our editor would be happy to hear from you and a postcard would do. Be sure to include your name and address, since in appreciation for a useful suggestion, we'd like to send you a free travel guide.

CONTENTS

4

CONTENTS

There's no place like London, a remarkably civilized metropolis elegantly poised between imperial traditions and a European destiny. From relics of the Romans to memories of the Blitz, history is everywhere. Yet London is as up-to-date as a portable phone, as trendy as next year's hairstyle.

This book was designed to complement the Berlitz London Travel Guide, to help you discover, at a glance and in detail, the best the capital has to offer—whether your interests lean towards art, music, good food, nightlife, or just an orgy of shopping.

We have sifted through and checked hundreds of addresses, covering everything imaginable from venerable monuments to the latest "in" nightspots, from museums to galleries of way-out art, from the City to the Home Counties. Need a hotel? We help you to find one, classy or budget. Where to have dinner? We let you choose between English and Ethnic, African and American, pub food and world-class cuisine. What about nightlife? There's an almost endless variety—theatre at its most innovative, concerts galore, cinema, jazz clubs, discos, nightclubs... We take you out of town, too, for the leisure parks, historic cities and stately homes.

With few exceptions, the London addresses are keyed to a large-scale street map; we give the nearest Underground (subway) station or, where valid, the railway station. You'll find information on public transport, along with other helpful guidelines, in a short section of Practical Information, just before the maps. In each chapter, the selections are listed in alphabetical order, but to help you find the sights quickly, there's a complete index at the back of the book.

No matter how long you stay in London, we sincerely hope our Little Black Book helps to make your visit even more enjoyable and memorable.

As so often happened, it was the Romans who really got things going. In the 1st century A.D., the invaders transformed an undistinguished ancient outpost called *Lyn-Din* (Celtic for "lake stronghold"), around the area we now know as the City, into a provincial capital. They called it *Londinium.*

From the new capital the Romans could control all of south-east England, with easy access to the country's heart. Soon London had all the trappings of a seat of government as well as the bare necessities of Roman life—public baths, a forum, a basilica and temples. Fortifications surrounded the town and highways fanned out in all directions. The Romans built the very first London Bridge. Then, after four centuries of occupation, the rulers beat a retreat; the rugged Angles and Saxons moved in and most Londoners moved out.

In 1066, the Normans invaded England. William the Conqueror had himself crowned in the newly built Westminster Abbey, then ordered **9** the construction of the Tower of London. As William I, he presided over the growth of the city into a powerful trading centre and bustling medieval metropolis.

Another boom time developed during the reign of the Tudor king, Henry VIII, whose colourful character has fascinated centuries of British schoolchildren. The king's lifestyle brought the chronic conflict between Church and Crown to a head; when Henry sought an annulment of his first marriage to the long-suffering Catherine of Aragon, the Pope refused to cooperate. So the headstrong king broke with the Church, dissolved the monasteries and confiscated Church property—and income. The resulting change in the real estate market spurred new expansion for London. As for the notorious Henry, he collected palaces the way he collected wives—of whom he had six in all. He commuted by barge between the Tower of London and the palaces of Greenwich, St. James's, Hampton Court and Whitehall.

With his daughter, Elizabeth I, on the throne, Britain celebrated a glorious golden age. Sir Francis Drake humbled the supposedly invincible Spanish Armada and explored the globe, and the dashing Sir Walter Raleigh helped to colonize the New World. At home, the finer things in life flourished: this was the age of Ben Jonson, Christopher Marlowe and a promising playwright named William Shakespeare, stationed at the Globe Theatre, not far from the present-day South Bank Arts Centre.

In ceremonial dress, Chelsea Pensioners wear medals and smiles.

Little of Tudor London escaped the Great Fire of 1666. More than 13,000 buildings, including 87 churches, went up in smoke. But the catastrophe inspired the most ambitious building programme London had ever seen, with the great Sir Christopher Wren at the helm. He designed over 50 churches, of which St. Paul's Cathedral was the crowning achievement. Before the Fire, the city had already begun to spread westwards. Covent Garden, built in the 1630s in the neoclassical style, was one of London's first planned squares, and its success started a trend. Its designer, Inigo Jones, was also responsible for Banqueting House, the last surviving part of Whitehall Palace and the scene of Charles I's execution in 1649.

The next great era for London's development began with the Hanoverians, monarchs of German descent, who reigned from 1714 to 1837. The family's four reigning Georges gave their name to the new style of architecture, Georgian, springing up all over town. Thanks to the riches flooding in from the colonies and the budding Industrial Revolution, London was fast becoming the economic capital of the world.

10

In 1837, Queen Victoria inherited an empire that was to cover one-fifth of the globe. Prosperity, though, had a bitter after-taste. Before long, people were pouring into the city in search of work, spawning teeming slums. Property speculators bought up whole tracts of land, erecting miles of cramped, terraced houses. The infrastructure, on the other hand—from the underground railway network to the sewers—still keeps London running.

The once-elegant mansions around the West End were split up into apartments after World War I, symbolizing the disintegration of the British Empire. But what changed London forever were the *Luftwaffe's* air raids in World War II; whole areas of the metropolis were all but flattened. The post-war years saw the demolition of terraced houses in the poorer areas and their replacement by inhuman tower blocks, the new dream of town planners. It turned out to be a disastrous experiment, destroying many of the distinctive characteristics of London's village-like, local communities.

In the 1980s a more manageable building boom, often in a post-Modern style, renewed much of London. Towering office buildings—skyscrapers by local standards—revolutionized the skyline, especially in the City. And great tracts of derelict land in the Docklands area were brought back to life.

Today's Londoners have developed a strong commitment to conserving good buildings of the past, as well as a passionate public interest in the future quality of life in this enormous and vital city.

A CITY OF VILLAGES

As glamorous as it is, sprawling London is no more than a conglomeration of villages, each with its own character. Here are mini-profiles of the best-known neighbourhoods, arranged alphabetically.

Camden. Now a chic area. The Grand Union Canal threads its way from Little Venice via Regent's Park and past London Zoo to Camden Lock, a hive of activity at weekends with its outdoor markets and shops.

Chelsea has a dual personality—part bohemian with artists and writers, part dignified with desirable residences. Swings from trendy fashion shops in the King's Road to peace and quiet along the river bank.

The City. The original London, all historic buildings and tradition—the Tower, St. Paul's Cathedral, the Inns of Court. Also, the business centre, home of the Bank of England, Lloyds and the Stock Exchange.

11

The Docklands. The former golden gateway to Britain's colonies, its death knoll was tolled by both the Blitz and commercial aviation. Now it's reconquered by modern apartment blocks, marinas and industrial buildings, with access via the new Docklands Light Railway. Downstream are the 20th-century **Thames Flood Barrier** and the historical buildings of **Greenwich.**

Hampstead. The Heath is one of the glories of London, and Hampstead itself is an upmarket village, with tiny, expensive cottages, smart townhouses, chic fashion stores and restaurants catering for a privileged clientèle.

Kensington and Knightsbridge. Areas for the well-heeled, with elegant shops, residential streets and squares, and hotels. For the studious or simply curious, Kensington is museum corner.

Marylebone. Best known is Harley Street, colonized by distinguished doctors. On the great artery of Marylebone Road, young and old alike converge on Madame Tussaud's and the London Planetarium.

The West End. The real heart of London, despite its name, teeming with shopping crowds by day and entertainment-seekers by night. Covent Garden, Leicester Square and Shaftesbury Avenue are where the big names in show business hang out, and Soho feeds the capital, notably in throbbing Chinatown. A pleasant contrast is **Bloomsbury,** home of the influential intellectuals known as the Bloomsbury Group, and a mecca for highbrows at London University and the British Museum. Finally, **Mayfair, Piccadilly** and the area around **Green Park** and **St. James's Park** give the West End its tone. Luxury hotels, stately embassies, royal palaces, glorious gardens—and centuries-old ceremonies around Buckingham Palace and Horse Guards Parade.

ALL HALLOWS BY THE TOWER   27 U9   ☞ Tower Hill

Byward Street, EC3. Open Monday to Friday 9.30 a.m.–6 p.m.; Saturday and Sunday 10 a.m.–5 p.m.

Standing on the site of a former Saxon church (of which an arch is still visible), All Hallows has been rebuilt several times over the centuries— by Richards I and III among others. The latest restoration followed the bombing of 1940. A Roman pavement and some interesting Roman and Saxon relics can be seen in the undercroft (crypt), and there is a fine collection of 14th–17th-century brasses. All Hallows rates a couple of small footnotes to American history: William Penn, the founder of Pennsylvania, was baptized here, and the sixth President, John Quincy Adams, was married in the church in 1797.

12 ## BROMPTON ORATORY   30 F5   ☞ South Kensington

Brompton Road, SW7. Open daily 6.30 a.m.–8 p.m.

The Oratory of St. Philip Neri, to give it its Sunday name, is a white Baroque-style church designed by Herbert Gribble for Catholic priests of the Institute of the Oratory. An architectural oddity when built in late-Victorian times, this spacious, domed church features an Italian high altar and statues of the Apostles from Siena cathedral.

CHELSEA OLD CHURCH   36 F2   ☞ Sloane Square

Old Church Street, SW3. Open Monday to Friday 10 a.m.–1 p.m. and 2–5 p.m.; Saturday 10 a.m.–1 p.m.; Sunday 7.30 a.m.–7 p.m.

Christened "All Saints"—probably when founded in the 12th century— this old church has been rebuilt more than once, notably in 1528 by Sir Thomas More, who had a house nearby and whose statue still watches over the area. More's elegant south chapel, happily surviving the inevitable World War II bombing which gutted the rest of the church, is the main attraction of this tastefully restored building. The church has strong Tudor connections: here Henry VIII supposedly married Jane Seymour, his third wife, in a private ceremony.

SOUTHWARK CATHEDRAL   26 S8   ☞ London Bridge

Borough High Street, SE1. Open Monday to Friday 8 a.m.–6 p.m.; Saturday and Sunday 8 a.m.–5 p.m.

Southwark used to be beyond the city limits, the place to which criminals, actors and other undesirables were banished. This is the oldest Gothic building in London and an outstanding example of this style of architecture. Note its fine early-English choir and retro-choir, as well as the 15th-century transepts. The spacious nave was remodelled by the Victorian architect Arthur Blomfield in a neo-Gothic style. Originally a parish church, Southwark achieved cathedral status as recently as 1905.

ST. BARTHOLOMEW-THE-GREAT   **16** R11   ⊖ Barbican
West Smithfield, EC1. Open daily 8 a.m.–5 p.m.
Although added to and rebuilt over the centuries, this is reckoned to be one of London's oldest churches and includes parts of an Augustinian priory founded in 1123, as well as interesting Norman architecture and monuments. After Henry VIII confiscated church property in the 16th century, the building had a variety of uses—including offices where Benjamin Franklin worked in 1725—until the late 19th century, when Sir Aston Webb restored it as a church.

ST. CLEMENT DANES   **15** O/P9   ⊖ Temple **13**
Strand, WC2. Open daily 8 a.m.–5 p.m.
The church in the nursery rhyme—"Oranges and lemons, say the bells of St. Clement's"—has had some distinguished worshippers over the centuries, including Ben Jonson and Dr. Samuel Johnson. Thought to be the work of the Danes in the 9th or 10th century, it was completely rebuilt by Sir Christopher Wren in 1680–1, the only one of his designs to have an apse. The stone tower incorporates some of the earlier 12th-century structure. Another victim of World War II bombing, it is now the beautifully restored central church of the RAF, and features memorabilia from both British and foreign air forces.

ST. ETHELDREDA   **15** P11   ⊖ Chancery Lane
Ely Place, EC1. Open daily 8 a.m.–7 p.m.
After the Reformation, several denominations used this former bishop's residence as a place of worship, but in 1874 the Roman Catholics bought it back. The beautiful little church is named after its founder, St. Ethelreda, the 13th-century bishop of Ely. Also called **Ely Chapel**, it features a ghostly crypt containing Roman ruins, possibly a basilica, as well as tracery windows and fine post-war glass.

ST. GEORGE'S BLOOMSBURY   **14** N10   ⊖ Holborn
Bloomsbury Way, WC1. Open Monday to Friday 9.30 a.m.–3 p.m.; Sunday 10–11 a.m. and 3–7 p.m.
One of several churches built by the great Nicholas Hawksmoor (c.1661–1736), St. George's has an impressive Corinthian portico and unusual stepped spire topped by a statue of George I dressed in a toga. Although the church was paid for by commissioners appointed by the king, George was as surprised as the rest of the populace when the statue was unveiled.

ST. GEORGE'S HANOVER SQUARE   12 K9   ⊖ Oxford Circus

St. George's Street, Hanover Square, W1. Open Monday to Friday 8.30 a.m.–3 p.m.; Sunday for services at 8.30 and 11.30 a.m.

The scene of many "fashionable" weddings, including those of Shelley, Disraeli and George Eliot, St. George's was completed in 1724 to a design by John James. Its main attractions are a portico of Corinthian columns topped by a prominent pediment, a lantern-shaped tower and a fine altar painting, *The Last Supper*, by William Kent.

ST. GEORGE-IN-THE-EAST   ⊖ Whitechapel

Cannon Street Road, E1.

The 160-foot (49-m.) tower of St. George-in-the-East dominates the East End, as Nicholas Hawksmoor intended when he designed it in 1726. The church displays the typical Hawksmoor characteristics: the solidity of massed limestone in a pared-down neoclassical style. In the 19th century, the church was the scene of anti-Papist riots.

14

ST. HELEN'S BISHOPSGATE   17 T10   ⊖ Liverpool Street

Great St. Helen's, EC3. Open daily 9 a.m.–5 p.m. except weekends.

Originally part of a Benedictine nunnery founded in the 13th century, St. Helen's features two parallel naves—one for the parishioners and one for the nuns, who were also blessed with a "squint", or peephole, so that they could see without being seen. Note the 15th-century choir stalls, the memorial window to William Shakespeare (believed to have been a parishioner) and the many fine monuments to city dignitaries.

ST. JOHN CLERKENWELL   9 Q12   ⊖ Farringdon

St. John's Square, EC1.

Join a guided tour to view the crypt and priory church of the medieval Order of St. John of Jerusalem (or Knights Hospitaller, of Crusader and Rhodes fame). Incorporating bits from various centuries down to the 12th, the church and crypt have many interesting features, including a 15th-century Flemish altarpiece. A museum on the same site (see p. 50) exhibits memorabilia and manuscripts of the famous Order. For tours of the church (Tuesday, Friday and Saturday, 11 a.m. and 2.30 p.m., or by arrangement) ring (071) 253 6644.

ST MARGARET'S WESTMINSTER   33 N6   ⊖ Westminster

Parliament Square, SW1. Open daily 9.30 a.m.–5 p.m.

Glamorous weddings more than architectural merit account for the fame of this modest church overshadowed by Westminster Abbey. Built in the 16th century, St. Margaret's has long been a favourite of the great and the good: diarist Samuel Pepys, the poet John Milton, and the promising politician Winston Churchill were all married in this, the parish church of the House of Commons. William Caxton and Sir Walter Raleigh are buried within. The stained-glass windows are much admired, particularly the east window dating from 1501.

ST. MARTIN-IN-THE-FIELDS 23 N8 ⊖ Charing Cross
Trafalgar Square, WC2.
Belying the bucolic name, the church of St. Martin-in-the-Fields looks out on all the urban dynamism of Trafalgar Square. The orchestra associated with it has gone on to world fame, but the 18th-century church is worth a visit if only to admire its Baroque architecture. The Corinthian portico and prominent spire have been much copied on both sides of the Atlantic, notably in St. Paul's Chapel on New York's Broadway. The architect here was James Gibbs, a disciple of Sir Christopher Wren. Drop in for a lunchtime concert, or dive into the crypt to see relics as fascinating as an 18th-century whipping post.

15

ST. MARY-LE-BOW 16 R/S10 ⊖ St. Paul's
Cheapside, EC2. Open Monday to Friday 6.30 a.m.–6.30 p.m.
Ringing from their tall, graceful steeple, the famous Bow Bells— traditionally, a true Cockney must be born within range of their sound— belonged to this church. The bells were destroyed during World War II, but were recast, incorporating bits of the damaged ones. Again they call visitors back to London, as they are supposed to have recalled the medieval Lord Mayor, Dick Whittington. Dating back to the 11th century, the church has been rebuilt several times, notably by Sir Christopher Wren after the 1666 Great Fire and by Laurence King after the last war.

ST. MARY-LE-STRAND 24 O9 ⊖ Temple
Strand, WC2. Open Monday to Friday 11 a.m.–3.30 p.m.
Now marooned between lanes of speeding traffic, the lovely early-18th-century Baroque church was the first major work of James Gibbs, who went on to design St Martin-in-the-Fields (see above). Gibbs had spent some time in Rome and the interior of the church reflects the Italian influence. Since volunteers keep the church going, the building may occasionally be closed during the published visiting hours.

ST. OLAVE 27 U9 ⊖ Tower Hill
8 Hart Street, EC3.
King Olaf II, patron saint of Norway, accounts for the name. As for the skulls and crossbones over the gateway of this restored 11th-century church, they may be a tribute to the victims of the Great Plague of 1665. They impressed Charles Dickens who, in *The Uncommercial Traveller*,

dubbed it *St. Ghastly Grim*. One of the few buildings to escape the Great Fire, St. Olave's was Samuel Pepys' favourite church and his body lies down below.

ST. PAUL'S   14 N9   ⊖ Covent Garden

Bedford Street, Covent Garden, WC2. Open Monday to Friday 9 a.m.–4.30 p.m.; Sunday for service at 11 a.m.

Not to be confused with any other St. Paul's, this is known as the "Actors' Church". Its architect, Inigo Jones, called it "the handsomest barn in Europe". He designed it in 1633 as part of a grand scheme for Covent Garden, but the present version dates from 1795 after a fire had damaged the original building. The church's long association with the theatre is commemorated by plaques to actors and playwrights, as well as by the odd casket of their ashes. Its secluded churchyard provides a surprisingly quiet corner just a stone's throw from the bustle of The Piazza.

16

SIR CHRISTOPHER WREN

London's skyline and architectural appearance owe much to one particular artistic genius—Sir Christopher Wren (1632–1723). The magnificent dome of St. Paul's Cathedral was the culmination of the career of a man who not only produced many fine buildings, but also held chairs in astronomy at the universities of both London and Oxford. Born (plain mister—the knighthood was a later reward for his contribution to London town planning) in 1632, he showed his extraordinary design talent at an early age. After the city had been virtually razed by the Great Fire of 1666, Wren, aged only 34, produced a new town plan, with St. Paul's at its heart. His cathedral was finally completed in 1711, and over 50 churches rose up majestically to pierce the skies alongside the cathedral's dome.

A royal favourite and towering figure of his age, Sir Christopher Wren also designed a new palace at Hampton Court and the Royal Naval Hospital and Old Royal Observatory—another domed affair—at Greenwich for William and Mary. Other monuments include the Sheldonian Theatre and Queen's College Library at Oxford.

Partly inspired by French ecclesiastical design, Wren's influence on his own and subsequent generations was enormous. Not only do his creations still dominate the London scene, but his style was copied far and wide. When he died in 1723 at the ripe old age of 91, he had had the satisfaction of seeing his masterpieces completed and was fittingly buried in the memorial he himself had designed. The Latin epitaph on his tomb in St. Paul's Cathedral translates: "Reader, if you seek his monument, look around you".

ST. PAUL'S CATHEDRAL 16 R10 ⊖ St. Paul's
Ludgate Hill, EC4; tel. (071) 248 2705. Open Monday to Friday 7.30 a.m.–6 p.m.; Saturday and Sunday 8 a.m.–6 p.m. Galleries, crypt and ambulatory Monday to Saturday 10 a.m.–4.15 p.m.
After the Great Fire of 1666, which destroyed more than two-thirds of the City, an immense crash programme of reconstruction was ordered. From the ashes of a giant Gothic church known as Old St. Paul's rose a new cathedral, the crowning achievement of Sir Christopher Wren. Its massive lead-covered dome, which has dominated the cityscape for well over three centuries, is only now being surpassed in height by a number of meritless modern office blocks. Wren had the honour and privilege of seeing his masterpiece completed (in 1711), and of lying forever within its walls.

Balance and clarity distinguish Wren's design. The Gothic plan of a Latin cross harmonizes with the classical dome and Baroque west **17** towers, the whole adorned with superbly carved statues and reliefs. The interior is awesome and features many superb carved and painted elements. High overhead runs the self-explanatory Whispering Gallery, and higher still the Golden Gallery at the base of the lantern gives dizzying views of the City. A treasury in the crypt contains models Wren made of the cathedral, as well as vestments and other church valuables.

ST. STEPHEN'S WALBROOK 17 S9 ⊖ Bank or Cannon Street
Walbrook, EC4. Open Monday to Friday 9 a.m.–4 p.m. (until 3 p.m. Friday).
Regarded as one of Sir Christopher Wren's masterpieces, the church is based on a cross-in-square plan with a large central dome—a mini version of St. Paul's Cathedral. The dome is supported by eight arches on Corinthian columns, the whole beautifully restored after the wreckage of World War II.

TEMPLE CHURCH 15 P9 ⊖ Temple
Inner Temple Lane, EC4. Open Monday to Saturday 10 a.m.–4 p.m.
This 12th-century church is one of only five round churches left in England. Originally the headquarters of the Order of Knights Templar, the Temple Church ended up, thanks to James I, in the hands of the lawyers, who used to meet their clients in the crypt. The church, in fact, belongs to the Inns of Court.

Much added to, by Christopher Wren among others, heavily "restored" last century, and damaged by bombs during World War II, the church has now been artfully repaired and succeeds in retaining some of the atmosphere of the original structure.

WESTMINSTER ABBEY **33** N6 ⊖ Westminster
Parliament Square, SW1; tel. (071) 222 5152. Open: nave only, Monday to Saturday 8 a.m.–6 p.m. (Wednesday until 7.30 p.m.) and Sunday between services; Royal Chapels, Monday to Friday 9 a.m.– 4.45 p.m., Saturday 9 a.m.–2.45 p.m. and 3.45–5.45 p.m.

There may have been an abbey at Westminster as early as the 7th century, but it was Edward the Confessor who laid the foundations of the church as we know it. (Edward's church is depicted in the Bayeux Tapestry.) In 1200, Henry III took Edward's creation and built it anew in grand Gothic style. Then, in 1519, Henry VII contributed the magnificent fan-vaulted chapel that bears his name. Because the abbey was the coronation church as well as the burial chamber of the kings and queens of England, Henry VIII spared it when he secularized the other religious edifices after breaking with Rome. Throughout the centuries, it has continued its role as royal mausoleum (most of the monarchs' tombs are to be found behind the altar in the Chapel of Edward the Confessor), as well as becoming a shrine to the nation's famous sons; here lie the bones of eminent statesmen (Gladstone and both Pitts), men of science (Newton, Darwin) and, in Poet's Corner, great men of letters (Chaucer, Dickens, Browning).

The most French of all English Gothic places of worship, with its soaring nave, ornate side-chapels, tracery windows and flying buttresses, it is more of a cathedral than a church (as which it functions regularly on Sundays). The Coronation Chair, surprisingly small and made of oak rather than precious metals, has been out of the abbey only once since 1302, and that was on the orders of Oliver Cromwell who had it moved to Westminster Hall for his installation as Lord Protector.

A guided tour takes you to the nave, choir, Royal Chapel, Poets' Corner and Statesmen's Aisle—special charge; book in advance on (071) 222 7110. There is also a brass rubbing centre in the north cloister (Monday to Saturday 9 a.m.–5 p.m.; tel. (071) 222 2085. Admission: small charge for entrance to the Royal Chapels.

WESTMINSTER CATHEDRAL **32** L5 ⊖ Victoria
Ashley Place, off Victoria Street, SW1. Open daily 7 a.m.–8 p.m. Campanile Wednesday to Sunday 9–11 a.m. and 2–4.50 p.m.
Though it looks terribly historic, the principal Roman Catholic Church in England was built at the dawn of the 20th century. The style is early-Christian Byzantine, the architect J. F. Bentley. The workmanship in the marble interior is superb, and the exterior brickwork is particularly fine. You can climb the campanile for one of the best views over the rooftops of London. (Small charge.)

MONUMENTS

ADMIRALTY ARCH **23** M8 ⊖ Charing Cross
The Mall, SW1.
Majestically straddling the Mall where it sweeps into Trafalgar Square, Sir Aston Webb's Admiralty Arch is one of a string of memorials erected in honour of Queen Victoria early in the century. It opens a perfect view of London's most elegant thoroughfare, The Mall (rhymes with "pal"). Traffic is restricted to the two side arches, with the central gates locked except for royal vehicles on ceremonious occasions.

BANK OF ENGLAND **17** S10 ⊖ Bank
Threadneedle Street, EC2; tel. (071) 601 4444.
The "Old Lady of Threadneedle Street" has watched over the capital's capital since 1694 when the Bank of England was incorporated by Royal Charter. **19**

Parts of the present building, including the symbolically unwelcoming curtain walls, go back to 1788, the year the great Sir John Soane was appointed to design the neoclassical stronghold. (The only other Soane masterpiece still standing is Dulwich College Picture Gallery— see p. 57; see also Sir John Soane's Museum—p. 42). The Bank of England was originally established as a means of raising money for the state on "perpetual interest" and is the only bank in England with a licence to print money. To learn the fascinating story of the bank, visit the Bank of England Museum, whose entrance is in Bartholomew Lane (see p 48).

BANQUETING HOUSE **24** N7 ⊖ Charing Cross or Westminster
Whitehall, SW1; tel. (071) 930 4179. Open Tuesday to Saturday 10 a.m.–4.30 p.m.; Sunday (summer only) 2–5 p.m.
Nestling amongst the many Government office buildings familiarly lumped together under the name of "Whitehall" (after the Palace that once stood here), Banqueting House is one of London's architectural gems. Inigo Jones designed it for James I early in the 17th century. James's son, Charles I, assigned Rubens to paint the ceiling, which remains a masterpiece of Baroque colour and movement. Notwithstanding his good taste in art, in 1649 Charles lost his head on a scaffold outside this building, under the executioner's axe. They've since abandoned public beheadings but the building is sometimes closed for private banquets or ceremonies, so it's best to check before visiting.
Admission: small charge.

OFF WITH HIS HEAD
The dashing cavaliers of school history books who lost the English Civil War to Oliver Cromwell's more sober—and shorter-haired—Roundheads were Royalists loyal to Charles I, the last British monarch to be executed.

Charles I (1600–49) was a well-meaning but unpopular king, who made the mistake of attempting to rule without Parliament. It didn't help that he was a Stuart and a Scot, whose father had succeeded to the English throne when Elizabeth I died childless.

An inevitable result of the conflict between a monarch who believed in the divine rule of kings and a country which couldn't and wouldn't accept such autocracy, the Civil War (or Wars), begun in 1642, lasted for seven years. Defeated, Charles was tried for treason and executed on January 30, 1649. The king walked out of one of the first-floor windows of the Banqueting House in Whitehall on to the scaffold, and addressed the crowd before being beheaded. He lies buried in St. George's Chapel in Windsor.

BIG BEN   **33** N6   ⊖ Westminster
Houses of Parliament, Bridge Street, SW1.
The chimes of Big Ben are heard all over the world via the BBC World Service. This majestic clock tower, which is part of the Houses of Parliament, has recently been cleaned and restored, and gleams so that even hardened Londoners have been known to look up at it in wonder. Legend says the bells were pointedly nicknamed after Sir Benjamin Hall, a rather rotund Commissioner of Works.

BUCKINGHAM PALACE   **32** K/L6   ⊖ St. James's Park
St. James's Park, SW1.   or Victoria
The 600-room London residence of British monarchs was built in the first half of the 19th century, thanks to King George IV. Much to the chagrin of the parliament of the day, Buckingham Palace cost about £700,000, a whopping figure in that era. Designed by John Nash, the king's favourite architect, it took nearly a quarter of a century to build; by the time it was ready, both the king and the architect had died. The first monarch to live there was Queen Victoria, who initiated the practice of waving to her faithful subjects from the central balcony. Open to the public are the Queen's Gallery (see p. 58) and the Royal Mews, where the ceremonial carriages and horses can be seen if they're not busy elsewhere (see p. 172). At 11.30 a.m. every day in summer (and on alternate days during the rest of the year) the colourful ceremony of the Changing of the Guard unfolds in the forecourt. (See p. 170)

CENOTAPH 24 N7   ⊖ Westminster
Whitehall, SW1.
This memorial to the dead of World War I, designed by Sir Edwin Lutyens, was erected in 1920. It now commemorates the fallen of all 20th-century military conflicts and on the Sunday nearest Armistice Day (11th November) a moving Remembrance Service, attended by the monarch, politicians and diplomats, is held here.

CHISWICK HOUSE   ⊖ Turnham Green ⇌ Chiswick
Burlington Lane, W4; tel. (081) 995 0508. Open daily 10 a.m.–6 p.m. (until 4 p.m. in winter).
The influence of the 16th-century Italian architect Andrea Palladio took well over a hundred years to reach England. Chiswick House, designed by William Kent in the 1720s for Lord Burlington, is inspired by Palladio's Villa Rotunda in Vicenza but has four asymmetrical sides. Kent also laid out the grounds, amongst the first in the English landscape style. On some days Chiswick (rhymes with "physic") House closes between 1 p.m. and 2 p.m.
Admission: small charge (includes guided tours and video).

21

CLEOPATRA'S NEEDLE 24 O8   ⊖ Embankment
Victoria Embankment, SW1.
If you're wondering how this massive granite obelisk, the gift of the Egyptian Viceroy in 1819, was transported all the way from Egypt, you are not the only one to puzzle over the problem. It foxed the minds of 19th-century engineers for nearly 60 years before they came up with an ingenious solution—towing it (not without difficulty) on an iron pontoon to its final resting place on the Embankment. Despite the name and the legends, the Needle has nothing to do with Cleopatra. The hieroglyphics, however, are authentic ancient Egyptian—inscribed in the 13th century B.C.

CROSBY HALL 36 F2   ⊖ Sloane Square
Cheyne Walk, SW3; tel. (071) 352 9663. Open Monday to Friday 10 a.m.–12 p.m. and 2.15–4 p.m.
There's been a change of site here. Crosby Place, the home of a wealthy medieval merchant, stood in Bishopsgate in the City of London until destroyed by fire in the 17th century. All that remained was the great hall, with memories of personalities like Sir Walter Raleigh and Sir Thomas More. In 1910 Crosby Hall was dismantled and moved to its present position in Chelsea, once part of More's garden. The most interesting features of the hall, now used as the dining room of a post-graduate hall of residence, are the high scissor-beam ceiling and oriel window.

DAILY EXPRESS BUILDING   **15** Q10   ⊖ Temple
Fleet Street, EC4.
London has few modern architectural masterpieces. But the Daily Express Building, designed by Owen Williams and completed in 1932, is a superb and innovative structure. The sleek chrome and black glass curtain wall was a pioneering example of the technique. The interior, with its Art Deco foyer and staircase of black marble, chrome and ebony by Robert Atkinson, is in lavish contrast to the simplicity of the façade. The Daily Express, perhaps reluctant to leave such a splendid home, was the last national newspaper to move out of the traditional media location, Fleet Street (to the best of the new press headquarters, another black and glass striped structure on the other side of Blackfriar's Bridge).

22   EROS   **23** L/M9   ⊖ Piccadilly Circus
Piccadilly Circus, W1.
The elegant Eros, God of Love, was intended by its sculptor, Sir Alfred Gilbert, to be the Angel of Christian Charity, a fitting memorial to the generosity of the 7th Earl of Shaftesbury. But it was soon seen in a more romantic light and became a symbol of London. Recently restored, the statue is protectively boarded up for New Year's Eve and other riotous celebrations.

GUILDHALL   **17** S10   ⊖ Bank
Gresham Street, EC2; tel. (071) 606 3030. Open Monday to Saturday 10 a.m.–5 p.m. (during office hours).
Originally built in 1411, this great survivor of a building (originally the home of the London "Guilds", or old-time trade unions) has withstood every disaster from the Great Fire of 1666 to World War II. Despite much renovation, the Great Hall, with its minstrels' gallery, Gothic stonework and livery company banners, is living history and a suitable backcloth for the traditional functions and dignified ceremonies of the Corporation of London which is based here. Every third Thursday of the month, at 1 p.m. (from September to June), the Court of Common Council meets in the Great Hall and the public is admitted. Otherwise the Guildhall, the crypt and the Clockmakers' Company Museum (see p. 40) can also be visited.

HOUSES OF PARLIAMENT   **33** N6   ⊖ Westminster
Parliament Square, SW1; tel. (071) 219 4272.
In London's history-soaked environment, it would be easy to mistake the Houses of Parliament for a Gothic masterpiece several centuries old. The truth is that the project is a mid-19th-century fantasy. The

architects, Sir Charles Barry and Augustin Pugin, were ardent neo-Gothicists who won a competition for a Thames-side building "in the Gothic or Elizabethan style". The building's official title, the Palace of Westminster, commemorates the royal palace that stood on this site, the main residence of English monarchs from the 11th century until the reign of Henry VIII. When the palace went up in flames in 1834, the only part that survived was Westminster Hall; it was incorporated into the Barry-Pugin building. The hall, which features a massive hammer-beam ceiling, served as the Law Courts for centuries—Sir Thomas More, Charles I and Guy Fawkes were all condemned to death here. For security reasons, the hall is not open to the public, but people are admitted to the Visitors' Galleries of the House of Commons and House of Lords when Parliament is sitting (November to July; apply to your Member of Parliament or embassy for tickets, or join the queues). Guided tours are also available, but must be arranged through a Member of Parliament.

23

INNS OF COURT 15 O/P9, 10 & 11   ⊖ Holborn or Chancery Lane
Fleet Street, EC4.
The inner sanctum of legal London is hidden from view on either side of Fleet Street. The four Inns of Court—Gray's Inn, Lincoln's Inn, the Inner Temple and the Middle Temple—have been associated with the legal profession since the 14th century, first as a law school and then as a professional society for bewigged practitioners.

You can gawk at the medieval buildings from afar, or enter the gardens of Lincoln's Inn. Also open to the public is the Norman Templar church (named after the crusading Knights Templar, who first occupied the building—see p. 17).

It's one of the few surviving medieval churches with a distinctive circular nave. In 1601 Shakespeare reputedly performed *Twelfth Night* in Middle Temple Hall, which dates from 1573.

KARL MARX'S GRAVE   ⊖ Highgate
Highgate Cemetery, Swain's Lane, N6; tel. (081) 340 1834. Open Monday to Friday 10 a.m.–5 p.m., Saturday and Sunday 10 a.m.–4 p.m.
Karl Marx, who wrote *Das Kapital* in this capital, lived in exile in London for the last 34 years of his life. At his tomb in the eastern, and more conventional, part of Highgate Cemetery, the granite slab topped by his bust is engraved with the last line of his Communist Manifesto, "Workers of All Lands Unite". The atmospheric western section of the cemetery, with its ornate tombs and catacombs, is known as the "Egyptian" cemetery. Admission is with a guided tour—ring for details. Admission: small charge.

KENSINGTON PALACE   19 D7   ⊖ Queensway
or High Street Kensington
Kensington Gardens, W8; tel. (071) 937 9561. Open Monday to Saturday 9 a.m.–5 p.m.; Sunday 1–5 p.m.
This elegant royal palace on the edge of Kensington Gardens is much older than Buckingham Palace. The Prince and Princess of Wales, Princess Margaret, and Prince and Princess Michael of Kent all have apartments here. Kensington Palace is a Jacobean house that was remodelled by Sir Christopher Wren and Nicholas Hawksmoor for William of Orange and Mary, who preferred the air in Kensington to riverside Whitehall. This is the birthplace of many a British monarch, including Queen Victoria. Here she learned of her accession to the throne, but later abandoned Kensington in favour of Buckingham Palace. Open to the public are the historic State Apartments, including the King's Gallery with its rare wind dial, and the Court Dress Collection, a priceless display of costumes ranging from servants' livery to full-dress uniforms and elaborate wedding dresses.

24

LAMBETH PALACE   33 O5   ⊖ Lambeth North
Lambeth Palace Road, SE1; tel. (071) 928 8282. Visits by appointment only.
For over seven hundred years, Lambeth Palace has been the official home of the Archbishop of Canterbury, head of the Church of England. The oldest part of the building, dating from the 12th century, is the vaulted crypt underneath the chapel, while the gatehouse is Tudor. The attractions of the Palace include some fine portraits, old books and manuscripts. The scene of some of the dramatic moments in English history, the palace has been attacked by both Wat Tyler's followers during the Peasants' Revolt of 1381, and the *Luftwaffe* during World War II. To view, write to the Bursar.

LAW COURTS   15 P10   ⊖ Chancery Lane or Holborn
Strand, WC2; tel. (071) 936 6000. Open during sessions, Monday to Friday, 10.30 a.m.–1 p.m. and 2–4.30 p.m.
If you're looking for a sensational murder trial, try the Old Bailey instead. The Law Courts, officially called the Royal Courts of Justice, specialize in civil—that is, non-criminal—cases. One of the best and most overlooked Victorian architects, G. E. Street, designed this neo-Gothic building with a bold complexity of elevations and innovative variety of skyline. Pomp replaces pleas and petitions at the Law Courts once a year: on the second Saturday in November, a new Lord Mayor is sworn in here after riding in procession from the Guildhall (see p. 22) through the streets of the City.

LLOYD'S BUILDING   **17** T9/10   ⊖ Bank or Monument
Lime Street, EC3; tel. (071) 623 7100. Open Monday to Friday 10 a.m.–2.30 p.m.
The architect Richard Rogers, of Pompidou Centre fame, regularly challenges the conservative tenets of contemporary British style. His new Lloyd's Building—all high-tech., chrome and glass with elevators and pipework on the outside—has raised the hackles of traditionalists. It's a far cry from Edward Lloyd's original coffee house where the Lloyd's of London insurance institution began more than three centuries ago.

A truly distinguished modern structure in a forest of concrete towers, Roger's creation dominates the cityscape. You can't miss it, particularly at night when it's awash with coloured lights. From the public gallery you can watch the underwriters at work conducting much of the world's insurance business.

25

MARBLE ARCH   **11** H9   ⊖ Marble Arch
W1
Marble Arch is not a true victory arch celebrating the glorious victories of Trafalgar and Waterloo, although that was its original conception.

Designed by John Nash and sculpted by Flaxman, Westmacott, Rossi and Baily, the final version represents the *Spirirt of England* inspiring *Youth, Valour and Virtue* and *Peace and Plenty*. At first it was erected in front of Buckingham Palace, but in 1851 was moved to its present location at the north-east corner of Hyde Park, until then the gruesome but popular site of Tyburn gallows. Now it's surrounded by fast-moving traffic, and discoloured by exhaust fumes.

MONUMENT   **27** T9   ⊖ Monument
Monument Street, EC3; tel. (071) 626 2717. Open (April to September) Monday to Friday 9 a.m.–6 p.m., Saturday and Sunday 2–6 p.m.; (October to March) Monday to Saturday 9 a.m.–4 p.m.
If you're fit enough, you can see London from a new perspective: climb to the top of the 202-foot (62-m.) column via a spiral staircase consisting of a mere 311 steps. On a clear day, the view from the summit of the tersely named Monument is predictably glorious. Designed by Sir Christopher Wren, the hollow, fluted column commemorates the Great Fire of 1666, which destroyed most of London. The fire is said to have started in a bakery exactly 202 feet east of the monument.
Admission: small charge.

ON THE SQUARE

Originally a Continental invention, the town square was taken over and perfected by London architects in Renaissance days. The 17th century saw London's first squares—Inigo Jones' **Covent Garden Piazza** in the 1630s and **Leicester Square** in 1670. Originally lined with great houses and formal gardens, they were fashionable addresses right through the 18th century until merchants and traders moved in, followed by cinemas and entertainment.

The word "square" is a misnomer, for few, if any, are geometrically true. Architecturally uniform, a typical square will have elegant, terraced houses built round a central garden filled with lawns, trees and the occasional statue, to which the front, or grand, entrance (and perhaps a key) gives access; the mews and servants' and trade entrances are discreetly hidden round the back.

26

Nowadays, they are oases of calm in traffic-jammed London. Among the best-known squares: **Berkeley** (pronounced Barclay) **Square**, where the nightingale is supposed to sing; **Grosvenor Square**, home of the American Embassy; **Russell Square**, a good place to relax after the rigours of a central visit to the nearby British Museum; and **Sloane Square**, which gave its name to the Sloane Rangers, an amusing media title for rich and trendy young people.

Most famous of all is **Trafalgar Square**—the traditional place for celebrations and demonstrations. Dominated by Nelson's Column and surrounded by fine neoclassical buildings such as the National Gallery and those tributes to the British Empire's former glory, Canada House and South Africa House, this centre of London activity has an air of elegance and timeless dignity, like an elderly aunt.

Whatever their names (and many are called after famous people), London's squares are an essential and vital feature of the landscape. That is, if they are not—like **Piccadilly** and **Oxford**—circuses.

NELSON'S MONUMENT   23 M8   ⊖ Charing Cross

Trafalgar Square, WC2.

Admiral Lord Nelson, the hero of the 1805 Battle of Trafalgar when he put paid to Napoleon on the high seas, stands atop a fluted granite column decorated with a Corinthian capital. Known familiarly as "Nelson's Column", the 185-foot. (56-m.) monument was erected in 1839–42 to the design by William Railton. The four bronze reliefs at its base depicting various battle scenes were cast from captured French cannon. The Landseer lions that guard the monument appeared belatedly some 25 years later.

NUMBER 10 DOWNING STREET   23 N7   ⊖ Westminster
Downing Street, SW1.
Margaret Thatcher had this celebrated street fenced off with heavy gates. As well as being critized for this regal gesture, the former prime minister annoyed the police who have to manhandle the ill-fitting ironwork whenever an official or petitioner wants to pass.

Number 10 has been the official residence of British prime ministers since 1732. All the terraced houses in this cul-de-sac were built in 1680 by Sir George Downing, a Member of Parliament.

Traditionally, the Chancellor of the Exchequer lives at Number 11, and the Party Whips' office is at Number 12. Gate-crashers without an invitation are turned away, so the only way to observe the comings and goings at the seat of power is to loiter in Whitehall.

OLD BAILEY   16 Q10   ⊖ St. Paul's
Old Bailey, EC4; tel. (071) 248 3277. Open during trials, Monday to Friday, 10.15 a.m.–1 p.m. and 2–4 p.m.
The galleries of the courtrooms are open to the public, but long queues tend to form when juicy trials are under way. Officially known as the Central Criminal Court of London, the Old Bailey is built on the site of the notorious Newgate Prison. The jail, where many famous prisoners as distinguished as William Penn and Daniel Defoe were incarcerated, was a cesspit of despair and disease.

As a precaution against the deadly fever that stalked its corridors, sweet-smelling herbs were strewn around the courtrooms, a tradition still observed by today's judges, who carry posies of flowers and herbs on occasion. The bronze figure of Justice, holding a pair of scales, crowns the dome above the area where those found guilty were once executed.

OLD ROYAL OBSERVATORY   ≈ Greenwich or Maze Hill or by river to Greenwich
Greenwich Park, Greenwich SE10; tel. (081) 858 1167. Open Monday to Saturday 10 a.m.–6 p.m., Sunday noon–6 p.m. (March to October); Monday to Saturday 10 a.m.–5 p.m., Sunday 2–5 p.m. (November to February).
A brass strip marks the spot where the momentous Greenwich meridian, the standard by which longitude and time are measured the world over, passes through this lovely circular building.

The former observatory, now part of the National Maritime Museum (see p. 37), is yet another project of Sir Christopher Wren. Admission: small charge.

PRINCE HENRY'S ROOM   **15** P9/10   ⊖ Temple

17 Fleet Street, EC4; tel. (071) 353 7323. Open Monday to Friday 1.45–5 p.m.; Saturday 1.45–4 p.m.

Perched above a small archway in Fleet Street, an old timbered building miraculously escaped the Great Fire of 1666. Earlier in the 17th century, it had been used as an inn, known as the Prince's Arms. The main room is lined with fine oak panelling, and visible on the plaster ceiling are the initials P.H. (for Prince Henry, elder son of James I and Prince of Wales), as well as his three-feather coat of arms. The house contains an interesting collection of memorabilia of the diarist Samuel Pepys.

QUEEN'S HOUSE   ⇌ Greenwich or Maze Hill
or by river to Greenwich

Romney Road, SE10; tel. (081) 858 4422. Open Monday to Saturday 10 a.m.–6 p.m.; Sunday 2–6 p.m. (May to September).

28

The queen in question was Anne of Denmark, wife of James I, although she did not live to see the completion of the house designed for her by Inigo Jones in 1616. By royal command, its superb view of the river (and the river's superb view of the house) was preserved when the nearby Royal Naval Hospital was built at the end of the 17th century. Admission: small charge.

ROYAL EXCHANGE   **17** S10   ⊖ Bank

Threadneedle Street and Cornhill, EC3; tel. (071) 623 0444. Open Monday to Friday 11.30 a.m.–2 p.m.

London merchants did most of their wheeling and dealing on the streets until the 1560s, when Sir Thomas Gresham built the first Royal Exchange, modelled on the Antwerp Bourse. The building was destroyed in the Great Fire of 1666 and replaced by a larger structure designed by the City surveyor, Edward Jarman. This was occupied by banks and insurance agents until it, too, was burned down. The present Royal Exchange, with its massive classical portico, was inaugurated in 1844. The Visitors' Gallery, open to the public, looks out over the trading floor of the London International Financial Futures Exchange, where all the excitement going on is inspired by intangibles like interest and exchange rates. Admission: free.

ROYAL HOSPITAL, CHELSEA   **37** H3   ⊖ Sloane Square

Royal Hospital Road, SW3; tel. (071) 730 5282. Open Monday to Saturday 10 a.m.–noon; Sunday (April to September only) 2–4 p.m.

About 400 Chelsea pensioners, in bright scarlet and navy uniforms, live out their days in this fine masterpiece of 17th-century architecture. Charles II's idea to build a home for his veteran soldiers was probably

inspired by the Hôtel des Invalides in Paris. The greatest architect of his day, Sir Christopher Wren, had the task of designing Chelsea Hospital (completed in 1692) but Robert Adam made some minor alterations 70 years later, and Sir John Soane, no less, was responsible for the stables. The Chelsea Flower Show is held in the hospital grounds every May. Otherwise, museum, chapel, Great Hall and grounds are open to the public.
Admission: free.

ROYAL NAVAL COLLEGE

≠ Greenwich or Maze Hill or by river to Greenwich

King William Walk, Greenwich SE10; tel. (081) 858 2154. Open daily except Thursday, 2.30–5 p.m.
This fine group of buildings with twin domes was principally the work of Sir Christopher Wren. Built on the site of one of **29** Henry VIII's palaces, the College was first used as a hospital for old and disabled seamen. The painted hall and chapel are open to the public.

ST. JAMES'S PALACE   23 L7

Θ St. James's

The Mall, SW1.
Although no monarch has lived here since 1837, ambassadors to Britain are still accredited to the "Court of St. James", the picturesque palace built by Henry VIII on the site of a medieval hospital for "maidens that were leprous". Henry intended the palace to be a gift to No. 2 wife, Anne Boleyn—their initials are carved over a mantel and two small doorways—but a few years after it was finished, he got rid of her. The palace is closed to the public, but it's worth entering the courtyards to view the outside of one of London's few remaining Tudor brick buildings. The Queen Mother lives in nearby Clarence House, also closed to the public. It was built in 1825 to a design by John Nash.

ST. PAUL'S CATHEDRAL
See SIGHTS p. 17.

ST. THOMAS'S HOSPITAL   27 S8
OPERATING THEATRE MUSEUM

Θ London Bridge

91 St. Thomas Street, SE1; tel. (071) 955 4791. Open Monday, Wednesday and Friday 12.30–4 p.m.
Surprisingly situated in the loft of a Wren church is this early-19th-century operating theatre, where women patients enjoyed the primitive facilities on display. A small exhibition is devoted to the medicinal herbs that were stored in the loft for use in the 13th-century hospital on the site. Access involves a rather tricky staircase.
Admission: small charge.

STAPLE INN   **15** P10   ⊖ Chancery Lane
High Holborn, WC1.
Built in 1378 as a hostel for wool "staplers", or merchants, Staple Inn
served as an Inn of Chancery (see Inns of Court, p. 23) from the
15th century until Victorian times. The picturesque timber-
framed façade, dating back to the late 16th century, is a rare
survivor in London. After bomb damage in World War II, the
building was restored incorporating much of the old material. It's
closed to the public, but the exterior is worth a look.

STOCK EXCHANGE   **17** T10   ⊖ Bank
*Old Broad Street, EC2; tel. (071) 588 2355. Open Monday to Friday
9.30 a.m.–3.30 p.m.*

The London Stock Exchange has come a long way from its modest
beginnings in the 17th century, when much of the business was done
in the coffee houses that were the forerunners of today's pubs. At the
computerized modern centre (erected in the 1970s to replace the
original 1802 edifice), shirt sleeves are replacing top hats, and modern
technology has killed off much of the former high drama. You can watch
the intense activities from the visitors' gallery overlooking the trading
floor, where there is also a display explaining how the market works and
regular cinema presentations.

TOWER BRIDGE   **27** U8   ⊖ Tower Hill
*SE1; tel. (071) 407 0922. Open daily 10 a.m.–6.30 p.m. (4.45 p.m. in
winter).*
The drawbridges of Tower Bridge, each weighing 1,000 tons, are
raised so that tall ships can pass, an operation taking only 90 seconds.
Inside the twin towers of this ornate mock-Gothic landmark (connected
by glassed-in walkways giving wonderful views up and down the river)
are exhibitions depicting the history and construction of the bridge,
opened in 1894.
Admission: small charge.

TOWER OF LONDON   **27** U8/9   ⊖ Tower Hill
*Tower Hill, EC3; tel. (071) 709 0765. Open (March to October) Monday
to Saturday 9.30 a.m.–5 p.m., Sunday 2–5 p.m; (November to February)
Monday to Saturday 9.30 a.m.–4.30 p.m., closed Sunday.*
This great medieval fort has been a stronghold, palace, prison and
place of execution for more than a thousand years—Sir Thomas More,
Sir Walter Raleigh and Anne Boleyn are among the best-known victims.
The aptly named Bloody Tower was the scene, in 1483, of one of the
great unsolved murder mysteries, that of the little princes, the two sons

of Edward IV, reputedly on the orders of their uncle, Richard, Duke of Gloucester.

Surrounded by a moat—drained in the 1840s—the massive walls of the fort are between 11 and 15 foot (3.5 and 4.5 m.) thick. The oldest existing part of the palace is the White Tower, begun in 1078 by William I and much expanded during Henry III's reign (1216–72). On an upper floor, the solemnly simple St. John's Chapel claims to be one of London's oldest churches (1080) and the city's only Norman sanctuary. Across the green, the Chapel of St. Peter ad Vincula, completed in the first half of the 12th century, is the burial site of many of those beheaded nearby.

Apart from its gory and glorious history, the Tower is the repository of the Royal Armouries and the Crown Jewels. Defended by Yeomen Warders—about 40 men in Tudor costume, known as Beefeaters—this is one of the most popular and colourful tourist stops in London; at the height of the season you may have a very long wait.
Admission: small charge.

31

London Bridge is falling down...

There has pretty certainly been a bridge across the Thames since Roman times. Today's bridges are still strong on history; beauty, too.

The original **London Bridge** of the nursery rhyme was a medieval structure of wood lined with shops, somewhat like the Ponte Vecchio in Florence. Furnished with a waterwheel that supplied river water to the City, it must have been much more picturesque than the present concrete affair dating from London's "Swinging Sixties".

Probably the most famous and certainly most photographed of the capital's bridges is **Tower Bridge**. It's often been mistaken for the subject of the nursery rhyme, most notably by the American millionaire who bought the 19th-century predecessor of the present London bridge, demolished it stone by stone, and re-erected it in the Arizona desert in 1967.

Upstream, alongside the Houses of Parliament, **Westminster Bridge** is the one immortalized by William Wordsworth. Like the poet, pre-war film directors appreciated its generous width, the sweeping lines of its curved, cast-iron structure and above all the magnificent backdrop of Big Ben and company.

Perhaps the prettiest bridge, the **Albert Bridge** gracefully links Chelsea and Battersea. Named after Queen Victoria's husband, the mini-Golden Gate span is a rousing sight, especially when they switch on its necklace of lights.

Forget the reluctant museum-goer's nightmare scenario: rainy days among fuddy-duddies and suffering schoolchildren, traipsing through endless, faintly lit rooms overflowing with musty old collections. Instead, imagine a light, agreeable and stimulating environment with priceless exhibits presented in novel ways. Many museums in London have been redesigned, taking advantage of modern technology. Tradition hasn't been abandoned, though. Some of the collections are housed in beautifully restored buildings, enhancing London's historical atmosphere.

The museums on our list have something for everyone, from academics to casual tourists. The new emphasis on visitor participation is good news for people travelling with children, who might have shuddered at the thought of hyperactive kids running riot among priceless antiques. Choose your objective to take in plenty of interactive displays with knobs to pull and buttons to push, and you'll keep even the wildest kids amused. (See also CHILDREN, pp. 165-8.)

We begin with a list of the most monumental museums, in the class of the British Museum and the Victoria & Albert. Don't be put off by their size. Even a short visit to glance at the highlights can be an unforgettable experience. Next on our list is the pick of the crop of London's smaller, specialized museums—from ultramodern to charmingly traditional. Whatever your interests, something is bound to appeal.

In the major museums, lectures, usually free of charge, are given regularly on specific themes and exhibits; details can be obtained at the museum reception desk or by telephone. Note, too, that opening hours may vary on public (bank) holidays.

In the good old days, public museums were always free. What with hard times and soaring costs, though, most of them have reluctantly introduced a small admission charge, in some cases euphemistically called a "donation". Whatever the word, it's a small price to pay to see the treasures on display.

33

Dining by dinosaur, tourists take a tea break in the Natural History Museum.

MAJOR MUSEUMS

BRITISH MUSEUM **14** N10 ⊖ Holborn
or Tottenham Court Road

Great Russell Street, WC1; tel. (071) 636 1555; recorded information (071) 580 1788. Open Monday to Saturday 10 a.m.–5 p.m.; Sunday 2.30–6 p.m.

Don't be overawed by its size. Although it would take years to do justice to the British Museum, you can see the really essential highlights in a single visit. That will still leave something important for the next time—and the next.

Enter through the main gates, pausing to regard the imposing building (designed by Sir Robert Smirke, built 1823–47), with its massive Ionic columns propping up the portico bearing the apt inscription, "The Progress of Civilization". In the ever-busy front hall, floor plans and the information desk can help you to find your way among the galleries of antiquities that make this perhaps the greatest of all the world's national museums.

34

Greek and Roman antiquities: sculptures, temple friezes, pottery, glass, jewellery, covering almost every aspect of art and life, from the early Greek Age to the late Roman Empire. Among the many star exhibits are the 5th-century B.C. "Elgin Marbles" from the Parthenon, the superb blue-glass Portland Vase (c. 15 A.D.), the Nereid Monument, the beautiful bronze head from Cyrene (c. 350 B.C.), and Exekias' 6th-century B.C. wine-jar. The lower galleries include the Roman portrait room, with representations of the famous and infamous of this ancient civilization.

Egyptian antiquities: the highlight of this wonderful collection is the Rosetta Stone (196 B.C.), the scholar's key to deciphering Egyptian hieroglyphics. Note, too, the vivid Theban tomb paintings and the lifelike statuary. Most popular of all (in the huge gallery on the upper floor) are the mummies, as well as exhibits depicting everyday life in ancient Egypt.

Western Asiatic collection: from the ancient Assyrian, Mesopotamian and Syrian empires, art treasures dating back to thousands of years before Christ, reflecting the growth of primitive societies into mature cultures. Prehistoric pottery, religious artefacts, sculptures and jewellery. Note especially the lion hunt reliefs from the palace of Nineveh, the Black Obelisk, the human-headed bull and the Nimrud ivories—all thousands of years old.

Oriental collections: covering cultures of the Middle and Far East, from the neolithic period to the 19th century. Outstanding Chinese bronzes and ceramics; Japanese lacquer work; Indian and South-east Asian intricate figures.

Islamic arts: early metalwork and artefacts and an unrivalled collection of 16th-century Turkish pottery from Iznik.

Prehistoric and Romano-British collections: a wealth of exhibits spanning early human achievement up to the Christian era, featuring a fine collection of Palaeolithic and Mesolithic flints and tools, Bronze- and Iron-Age relics, Celtic artefacts (decorated shields and jewellery) and, the star attraction, "Lindow Man" (c. 300 B.C.), found preserved in a Cheshire peat-bog.

Roman glassware and the Mildenhall Treasure—4th-century silver tableware—provide the highlights of the remarkable Roman collection covering the period of their occupation of Britain, the first five centuries A.D.

Medieval, Renaissance and Modern collections: tiles, pottery, jewellery, a collection of 3,000 clocks and watches, and beautifully crafted objects of all kinds, but the real highlight is the Sutton Hoo Treasure, a dazzling array of ancient gold and silverware from the 7th-century burial ship of King Raedwald of the Angles.

Coins and medals: over half a million coins, notes and medals, providing an international monetary history from around 625 B.C. to the present. Selections are displayed in separate galleries, with British coins, representing royal and military history, on permanent display.

Prints and drawings: a storehouse of over two million items, including works by Dürer, Rubens, Rembrandt and Turner, selections from which are shown in temporary exhibitions throughout the year.

British Library: rare and historic documents, manuscripts and first editions, notably a copy of the *Magna Carta* (1215), Shakespeare's *First Folio* (1623), a Gutenberg Bible (1453), the beautifully illuminated 7th-century *Lindisfarne Gospels* and early examples of printing from Britain, Germany, Sweden and China. (The famous Round Reading Room is restricted to reader membership only.)

Admission: free, but donation requested. Tickets for guided tours (90 minutes, extra charge) and details of temporary exhibitions and lectures available from front hall information desk.

IMPERIAL WAR MUSEUM

⊖ Elephant & Castle
or Lambeth North

Lambeth Road, SE1; tel. (071) 416 5000; recorded information (071) 820 1683. Open daily 10 a.m.–6 p.m.

On the site of the old "Bedlam" lunatic asylum, the last word about war—or at least the military operations involving British and Commonwealth troops since 1914. Recently reopened after a drastic redevelopment programme, the Imperial War Museum wins for high-tech. design and an imaginative approach to museum-keeping. Military machinery and paraphernalia, paintings and documentation illuminate the human as well as technical aspects of war. Some of the exhibits are enormous: submarines, V2 rockets, tanks and fighter planes. Interactive displays re-create the sights, sounds and emotions of war, from the London Blitz (complete with Anderson shelter) to the Far East campaigns. And you can test your flying nerves and skill on the flight simulator (extra charge).

36 The spacious art galleries contain works by Sutherland, Wyndham Lewis and Nash, amongst others. Temporary exhibitions feature archive material—photographs, posters, treaties and proclamations, as well as personal letters and diaries. The newest galleries (opened in 1990) are devoted to World War I, with interactive effects of the Western Front. Frequent film shows are given, as well.

Admission: small charge, but free on Fridays.

MUSEUM OF LONDON   16 R10

⊖ Barbican or St. Paul's

150 London Wall, EC2; tel. (071) 600 3699. Open Tuesday to Saturday 10 a.m.–6 p.m.; Sunday 2–6 p.m.; closed Monday except public holidays.

Appropriately set next to the remains of the old city wall, this modern museum (part of the Barbican Centre) tells the history of London from prehistoric swamp to present-day conurbation. See a room in Roman London, a 17th-century merchant's house, a Newgate Prison cell in Georgian times and a Victorian grocer's shop. One of the best audiovisuals in London re-creates the spread of the Great Fire of 1666. Some exhibits showcase new material from archaeological digs all over the city, such as the 2nd/3rd-century marble head of Mithras. Small items are as telling as large (a plague bell, gambling chips from gentlemen's clubs, a Stuart calculator). But a big attraction is the ornate gilt Lord Mayor's State Coach of 1757, still brought out annually for the Lord Mayor's Show.

The museum has an active research department and organizes lectures and workshops (ring for details).

Admission: free.

MUSEUM OF MANKIND   22 L9   ⊖ Green Park
or Piccadilly Circus

6 Burlington Gardens, W1; tel. (071) 437 2224; recorded information (071) 580 1788. Open Monday to Saturday 10 a.m.–5 p.m.; Sunday 2.30–6 p.m.

In fashionable Burlington Gardens, the Ethnography Department of the British Museum, alias the Museum of Mankind, can be a haven of peace as well as a feast for the eye and mind. A genuine Easter Island statue greets you in the foyer. The enormous collection comes from Africa, Australia, the Pacific Islands, North and South America, and parts of Asia and Europe. Regularly changing exhibitions of artefacts, clothing and even housing complement the permanent display of the museum's finest artistic treasures. Among the exhibits of ornate craftsmanship in every conceivable form, don't miss the exquisite Aztec turquoise mosaics.

Admission: free, but donations requested.

NATIONAL MARITIME MUSEUM   ⇌ Greenwich or Maze Hill **37**
or by river bus to Greenwich

Romney Road, SE10; tel. (081) 858 4422. Open Tuesday to Saturday 10 a.m.–6 p.m.; Sunday 2–6 p.m. (closes daily 5 p.m. November to February).

Unless you get seasick just thinking about boats, you won't regret an outing to the National Maritime Museum. Even the most fanatical landlubbers admire the lovely buildings by Sir Christopher Wren and Inigo Jones, splendidly set on the river bank in Greenwich Park. The museum contains Britain's largest collection of nautical artefacts, relating maritime history through navigational instruments, models of ships, barges, and weaponry. There are striking relics of distinguished British sailors like Nelson, Cook and Bligh—paintings and prints, charts and manuscripts. In Neptune Hall you can see the paddle tug *Reliant*, a boat-building shed and barge house, and a Battle of Trafalgar display with a gory highlight, Admiral Lord Nelson's bloodstained uniform.

A walk up the hill leads to Wren's delightful Flamsteed House, the Old Royal Observatory, with its distinctive red time ball (see it drop at 1 o'clock, as sailors did in the days before watches) and lofty Octagon Room. Here is the prime (0°) meridian and an exhibition of chronometry and timekeeping, from sundials to atomic clocks. The newly opened East Wing (separate admission charge) stages special exhibitions (ring for details). Finally, you can relieve all that seasickness by visiting Inigo Jones' Queen's House (small charge), now restored to its original beauty, with a fine display of furniture and paintings.

Admission: small charge.

NATURAL HISTORY MUSEUM   **29** E5   ⊖ South Kensington
*Cromwell Road, SW7; tel. (071) 938 9123. Open Monday to Saturday
10 a.m.–6 p.m.; Sunday 11 a.m.–6 p.m.*
If you're dreading dusty cabinets crammed with fossils, you're due for
a pleasant surprise. The extensive national collection of plants,
minerals, animals, insects, and, yes, fossils has been transformed with
new galleries and computerized interactive audio-visual displays
telling the story of evolution with imaginative flair.

The building itself, opened in 1881, is a Romanesque-style
masterpiece specially designed by Alfred Waterhouse especially for
the British Museum's natural history collections. (It houses a scientific
research department of world renown.) The great façade of beige and
blue terracotta sports animal and plant decorations and the Central
Hall is as lofty as a cathedral nave. Here graze the dinosaurs, or at least
lifelike models of them, always a hit with visitors; side displays consider
their lifestyles and extinction theories. Other highlights include the Hall
of Human Biology, where mechanical devices and computer games
reveal all about your nervous system and muscles, and the Mammal
Diversity Hall, with a full-scale model of a huge blue whale as its
centrepiece. The newest of the galleries, reflecting current concern, is
devoted to man's effect on the environment and an explanation of eco-
systems.

38

Geological Museum: now a department of the Natural History Museum,
it encompasses a massive collection of gems, ores, minerals and just
plain rocks (and a not-so-plain rock brought back from the moon which
reveals a wonderful cross-section of lunar geology). With the help of
clear displays, models and dramatic audio-visual effects, you can
trace the history of the Earth from its birth to the present. A popular
attraction is the simulator platform, the closest thing to experiencing a
real earthquake.
Admission: small charge, free after 4.30 p.m. (Sunday 5 p.m.).

SCIENCE MUSEUM   **29** F5   ⊖ South Kensington
*Exhibition Road, SW7; tel. (071) 589 3456. Open Monday to Saturday
10 a.m.–6 p.m.; Sunday 11 a.m.–6 p.m.*
Britain's foremost museum of science and industry has led the way in
exciting, "visitor-friendly" museum presentation. The ingredients of this
success are the legacy of Britain's 19th-century industrial and scientific
pre-eminence, plus the latest international achievements in technology. Understanding the wonders of science is within your grasp—
literally, if you push all the buttons and pull all the levers they've
provided.

Every aspect of science and technology, of physics and engineering, of chemistry and medicine has its own comprehensive section (or gallery) here, and many history-making "firsts" in transport, manufacture and communications have come to rest in this venerable building. You can see *Puffing Billy*, the oldest surviving steam locomotive, Stephenson's famous *Rocket* (1829), Fox's first camera, Arkwright's original spinning machine (1769), Edison's phonograph, and Amy Johnson's *Gypsy Moth* aircraft. Among the reconstructions, you can get a taste of life in a steel furnace, a Victorian kitchen or on an off-shore oil rig.

Newly opened galleries cover the fields of plastics, chemical engineering and industry, and there is a big space-exploration section featuring full-sized replicas of space capsules (though lunar command module, Apollo 10, is the genuine article). The interactive displays in the Launch Pad gallery let you share the excitement of an astronaut; you can measure your heartbeat to gauge the tension.

Dramatized talks, free films and lectures complement the exhibits (ring for details).

39

It all adds up to one of London's most exciting (and crowded) museums.

Admission: small charge, but free after 4.30 p.m.

VICTORIA & ALBERT   29 F5   ⊖ South Kensington

Cromwell Road, SW7; tel. (071) 938 8500; recorded information (071) 938 8441. Open Monday to Saturday 10 a.m.–5.50 p.m.; Sunday 2.30–5.50 p.m.

Officially, it's the National Museum of Art and Design, but everybody calls it the V & A. By any name, it's the world's greatest museum of the decorative arts.

Where to start? As with the British Museum, it would take years to explore all the displays in all the endless stretches of galleries and walkways. Guided tours are recommended, as are the free gallery talks (daily 2.30 p.m.). See the superb collection of religious and secular masterpieces from early Christian times to the present. Exhibits which should not be missed: the Rodin sculptures, the Raphael Cartoons, the medieval tapestries, the musical instruments, the Gothic Rooms and the dress collection. Also outstanding: treasures from India, China, Japan and the Middle East.

In spite of the crowds, the atmosphere can be relaxing, and even romantic in the quiet corners conveniently situated throughout the building. If you've time, pop into the well-stocked shop and attractive tea rooms—the latter designed by William Morris no less.

Admission: free, but donation suggested.

ARTS MUSEUMS

CLOCKMAKERS' COMPANY COLLECTION   **17** S10   ⊖ Bank
or Moorgate
Guildhall Library, Aldermanbury, EC2; tel. (071) 606 3030. Open Monday to Friday 10 a.m.–4.45 p.m.
Several hundred magnificent examples of the clock- and watchmakers' art, collected by members of the Clockmakers' Company since its foundation in 1631, although some exhibits go back to an even earlier date. Exquisite pocket watches, self-winding escapements, marine chronometers and long-case (grandfather) clocks are displayed in well-appointed rooms; in addition, there is a horology library, off the Guildhall Library foyer. Many delightful chimes to be heard, especially at noon or earlier.
Admission: free.

40 **DESIGN MUSEUM**   ⊖ Tower Hill or London Bridge
Butler's Wharf, SE1; tel. (071) 403 6933; recorded information (071) 407 6261. Open Tuesday to Sunday 11.30 a.m.–6.30 p.m.
As one might expect, a well-planned, light and airy modern museum, featuring the best and worst designs that mass production has to offer. Also stages temporary exhibitions and regular previews of new products.
Admission: small charge.

FENTON HOUSE   ⊖ Hampstead
Hampstead Grove, NW3; tel. (071) 435 3471. Open Saturday to Wednesday 11 a.m.–5 p.m. (April to October).
A peaceful, walled garden surrounds this attractive, late-17th-century house stocked with period furniture and 18th-century porcelain. But most notable of all is the collection of early keyboard instruments, including a 1612 harpsichord. Baroque music recitals are given on certain summer evenings (ring for details).
Admission: small charge.

FORTY HALL MUSEUM   ⇌ Enfield Town
Forty Hill, Enfield, EN2; tel. (081) 363 8196. Open Tuesday to Sunday 10 a.m.–6 p.m. (5 p.m. October to Easter).
This mansion, with splendid plasterwork and panelling, was the home of a 17th-century Lord Mayor of London, Sir Nicholas Raynton. It contains a fine collection of 17th- and 18th-century furniture and paintings, as well as documents and prints recounting local history.
Admission: free.

GEFFRYE MUSEUM ⊖ Bethnal Green
Kingsland Road, E2; tel. (071) 739 9893; recorded information (071) 739 8543. Open Tuesday to Saturday 10 a.m.–5 p.m.; Sunday 2–5 p.m.

The "typical British home" from Elizabethan times to the present day is on view in a fascinating series of reconstructed period rooms, complete with contemporary furniture and fittings, prints, paintings and costumes that capture the atmosphere of their epoch; harmoniously sited in a terrace of former 18th-century almshouses.
Admission: free.

HORNIMAN MUSEUM ⇌ Forest Hill
London Road, SE23; tel. (081) 699 2339. Open Monday to Saturday 10.30 a.m.–6 p.m.; Sunday 2–6 p.m.

In 1901 the tea merchant, Frederick John Horniman, presented this Art Nouveau building and its park to the people of London. The bequest included his extraordinary private collection, on view within: everything from Egyptian mummies and stuffed birds to native headdresses, and **41** musical instruments numbering thousands. The vast grounds include nature trails and a sunken garden.
Admission (and parking): free.

MUSEUM 24 O8 ⊖ Waterloo
OF THE MOVING IMAGE (MOMI) or Embankment
South Bank, SE1; tel. (071) 928 3535; recorded information (071) 401 2636. Open Tuesday to Sunday 10 a.m.–8 p.m.

All about moving pictures. This award-winning museum, part of the South Bank Arts Centre, takes a fresh, invigorating look at the history of film and TV. Going back to magic lantern shows and forward into space-age technology, its 50 exhibition areas are packed with working studios, TV and film clips, and interactive features. Become "Superman", read the news from an autocue, or try out your acting talent with the help and encouragement of the actor-guides.
Admission: charge.

PERCIVAL DAVID FOUNDATION 7 M12 ⊖ Russell Square
OF CHINESE ART or Euston Square
53 Gordon Square, WC1; tel. (071) 387 3909. Open Monday to Friday 10.30 a.m.–5 p.m.

A delight for devotees of Chinese ceramics: a comprehensive collection of Chinese vases, pots and amphorae, starting with specimens from the 10th century Song Dynasty and going on up to the 18th century of the Manchu era. The whole hoard was presented to London University by the Oriental scholar, Sir Percival David.
Admission: free.

ROYAL COLLEGE OF MUSIC   **29** E6   ⊖ South Kensington
MUSEUM OF INSTRUMENTS
Prince Consort Road, SW7; tel. (071) 589 3643. Open Wednesday only 2–4.30 p.m.
If you can tailor your schedule to this museum's uncommonly restrictive visiting hours, you can glimpse more than 500 keyboard, wind and string instruments from the late 15th century to the present. Celebrity honours go to a Haydn clavichord and a Handel spinet.
Admission: free (donation requested).

ST. BRIDE'S CHURCH   **15** Q9/10   ⊖ Blackfriars
CRYPT MUSEUM
St. Bride's Church, Fleet Street, EC4; tel. (071) 353 1301. Open Monday to Sunday 9 a.m.–5 p.m.
Go below ground into this spooky crypt to view the archaeological remains of all the buildings that have stood on this site from Roman times onwards. Brought to light during recent redevelopment, they include a real Roman pavement. This being Fleet Street, there's also a small exhibition on the newspaper and printing industry.
Admission: free.

SHAKESPEARE GLOBE MUSEUM   **26** R8   ⊖ London Bridge
or Mansion House
1 Bear Gardens, Bankside, SE1; tel. (071) 928 6342. Open Monday to Saturday 10 a.m.–5 p.m.; Sunday 2–5 p.m.
On the site of the last bear-baiting ring on Bankside, close to the original Globe Theatre, but not quite as exciting as it sounds. On display are models of Shakespearian theatre, finds from the recently excavated Rose Theatre and plans of the working reconstruction of the Globe, now being built from the original 16th-century designs.
Admission: small charge.

SIR JOHN SOANE'S MUSEUM   **14** O10   ⊖ Holborn
13 Lincoln's Inn Fields, WC2; tel. (071) 405 2107. Open Tuesday to Saturday 10 a.m.–5 p.m.
On the north side of the historic gardened square of Lincoln's Inn, Britain's smallest national museum occupies the early-19th-century house built by and for the architect and art connoisseur, Sir John Soane. On show are Soane's furniture, his library and the treasures he collected, just as he left them when he died in 1837. The many paintings and drawings (literally thousands of architectural drawings alone) include Hogarth's *Rake's Progress* and *Election* series and works by Watteau and Canaletto, Piranesi and Turner. Among the

42

innumerable Roman relics, the 18th- and 19th-century casts, the sculpture (especially by Flaxman) and the natural history objects, pride of place goes to the sarcophagus of Pharaoh Seti I (14th century B.C.). Admission: free. Guided tours Saturday 2.30 p.m.

THEATRE MUSEUM   14 N9   ⊖ Covent Garden
Russell Street, WC2; tel. (071) 836 7891; recorded information (071) 836 7624. Open Tuesday to Sunday 11 a.m.–7 p.m.
A branch of the V & A, Britain's first national museum dedicated to the performing arts is situated in Covent Garden's old flower market. It has a fascinating array of props, set models, costumes and theatrical memorabilia covering every form of show business—from theatre, ballet and opera to circus, puppets and pop shows. There's also an art gallery and studio theatre.
Admission: charge, but family reduction.

THOMAS CORAM FOUNDATION   8 O12   ⊖ Russell Square   **43**
FOR CHILDREN
40 Brunswick Square, WC1; tel. (071) 278 2424. Open Monday to Friday 10 a.m.–4 p.m.
The orphans have long since moved out but you can still see the art treasures that helped to support the foundlings' hospital established here in the 18th century. There are distinguished paintings by Gainsborough and Reynolds and a cartoon by Raphael; also an original score of Handel's *Messiah,* as well as a collection of period furniture, clocks and watches. The kindly old gentleman looking down at you from the first floor (in the painting by William Hogarth) is Captain Thomas Coram, founder and benefactor of the charity.
Admission: small charge.

WILLIAM MORRIS GALLERY   ⊖ Walthamstow Central
Lloyd Park, Forest Road, E1; tel. (081) 527 3782. Open Tuesday to Saturday 10 a.m.–1 p.m. and 2–5 p.m.; first Sunday in month 10 a.m.–noon and 2–5 p.m.
An inspiration to all arts and crafts lovers is this attractive mid-18th-century house where William Morris, the architect, designer and social reformer, lived as a youth from 1848 to 1856. Featuring all aspects of his work (textiles and wallpapers, tiles, stained glass, carpets and furniture), it also displays treasures by other l9th-century craftsmen and artists: ceramics by William de Morgan and the Martin brothers and Pre-Raphaelite paintings and sculpture, with works by Rodin, Rosetti, Sickert and Burne-Jones.
Admission: free.

MILITARY, TRANSPORT AND SCIENTIFIC MUSEUMS

CABINET WAR ROOMS   **23** M7   ⊖ Westminster
Clive Steps, King Charles Street, SW1; tel. (071) 930 6961. Open 10 a.m.–6 p.m. daily.
Like millions of Londoners allergic to bombs, Winston Churchill and the British Government went underground during World War II. They ran Britain and the war effort from a network of blastproof rooms handy for Whitehall. Now the subterranean seat of government has been restored to its original spartan 1940 state. You can see Churchill's office-bedroom, from which he made many of his inspiring broadcasts, the Telephone Room, with a direct line to President Roosevelt in the White House, the Map Room, with markers still delineating the war fronts, and the Cabinet Room, ready for the day's 5 p.m. meeting.
Admission: charge.

44 CUTTY SARK   ⇌ Greenwich or Maze Hill
                                     or by river bus to Greenwich
King William Walk, SE10; tel. (081) 858 2698. Open Monday to Saturday 10.30 a.m.–5 p.m.; Sunday noon–5 p.m. (earlier in winter).
Wander around the last and fastest of the great tea-carrying clipper ships. A beautiful final flutter of the age of sail, the *Cutty Sark* was launched in 1869, after steamships had already proved their reliability. Above decks, marvel at the array of masts and riggings designed to exploit wind power. Below, reconstructed cabins and cargo holds are filled with exhibitions of maritime relics and prints, and a unique collection of carved and painted figureheads. Alongside the *Cutty Sark* is the almost impossibly small ketch, *Gypsy Moth IV*, in which Sir Francis Chichester sailed single-handedly round the world in 1966–7.
Admission: small charge.

DARWIN MUSEUM   ⇌ Bromley South, then 146 bus
Down House, Luxted Road, Downe, Orpington, Kent; tel. (0689) 59119. Open Wednesday to Sunday and public holidays 1–5.30 p.m.
This is the house Charles Darwin lived in when he published *On the Origin of Species by means of Natural Selection* in 1859. His theory of evolution not only revolutionized scientific thinking but also shocked the churches. This museum, in the house that was his home for the last 40 years of his life, displays his collections of fossils, birds and butterflies, many gathered on his voyages to the Pacific and South Atlantic in *HMS Beagle;* also on show are some of his scientific instruments and personal belongings.
Admission: small charge.

FARADAY MUSEUM   **22** K9   ⊖ Green Park

The Royal Institution, 21 Albemarle Street, W1; tel. (071) 409 2992. Open Tuesday and Thursday 1–4 p.m.

Down in the basement of the Royal Institution, where he used to work, the pioneer 19th-century scientist, Michael Faraday, is honoured by a small museum. The son of a blacksmith, Faraday made historic discoveries in electricity, electromagnetism and electrochemistry and inspired generations of researchers. His laboratory is reconstructed here, with some of his experimental equipment and personal belongings.

Admission: small charge.

FLORENCE NIGHTINGALE MUSEUM   **33** 06   ⊖ Waterloo
or Westminster

St. Thomas's Hospital, 2 Lambeth Palace Road, SE1; tel. (071) 620 0374. Open Tuesday to Sunday 10 a.m.–4 p.m.

Honouring the founder of modern nursing, this small, award-winning museum charts the career of Florence Nightingale, the determined "lady with the lamp". Among well-presented exhibits of medical equipment and uniforms are reconstructed Crimean War hospital wards.

45

Admission: small charge.

GUARDS MUSEUM   **32** L6   ⊖ St. James's Park

Wellington Barracks, Birdcage Walk, SW1; tel. (071) 930 4466, extension 3271. Open Saturday to Thursday 10 a.m.–4 p.m.

Home of the soldiers who provide the spectacle of the "Changing of the Guard", Wellington Barracks also runs its own military museum. The history of the five Guards regiments (Grenadier, Coldstream, Scots, Irish and Welsh Guards) is documented here, from the English Civil War (1642–9) to the recent Falklands Campaign, with uniforms, weapons and memorabilia to engross any military enthusiast.

Admission: small charge, but family reductions.

KEW BRIDGE STEAM MUSEUM   ⇄ Kew Bridge

Green Dragon Lane, Brentford, Middx.; tel. (071) 568 4757. Open daily 11 a.m.–5 p.m.

Massive engines from the 19th-century industrial age, including the giant beam engines that pumped London's water supply for over 100 years. Many are still in good working order and can often be seen in action. Also on display are a working forge, a belt-driven machine shop, a set of traction engines and steam boats. A treat for budding engineers.

Admission: small charge, but family reductions.

LONDON TRANSPORT MUSEUM   **14** N9   ⊖ Covent Garden
Covent Garden, WC2; tel. (071) 379 6344; recorded information (071) 836 8557. Open daily 10 a.m.–6 p.m.
This compact collection, ranging from horse-drawn omnibuses and trams to prototype tube trains, shows how London's urban transport system developed, spurring the expansion of the city. Join the queue for your turn in the driver's seat for a simulated trip around the Circle Line.

Another highlight of this spotless museum: a sampling of the adventurous posters that brought London Transport fame as a patron of the arts.
Admission: charge, but family reduction.

MUSEUM OF ARTILLERY   ⇉ Woolwich Arsenal
46 *The Rotunda, Repository Road, SE18; tel. (081) 316 5402. Open Monday to Friday noon–5 p.m.; Saturday, Sunday 1–5 p.m. (closes daily 4 p.m. November to March).*
War buffs will want to zero in on this tribute to the romance of the heavy artillery. But first you have to run the gauntlet of field guns and tanks guarding John Nash's circular, tent-like building, moved here in 1819 from St. James's Park.

The collection, begun in 1778 by Captain Congreve, the father of military rocketry, contains items of world-shattering importance and mind-boggling size. Here you can learn how to cast and fire a cannon or manoeuvre an armoured vehicle. Even a pacifist could hardly avoid admiring the craftsmanship involved in producing some of these deadly weapons.
Admission: free.

NATIONAL ARMY MUSEUM   **36** H3   ⊖ Sloane Square
Royal Hospital Road, SW3; tel. (071) 730 0717. Open Monday to Saturday 10 a.m.–5.30 p.m.; Sunday 2–5.30 p.m.
Just next to the home of the Chelsea Pensioners, this purpose-built museum tells the story of the British Army across five centuries, largely from the soldier's point of view.

Exhibits range from the most mundane mementoes of war to the more vainglorious aspects (such as the Duke of Marlborough's 18th-century gold-embroidered saddle-cloth). There are regimental and

personal relics, extensive collections of uniforms and arms (from long bows to missiles), and, last but not least, an art gallery featuring works by Reynolds and Gainsborough.
Admission: free.

NORTH WOOLWICH
OLD STATION MUSEUM
⇌ North Woolwich

Pier Road, E16; tel. (071) 474 7244. Open Monday to Saturday 10 a.m.–5 p.m.
Restored to its former glory and complete with Victorian ticket-office, this old station documents the history of the Great Eastern Railway and docklands train network with models, photographs and relics. But the real attractions are the magnificent engines themselves, one of which is regularly under steam.
Admission: free.

47

ROYAL AIR FORCE MUSEUM
⊖ Colindale

Grahame Park Way, NW9; tel. (081) 205 2266. Open daily 10 a.m.– 6 p.m.
Historic planes, grounded in two huge hangars-turned-exhibition-halls, on the site of an old airfield, tell the story of the exploits and everyday life of the Royal Air Force, from World War I to the present day. The Battle of Britain Museum, with German and Italian aircraft, and the Bomber Command Museum both pay tribute to the courage and skill of World War II airmen.
   Films, photographs and memorabilia of all kinds supplement audio-visual displays and would-be fighter pilots can try their nerve at low-flying a Tornado on the flight simulator.
Admission: charge, but family reductions.

TELECOM TECHNOLOGY SHOWCASE
16 Q9   ⊖ Blackfriars
or St.Paul's

135 Queen Victoria Street, EC4; tel. (071) 248 7444. Open Monday to Friday 10 a.m.–5 p.m.
Two centuries of telecommunications history, from the birth of the telegraph to today's digital technology. Examine a reconstructed Victorian telephone exchange, displays of telephone handsets old and new, fibre optics and satellite technology. Try the interactive exhibits, and see what 21st-century technology holds in store.
Admission: free.

OTHER SPECIAL INTEREST MUSEUMS

BADEN POWELL HOUSE   **29** E5   ⊖ South Kensington
or Gloucester Road
Queen's Gate, SW7; tel. (071) 584 7030. Open daily 7 a.m.–11 p.m.
Lord Baden-Powell (1857–1941), whose statue stands outside, was a
British war hero better known worldwide as the founder of the Boy
Scouts and co-founder of the Girl Guides. In the hostel belonging to the
headquarters of the United Kingdom scout movement, a small
exhibition documents the life and work of Baden-Powell and the history
of scouting.
Admission: free.

BANK OF ENGLAND MUSEUM   **17** S10   ⊖ Bank
*Bartholomew Lane, EC2; tel. (071) 601 5545. Open Monday to Friday
10 a.m.–5 p.m., Saturday, Sunday and public holidays 11 a.m.–5 p.m.*
48 *(summer only).*
In this treasure trove you can learn about the history of money-making
and gaze (longingly) at gold bars, gold coins and bank notes galore.
Also interactive video displays.
Admission: free.

BETHNAL GREEN MUSEUM OF CHILDHOOD
See CHILDREN p. 165.

CRYSTAL PALACE MUSEUM   ⇥ Crystal Palace
Anerley Hill, SE19; tel. (081) 676 0700. Open Sunday 2–5 p.m.
The whole story of Joseph Paxton's glorious glass and iron building,
erected to house the Great Exhibition of 1851 but destroyed by fire in
1936. Surrounding the remains of the palace is a vast park, also
containing a sports centre, children's zoo and dinosaur park.
Admission: free (donation requested).

FREEMASONS' HALL   **14** N10   ⊖ Holborn or Covent Garden
*Great Queen Street, WC2; tel. (071) 831 9811. Open Monday to Friday
9 a.m.–5 p.m.; Saturday by appointment.*
The first-floor museum in this impressive building (erected 1927–33)
contains an extensive collection of the Freemasons' regalia, art and
china- and glassware.
   Masonic history is explained on the free guided tour and you can
speculate on the secret rituals that take place in the Grand Temple and
elegant ceremonial rooms.
Admission: free.

A SECRET GARDEN

Everone has heard of the Royal Botanical Gardens at Kew, on the outskirts of London (see p. 193). But there is an even older collection of plants in the city that few people know about. The **Chelsea Physic Garden**, 66 Royal Hospital Road, SW3; tel. (071) 352 5646 (map ref. p.36 H2), was established in 1673 by the Society of Apothecaries to grow plants for medicinal research. Much of the collection originated in the New World, and includes a number of rare herbs. Like Kew, the Physic Garden suffered severe storm damage in 1987, when some of its ancient trees were uprooted, but it is still worth a visit. Open Wednesday and Sunday 2–5 p.m. (April to October); small charge.

GUINNESS WORLD OF RECORDS

See CHILDREN p. 169.

GUNNERSBURY PARK MUSEUM ⊖ Acton Town 49

Gunnersbury Park, W3; tel. (081) 992 1612. Open Monday to Friday 1–5 p.m. (4 p.m. November to February); Sunday 2–6 p.m. (4 p.m. November to February).
Set in a spacious park, the 19th-century mansion once owned by the Rothschild family houses a wide-ranging collection covering local history, costume, transport and archeology. Also temporary exhibitions in the restored Victorian kitchens and Small Mansion art gallery.
Admission: free.

JEWISH MUSEUM 7 M12 ⊖ Russell Square or Euston Square

Woburn House, Tavistock Square, WC1; tel. (071) 388 4525. Open Tuesday to Friday, Sunday 10 a.m.–4.30 p.m. (October to March: shuts at 12.45 p.m. on Friday). Closed Jewish festivals.
A collection of many ritual and functional antiquities concentrating largely on Anglo-Jewish life, history and tradition. Among interesting ceremonial objects is an ornately carved, 16th-century Venetian Ark, intended to house sacred scrolls but found being used as a servant's wardrobe.
Admission: free (donation requested).

LONDON DUNGEON

See CHILDREN p. 171.

LONDON TOY & MODEL MUSEUM

See CHILDREN p. 166.

LORD'S CRICKET GROUND   4 F12   ⊖ St. John's Wood
St. John's Wood, NW8; tel. (071) 289 1611. Open Monday to Saturday 10.30 a.m.–3 p.m.
The Cricket Memorial Gallery at this celebrated ground attracts fans of the unique, if puzzling, national game to admire its display of mementoes, most notably the urn containing the original "Ashes". Open during the cricket season, Monday to Saturday 10 a.m.–3 p.m., with guided tours by arrangement.

MADAME TUSSAUD'S
For this, and the nearby LASERIUM and PLANETARIUM, see CHILDREN pp. 71-2.

MUSEUM OF GARDEN HISTORY   33 O5   ⊖ Waterloo
or Lambeth North
St. Mary-at-Lambeth, Lambeth Palace Road, SE1; tel. (071) 261 1891. March to mid-December: open Monday to Friday 11 a.m.–3 p.m.; Sunday 10.30 a.m.–5 p.m.
A charming little museum in a preserved church and churchyard where the Tradescants, who were plant collectors and gardeners to King Charles I, are buried, along with Admiral *Mutiny on the Bounty* Bligh. Inside are displays of antique tools and other aspects of garden history; outside, the gardens feature the descendants of plants brought here from the far corners of the world in the 17th century.
Admission: free.

MUSEUM OF THE ORDER OF ST. JOHN   16 Q11   ⊖ Farringdon
or Barbican
St. John's Gate, St. John's Lane, EC1; tel. (071) 253 6644. Open Monday to Friday 10 a.m.–5 p.m.; Saturday 10 a.m.–4 p.m.
The early 16th-century gatehouse of the long-gone Priory of the Order of the Hospital of St. John of Jerusalem contains a variety of items relating to the colourful history of this medieval knightly order. There are armour and arms, documents and fine early books, and a wealth of art treasures (notably an illuminated Rhodes Missal and panels of a 15th-century Flemish triptych). You can also visit the surviving 12th-century church crypt.
Admission: free (donation requested).

NATIONAL POSTAL MUSEUM   16 R10   ⊖ St. Paul's
or Barbican
King Edward Building, King Edward Street, EC1; tel. (071) 239 5420. Open Monday to Thursday 9.30 a.m.–4.30 p.m.; Friday 9.30 a.m.–4 p.m.

50

A philatelist's dream—drawers and drawers full of stamps, not only official Post Office material, but also private collections from Britain and all over the world. On permanent or temporary display are many priceless rarities (the complete sheet of *Penny Blacks* is a favourite), as well as a fascinating section on forgeries. Film and guided tours for groups.
Admission: free.

POLLOCK'S TOY MUSEUM
See CHILDREN p. 168.

PUBLIC RECORD OFFICE MUSEUM   15 P10   ⊖ Chancery Lane
Chancery Lane, WC2; tel (081) 876 3444. Open Monday to Friday 9.30 a.m.–5 p.m. Closed first two weeks in October (for stocktaking).
The national storehouse of the most significant state documents since Norman times (not to be confused with the register of births, deaths and marriages at St. Catherine's House). Among the treasures: the **51** *Domesday Book* (1086), a copy of the *Magna Carta* (1215), the logbook from Nelson's *H.M.S. Victory*, and many famous signatures.
Admission: free.

WIMBLEDON LAWN TENNIS MUSEUM   ⊖ Wimbledon Park
Church Road, SW19; tel. (081) 946 6131. Open Tuesday to Saturday 11 a.m.–5 p.m.; Sunday 2–5 p.m. During championship fortnight (spectators only): 11 a.m.–7 p.m.
Close to their famous Centre Court, the All England Lawn Tennis and Croquet Club runs a museum which traces the history of the club (founded in 1877), thereby providing a fascinating insight into society life over the past hundred years or more. As well as a collection of tennis memorabilia (including John McEnroe's trainers), it also has a reconstruction of the original men's changing room, a racquet-maker's workshop, and videos of great matches.
Admission: small charge.

WINDMILL MUSEUM   ⊖ Wimbledon
Windmill Road, off Parkside, SW19; tel. (081) 788 7655. Open (Easter to October) Saturday, Sunday and public holidays 2–5 p.m.
Wimbledon's wonderful weatherboard windmill, which dates from 1817, claims to be the only hollow-post flour mill in Britain. It was restored in 1975 and turned into a museum. The displays include working models, tools and machinery illustrating the history and workings of different types of windmill.
Admission: very small charge.

HOMES OF THE FAMOUS

APSLEY HOUSE 21 J7   ⊖ Hyde Park Corner
149 Piccadilly, Hyde Park Corner, W1; tel. (071) 499 5676. Open Tuesday to Sunday 11 a.m.–5 p.m.
Also known as the Wellington Museum. When Robert Adam built this grand house in the 1770s, it was the westernmost residence in the city, hence the traditional address, "Number One, London". The Iron Duke moved in two years after winning the Battle of Waterloo. In 1947 his descendant, the 7th Duke of Wellington, presented the building to the nation.

Superbly restored, Apsley House contains magnificent collections of art, silver and porcelain. Note a colossal statue of Napoleon by Canova (which Napoleon himself disliked), a Nollekens bust and a Goya portrait of the "Iron Duke".
Admission: small charge.

52

CARLYLE'S HOUSE 36 G2   ⊖ Sloane Square
24 Cheyne Row, SW3; tel. (071) 352 7087. Open Easter to October: Wednesday to Sunday, public holiday Mondays 11 a.m.–5 p.m.
Fans of Thomas Carlyle drift to this delightful, early-l8th-century terraced house, close to the Chelsea embankment, where the man of letters lived with his wife Jane from 1834 until his death in 1881. Many mundane items illustrate their daily domestic life (for example, his hat still hanging on its peg) and in the attic study can be seen various Victorian literary mementoes, as well as the writing table on which Carlyle penned *Frederick the Great* and *The French Revolution*.
Admission: small charge.

DICKENS' HOUSE 8 O12   ⊖ Russell Square
                                                          or Chancery Lane
48 Doughty Street, WC1; tel. (071) 405 2127. Open Monday to Saturday 10 a.m.–4.30 p.m.
A shrine to London's most famous novelist, this is where Charles Dickens, as a young married man, lived from 1837 to 1839 and where he worked on *Pickwick Papers*, *Oliver Twist* and *Nicholas Nickleby*. See his study and the drawing room where literary and artistic celebrities used to gather, as well as a fascinating array of memorabilia: manuscripts, furniture (including his portable reading desk), portraits, letters, personal records of his children (two of whom were born here) and an extensive Dickens library with valuable first editions.
Admission: small charge, with family reduction.

FREUD MUSEUM ⊖ Finchley Road

20 Maresfield Gardens, NW3; tel. (071) 435 2002. Open Wednesday to Sunday noon–5 p.m.

See the famous couch! Sigmund Freud brought it here when he and his daughter Anna fled from Nazi Vienna in 1938. The London home of the pioneer psychoanalyst is virtually as it was when he died in 1939, still filled with his personal effects. Also on display is his fine collection of antiquities and *objets d'art*. There are guided tours, plus archive films and lectures.

Admission: small charge.

DR. JOHNSON'S HOUSE   15 P10 ⊖ Temple or Blackfriars

17 Gough Square, EC4; tel. (071) 353 3745. Open Monday to Saturday 11 a.m.–5.30 p.m. (5 p.m. October to April).

The classically tall and narrow Georgian town house, newly refurbished, of larger-than-life Dr. Samuel Johnson, who compiled his famous dictionary in this very attic. On show are some of his letters, an early copy of the dictionary, and a portrait of his friend and biographer, James Boswell, by Joshua Reynolds.

53

Admission: small charge.

KEATS' HOUSE ⊖ Hampstead

Keats Grove, NW3; tel. (071) 435 2062. Open April to October: Monday to Friday 2–6 p.m.; Saturday 10 a.m.–1 p.m. and 2–5 p.m.; Sunday 2–5 p.m. November to March: Monday to Saturday 2–5 p.m.; Sunday 10 a.m.–1 p.m.

The Romantic poet's early-19th-century home where he wrote most of his greatest works and fell in love with Fannie Brawne, the girl next door. The two houses are now one and some fascinating mementoes and manuscripts are on display.

Admission: free.

JOHN WESLEY'S HOUSE AND METHODIST MUSEUM ⊖ Old Street

47–9 City Road, EC1; tel. (071) 253 2262. Open Monday to Saturday 10 a.m.–4 p.m.; 11 a.m. service, lunch, talk and guided tour.

The founder of Methodism lived here for the last dozen years of his life. The house contains an interesting collection of the preacher's personal effects.

Next door is the Chapel he opened in 1778, its crypt now a small museum devoted to Methodism, with such items as playing cards showing godly texts in place of suits.

Admission: small charge.

London's galleries embrace a whole world of painting and sculpture, a compendium of artists from Arp and Annigoni to Zurbarán. Superlative collections of Old and Modern Masters have made the National Gallery and the Tate world-famous, but don't forget the other worthy galleries, such as the Courtauld Institute, now transferred to Somerset House. Many of London's museums, too, contain art collections, notably the V & A and the British Museum, which between them hoard more than four million paintings and prints and thousands of sculptures.

Entrance is often free, though admission is charged for the large-scale international exhibitions. The smaller public and commercial galleries hold temporary exhibitions of high quality, covering art from antiquity to the present day. These galleries usually close for a short period between shows. The policy for opening on public holidays tends to vary from one establishment to another, so it's best to check first.

Our list starts with the prestigious public art galleries. The next section proposes a selection of London's commercial galleries. Don't expect to find the bargain of the century here, for London prices can be astronomical. But viewing is free and the works on show offer an insight into tastes and trends in the art world. In addition, many establishments hold temporary exhibitions open to the public, either as a continuous policy or once or twice a year.

55

Commercial galleries generally open from 10 a.m. to around 5.30 p.m. on weekdays, and from 10 a.m. to lunchtime on Saturdays. The top-flight commercial dealers are mainly clustered around Bond Street and St. James's Street.

For full details of current exhibitions all over town, consult the listings magazines, *Time Out* or *What's On*.

In a London gallery, turning three-dimensional art into two.

NATIONAL GALLERY 23 M8 ⊖ Charing Cross or Leicester Square

Trafalgar Square, WC2; tel. (071) 839 3321; rec. information (071) 839 3526. Open Monday to Saturday 10 a.m.–6 p.m., Sunday 2–6 p.m.

Britain's greatest collection of European painting covers all schools from the 12th to 20th centuries, with nearly all the Old Masters represented. The whole treasure is usually on show, in a series of well-arranged rooms. Look for famous masterpieces by the likes of van Eyck, Leonardo da Vinci, Rembrandt, Vermeer, Velazquez, Titian, Constable and Cézanne. If you're overwhelmed by this plethora of riches, you can pick up a list of outstanding paintings at the entrance. Or take advantage of the guided tours, audio-visual commentaries and free lectures. Otherwise, browse at your own pace through the thematically arranged galleries: Flemish and Dutch, Italian Renaissance and Medieval, post-Impressionists, etc. In addition, seasonal exhibitions focus on specific aspects of the collections.
Admission: free.

56

TATE GALLERY 33 N4 ⊖ Pimlico

Millbank, SW1; tel. (071) 821 1313; rec. information (071) 821 7128. Open Monday to Saturday 10 a.m.–5.50 p.m., Sunday 2–5.50 p.m.

Here on the embankment, on the site of a former prison, are housed both the National Collection of Historic British Painting (from the beginning of the 16th century to the present) and the National Collection of Modern Art (consisting of both British and foreign sculpture and painting). The Historic galleries include particularly fine examples of work by Blake, Hogarth, Stubbs, Constable and the Pre-Raphaelites, while Turner has the post-Modern Clore Gallery all to himself. Among the impressive Modern Collection is sculpture by Moore and Hepworth, and fine Cubist and Impressionist displays, with works by Picasso, Pollock, Degas, Chagall and Mondrian. Special exhibitions are held regularly (against a small charge), and guided tours and free lectures are also given.
Admission: free.

BARBICAN ART GALLERY 17 S11 ⊖ Barbican or Moorgate

Levels 8 & 9, Barbican Centre, Silk Street, EC2; tel. (071) 638 4141 ext. 306; rec. information (071) 588 9023. Open Monday to Saturday 10 a.m.–6.45 p.m., Sunday and public holidays noon–5.45 p.m.

A large gallery area on two floors presenting temporary (largely thematic) exhibitions which usually encompass international works of art of both contemporary and historic nature.
Admission: small charge.

COURTAULD INSTITUTE GALLERIES   24 O9   ⊖ Aldwych

Somerset House, Strand, WC2; tel. (071) 873 2526. Open Monday to Saturday 10 a.m.–6 p.m. (Tuesday till 8 p.m.), Sunday 2–6 p.m.

At last an appropriate setting for this small but splendid collection: Somerset House, Sir William Chambers' palatial 18th-century riverside building. Here's a crash course in art history from 14th-century altarpieces by Bernardo Daddi to the best of Manet, Renoir, Van Gogh and Gauguin. And there are paintings by living artists. A separate gallery specializes in prints, drawings and watercolours.
Admission: small charge.

DULWICH PICTURE GALLERY   ⇝ West Dulwich

College Road, SE21; tel. (081) 693 5254. Open Tuesday to Friday 10 a.m.–1 p.m. and 2–5 p.m., Saturday 11 a.m.–5 p.m., Sunday 2–5 p.m.

Designed by Sir John Soane in the early 19th century, this is one of Britain's most beautiful galleries. On display are handsome works by such famous names as Claude, Poussin, Rembrandt, Rubens, Van Dyck, Gainsborough and Canaletto. Free guided tours at weekends.
Admission: small charge.

57

HAYWARD GALLERY   24 O8   ⊖ Waterloo

Belvedere Road, South Bank, SE1; tel. (071) 928 3144; recorded information (071) 261 0127. Open Tuesday & Wednesday 10 a.m.–8 p.m., Thursday to Sunday 10 a.m.–6 p.m. Closed between shows.

Large-scale temporary art exhibitions of all kinds, including sculpture: British and foreign historical and contemporary works.
Admission: small charge, but half price for adults on Mondays.

INSTITUTE   23 M8   ⊖ Charing Cross
OF CONTEMPORARY ARTS (ICA)

Nash House, The Mall, SW1; tel. (071) 930 3647. Open daily noon–8 p.m.

Contemporary arts of all kinds, with changing innovative and experimental shows of paintings by British and international artists.
Admission: small charge.

IVEAGH BEQUEST, KENWOOD   ⊖ Golders Green, then 210 bus

Kenwood House, Hampstead Lane, NW3; tel. (081) 348 1286. Open daily April to September 10 a.m.–6 p.m.; October to March 10 a.m.–4 p.m.

On the north side of Hampstead Heath, this outstanding neoclassical stately home, with a glorious library designed by Robert Adam (1764–73), has a fine collection of Old Masters and English paintings (works

by Rembrandt, Vermeer, Hals, Reynolds, Gainsborough and Romney), as well as sculpture and 18th-century English furniture.
Admission: free.

LEIGHTON HOUSE   ⊖ High Street Kensington
12 Holland Park Road, W14; tel. (071) 602 3316. Open Monday to Saturday 11 a.m.–5 p.m. (until 6 p.m. during exhibitions).
Built in 1866, this splendid Eastern-inspired house, home of wealthy artist and collector, Lord Leighton, is fascinating for both its architecture (particularly the exotic domed Arab Hall) and contrasting collections of Islamic ceramics and late-Victorian paintings (works by Leighton himself, Burne-Jones, Watts and Millais). Sculpture by Leighton, Brock and Thorneycroft is also on view, some of the works displayed in splendour in the large garden. Changing exhibitions are held throughout the year.
Admission: free.

NATIONAL PORTRAIT GALLERY   23 M9   ⊖ Charing Cross
St. Martin's Place, WC2; tel. (071) 930 1552. Open Monday to Friday 10 a.m.–5 p.m., Saturday 10 a.m.–6 p.m., Sunday 2–6 p.m.

58 Devoted to the painted rather than the painter, the National Portrait Gallery contains thousands of familiar faces (paintings, photographs, sculptures, miniatures and engravings), which range from medieval times to the present day, providing a panorama of artistic, social and political history. Among the treasures arranged in chronological galleries are paintings of Shakespeare, Milton and Pepys, as well as Holbein's Henry VIII and Gheeraerts' Elizabeth I. In the 20th-century room, images of modern royals (including Bryan Organ's portrait of Princess Diana) appear alongside those of Andy Warhol, Bob Geldof and Sebastian Coe.
Admission: free.

QUEEN'S GALLERY   32 K6   ⊖ Victoria or St. James's Park
Buckingham Palace Road, SW1; tel. recorded information (071) 799 2331. Open Tuesday to Saturday 10.30 a.m.–4.30 p.m., Sunday 2–4.30 p.m. Closed between exhibitions (usually winter).
Changing exhibitions reveal facets of the magnificent Royal Collection, including celebrated Old Masters, mostly housed at Windsor Castle.
Admission: small charge.

ROYAL ACADEMY OF ARTS   22/23 L8   ⊖ Piccadilly Circus
or Green Park
Burlington House, Piccadilly, W1; tel. (071) 439 7438; recorded information (071) 434 996/7. Open daily 10 a.m.–6 p.m. during exhibitions.

Founded in 1768 as a free art school, the revered Royal Academy is now famous not only for its annual Summer Exhibition of selected works by living artists, but also for its highly popular temporary shows. These usually feature Old and Modern Masters, either on loan from other galleries, or chosen from the Academy's own collection, built up over the years from the compulsory gifts of members, and constituting a fascinating history of British art.
Admission: free.

SAATCHI COLLECTION ⊖ St. John's Wood
98a Boundary Road, NW8; tel. (071) 624 8299. Open Friday and Saturday noon–6 p.m.
Britain's largest contemporary art collection still in private hands, with works by Eric Fischl, Jennifer Bartlett, Elizabeth Murray, Kiefer and Warhol. Exhibitions change half-yearly.
Admission: free.

SERPENTINE GALLERY   20 E/F7 ⊖ South Kensington
Kensington Gardens, W2; tel. (071) 402 6075; recorded information (071) 706 0454. Open Monday to Sunday 11 a.m.–dusk. Closed between exhibitions.
Changing monthly exhibitions of contemporary British and foreign art, staged in a former tea pavilion, with lawns providing the setting for occasional displays of sculpture.
Admission: free.

59

WALLACE COLLECTION   12 J10 ⊖ Bond Street
Hertford House, Manchester Square, W1; tel. (071) 935 0687. Open Monday to Saturday 10 a.m.–5 p.m., Sunday 2–5 p.m.
A wonderful private collection bequeathed to the nation in 1897 by the widow of Sir Richard Wallace, M.P., art lover and philanthropist. It stars 17th- and 18th-century French paintings (Watteau, Fragonard and Boucher) and notable works by Rembrandt, Rubens, Guardi, Canaletto and Titian. There is also an excellent set of Bonnington oils and water colours, Sèvres porcelain, Limoges enamels, French furniture, and armour.
Admission: free (donation requested).

WHITECHAPEL ART GALLERY ⊖ Aldgate East
Whitechapel High Street, E1; tel. (071) 377 5015; recorded information (071) 377 0107. Open Tuesday, Sunday 11 a.m.–5 p.m., Wednesday 11 a.m.–8 p.m. Closed between exhibitions.
A long way from Bond Street, setting the pace in high-quality, temporary exhibitions of contemporary art, this is where the work of some of Britain's best present-day artists is likely to be seen.
Admission: free.

COMMERCIAL ART GALLERIES

AGNEW **22** L8 ⊖ Piccadilly Circus or Green Park
43 Old Bond Street, W1; tel. (071) 629 6176.
Old Master works of high quality (and prices) and an annual spring show of outstanding prints and drawings.

ALBEMARLE **22** K8/9 ⊖ Green Park
18 Albemarle Street, W1; tel. (071) 355 1880.
Well-informed on the contemporary scene, a gallery specializing in work by young British and overseas artists.

ANNE BERTHOUD **22** K/L9 ⊖ Oxford Circus or Green Park
10 Clifford Street, W1; tel. (071) 437 1645.
A small gallery with monthly shows of British and contemporary painters (figurative to abstract art), as well as interesting, quite inexpensive African and South American ceramics.

ANTHONY D'OFFAY **12** K9/10 ⊖ Bond Street
9 & 23 Dering Street, W1; tel. (071) 499 4100.
One of London's most important commercial galleries, featuring, at No. 23, international contemporary art and, at No. 9, early-20th-century British art (Camden Town school and post-Impressionism).

BERNARD JACOBSON GALLERY **22** K/L9 ⊖ Oxford Circus
14a Clifford Street, W1; tel. (071) 495 8575.
Prints and paintings by contemporary British artists, both well-established and up-and-coming.

COLNAGHI **22** L8 ⊖ Piccadilly Circus
14 Old Bond Street, W1; tel. (071) 491 7408.
Top-flight dealers, specializing in the finest Old Master paintings and drawings; they have also exhibited classic photographs.

FABIAN CARLSSON GALLERY **22** K9 ⊖ Green Park
or Bond Street
160 New Bond Street, W1; tel. (071) 409 0619.
European and American contemporary art, with a focus on young British artists.

GIMPEL FILS **12** K9 ⊖ Bond Street
30 Davies Street, W1; tel. (071) 493 2488.
A prominent gallery for innovative contemporary work by both established and younger British, European and American artists.

HAMILTONS GALLERY   **22** J9   ⊖ Green Park or Bond Street
13 Carlos Place, W1; tel. (071) 499 9493.
High-class photography covering a wide range of disciplines—advertizing, fashion and celebrity portraits—and also serious shows of work at serious prices.

MARLBOROUGH   **22** L8   ⊖ Green Park
6 Albemarle Street, W1; tel. (071) 629 5161.
An important gallery reflecting the contemporary British art scene and exhibiting not only many major artists at substantial prices, but also promising young artists.

PHOTOGRAPHERS' GALLERY   **14** M/N9   ⊖ Leicester Square
5 & 8 Great Newport Street, WC2; tel. (071) 831 1772.
London's foremost venue for artistic and experimental photography, including photo-journalism. The Print Room at No. 5 has a good selection of work by both famous and lesser-known photographers, at varying prices.

WADDINGTON GALLERIES   **22** K/L9   ⊖ Green Park
5, 11, 12 & 34 Cork Street, W1; tel. (071) 437 8611.
International modern and contemporary works of outstanding quality and range, including Picasso and Miro, Hoyland and Palidino, Ben Nicholson and Hockney. The galleries stretch along Cork Street, with monthly changing exhibitions of major artists. Also sculpture.

61

WADDINGTON GRAPHICS   **22** K/L9   ⊖ Oxford Circus
GALLERIES
16 Clifford Street, W1; tel. (071) 439 1866.
The Graphics Gallery in Clifford Street shows an equally illustrious range of prints.

WHITFORD & HUGHES   **23** L8   ⊖ Green Park
6 Duke Street, SW1; tel. (071) 930 9332.
A high-class gallery with fine paintings from the end of the 19th century to 1960—post-Impressionists, Salon and Academy, Modernists and post-War schools. Two major exhibitions a year.

Napoleon called England a "nation of shopkeepers" and it would seem that things haven't changed much since his day. Countless shops of all shapes and sizes abound and if you can't find what you want somewhere in London, it's probably not worth having anyway.

To make things easier, stores are now staying open longer: in the West End late-night shopping is Thursday, while in Knightsbridge, it's Wednesday. In Covent Garden, many shops continue trading in the evening every day and Sunday opening is rapidly gaining ground as well. As the Christmas season approaches, you may find that shops never seem to close at all. The best bargains can be had during the sales—July and after Christmas—but some discount shops and market stalls offer reasonably priced goods all the year round.

Visitors from abroad can be reimbursed for value-added tax (VAT) paid on purchases in the United Kingdom. Simply follow the procedure outlined on p. 207.

For toys and children's shopping, see under CHILDREN, pp. 177-80.

In such a large city, it's only natural that there should be a number of shopping areas which have their own particular character and specialities. In addition, residential areas usually have a main street lined with branches of well-known stores and supermarkets. To help you find your way around the main central commercial spots, they are described below.

The West End is the largest shopping area. Most of the major **63** department stores can be found in **Oxford Street, Regent Street** and **Piccadilly**. There is an amazing array of fashion shops here, and antiques, fine art and jewellery are on sale in **Bond Street** (New and Old), and **South Molton Street**.

Covent Garden blossomed as a chic shopping area during the 1970s when the market moved out and small smart shops and restaurants moved in.

Kensington High Street is a busy street with a good range of shops and the well-known department store, House of Fraser.

King's Road, Chelsea, is the place for the latest popular fashion, especially on Saturday when the young parade up and down.

Knightsbridge is the home of London's most expensive shops, including the world-famous department stores, Harrods and Harvey Nichols.

Glamour products come in glamorous packages.

ARCADES

BURLINGTON ARCADE **22** L8
Piccadilly, W1.

⊖ Piccadilly Circus
or Green Park

A charming covered passageway dating from the Regency era, lined with small exclusive shops which still retain their original Dickensian windows. The period atmosphere is enhanced by the presence of beadles in livery on guard at the entrance.

COVENT GARDEN MARKET **14** N9
Covent Garden, WC2.

⊖ Covent Garden

Set up during the 1970s in the attractive buildings of the former Covent Garden fruit and vegetable market, this has proved a great success and is always busy. There is a good range of small smart shops and cafés, and the added attraction of street musicians and entertainers.

HAY'S GALLERIA **27** T8
London Bridge City, Tooley Street, SE1.

⊖ London Bridge

There is an Underground station nearby, but why not take the pleasant Thames-side walk to one of London's newest shopping arcades, housed in tastefully transformed former warehouses close to the river. A wide selection of shops, stalls and cafés shelters under a glass dome of impressive scale, around a hypnotic kinetic water sculpture.

64

ROYAL OPERA ARCADE **23** M8
Pall Mall, SW1.

⊖ Piccadilly Circus

Designed by John Nash in 1816, this is London's oldest arcade. Its delightful bow-windowed specialist shops cater for the well-heeled.

THE PLAZA, OXFORD STREET **13** L10 ⊖ Tottenham Court Road
Oxford Street, W1. Open Monday to Friday 10 a.m.–8 p.m.; Saturday 10 a.m.–7 p.m.

This modern centre on three floors, with its small, intimate shops, makes a welcome change from the huge department stores. Fountainside Food Court offers varied refreshment facilities.

TOBACCO DOCK
Wapping Lane, Wapping; tel. (071) 702 9681. Open 7 days a week; Monday to Saturday until 8 p.m.

⊖ or DLR to Shadwell

As the name suggests, it's a former tobacco warehouse in the rejuvenated Docklands, transformed into a vast under-cover shopping village with unique Georgian malls and arcades. Branches of many chain stores, as well as specialist shops and cafés. Not far from the Tower, you can view historic ships if you get tired of shopping.

DEPARTMENT STORES

ARMY & NAVY   **32** L5   ⊖ Victoria or St. James's Park
101–105 Victoria Street, SW1; tel. (071) 834 1234. Open Monday to Saturday 9.30 a.m.–6 p.m.
The food hall and wine department are the best parts of this store, which is otherwise competent but unexceptional.

DEBENHAMS   **12** K10   ⊖ Bond Street
344–348 Oxford Street, W1; tel. (071) 580 3000. Open Monday & Saturday 9.30 a.m.–6 p.m.; Tuesday 10 a.m.–6 p.m.; Wednesday to Friday 9.30 a.m.–8 p.m.
A huge range of reasonably priced women's and men's fashions is this store's strong point, with noteworthy kitchenware and china departments, too. A redesigning venture a few years ago unfortunately did not enhance the interior of the shop.

DICKINS & JONES   **13** L9   ⊖ Oxford Circus
224 Regent Street, W1; tel. (071) 734 7070. Open Monday to Saturday 9.30 a.m.–6 p.m. (Thursday until 8 p.m.).
Strong on fashion, with good designer names and stylish accessories, this store has still not entirely shaken off its slightly staid image.

65

FENWICKS OF BOND STREET   **12** K9   ⊖ Bond Street
63 New Bond Street, W1; tel. (071) 629 9161. Open Monday to Saturday 9.30 a.m.–6 p.m. (Thursday until 7.30 p.m.).
Plenty of good-quality women's wear from middle-of-the-range to designer; wonderful lingerie department catering for all tastes and pockets. Also accessories and gifts.

FORTNUM & MASON   **23** L8   ⊖ Piccadilly Circus or Green Park
181 Piccadilly, W1; tel. (071) 734 8040. Open Monday to Friday 9 a.m.–5.30 p.m.; Saturday 9 a.m.–5 p.m.
A paradise for lovers of luxurious foods for over two centuries, this is the place to go for exotic (and expensive) gourmet gifts. Food hampers are a speciality. Less well-known are the store's non-edible goods, including classy women's and men's clothes.

HARRODS   **30** G6   ⊖ Knightsbridge
Brompton Road, Knightsbridge, SW1; tel. (071) 730 1234. Opens 9 a.m. Monday to Saturday; closes 6 p.m. except Wednesday (7 p.m.) and Saturday (5 p.m.).
Probably the world's most famous department store, patronized by many of London's wealthy. You can buy virtually anything here and the

store offers a wide range of services too—at a price. Wonderful for browsing as well as buying. Don't miss the fabulous food halls, still with their original tiling.

HARVEY NICHOLS   **21** H6   ⊖ Knightsbridge
109 Knightsbridge, SW1; tel. (071) 235 5000. Open Monday to Saturday 10 a.m.–7 p.m.
Renowned as Britain's most exclusive high-fashion department store, selling clothes by top British, Continental and US designers. Also stocks household goods and home furnishings.

HOUSE OF FRASER   **12** K10   ⊖ Bond Street or Oxford Circus
318 Oxford Street, W1; tel. (071) 629 8800. Open Monday to Saturday 9.30 a.m.–6 p.m. (Thursday until 8 p.m.).
A good general department store, but with no particularly outstanding qualities.
     There is another branch at 63 Kensington High Street, W8; tel. (071) 937 5432.

JOHN LEWIS   **12** K10   ⊖ Bond Street or Oxford Circus
278–306 Oxford Street, W1; tel. (071) 629 7711. Open Monday to Saturday 9 a.m.–5.30 p.m. (Thursday until 8 p.m.).
66 "Never knowingly undersold" is the motto of this chain of stores, and indeed all its merchandise is competitively priced and of good quality. It boasts a vast range of dress and furnishing fabrics, as well as good crafts, bedding and floor-covering departments.

LIBERTY   **13** L9   ⊖ Oxford Circus
210–220 Regent Street, W1; tel. (071) 734 1234. Open Monday to Saturday 9.30 a.m.–6 p.m. (Thursday until 7.30 p.m.).
Justly world-famous for its exclusive Liberty-print dress and furnishing fabrics, both traditional and modern. Notable also for designer clothes, accessories, unusual jewellery, glassware, china and gifts, all housed in a quaint, partly mock-Tudor building.

SELFRIDGES   **12** J9   ⊖ Marble Arch or Bond Street
400 Oxford Street, W1; tel. (071) 629 1234. Open Monday to Saturday 9.30 a.m.–6 p.m. (Thursday 10 a.m.–8 p.m.).
An outstanding range of household goods, great fashions, a comprehensive electronics department and a recently restyled food hall are among the attractions of this store, still trading in the original, turn-of-the-century building. Convenient for one-store shopping.

ANTIQUES AND COLLECTORS' ITEMS

When shopping for antiques, look for the seal of the professional associations: LAPADA and BADA. Centres like Grays Market (Davies Street, W1) and Bond Street Antique Centre, Antiquarius and Camden Passage gather scores of dealers under one roof. The weekly *Antique Trade Gazette* announces all the auctions and shows. For convenience, we have listed markets and dealers separately.

ANTIQUE MARKETS

ALFIES ANTIQUE MARKET   10 F11   ⊖ Edgware Road
13–25 Church Street, NW8; tel. (071) 723 6066. Open Tuesday to Saturday 10 a.m.–6 p.m.
Claiming to be the largest covered antique market in England, boasts more than 350 stands selling just about everything under the sun.

ANTIQUARIUS   36 G3   ⊖ Sloane Square
135–141 King's Road, SW3; tel. (071) 351 5353. Open Monday to Saturday 10 a.m.–6 p.m.
Probably London's best-known indoor market, housing stalls selling a wide variety of antiques, including china and glass, books, prints and jewellery. Particularly worth visiting for its period clothing.

67

BERMONDSEY MARKET   ⊖ London Bridge
New Caledonian Market, SE1. Open Friday 5 a.m.–2 p.m.
You have to be an early riser to catch the best bargains in this out-of-town street market, the source of stock for many of the capital's antique shops. Haggling is the order of the day.

CAMDEN PASSAGE ANTIQUES MARKET   ⊖ Angel
Camden Passage, Islington, N1; tel. (071) 359 0190. Open Wednesday and Saturday 9 a.m.–4 p.m.; Thursday 7 a.m.–4 p.m.
350 dealers sell at this market: general antiques on Wednesdays and Saturdays; books, prints and drawings on Thursdays.

GRAYS ANTIQUE MARKET   12 J/K9   ⊖ Bond Street
58 Davies Street and 1–7 Davies Mews, W1; tel. (071) 629 7034. Open Monday to Friday 10 a.m.–6 p.m.
Two covered antique markets full of fascinating stalls, where goods are sold under the Grays' guarantee that they are all they are claimed to be.

SHOPPING

PORTOBELLO ROAD MARKET   ⊖ Ladbroke Grove
Portobello Road, Westbourne Grove to Colville Terrace, W11. Open Saturday 7 a.m.–5 p.m.
Antique and bric-à-brac stalls occupy a fair-sized section of Portobello Road's bustling general market. You're no longer likely to discover the bargain of the century, but it's great fun nevertheless.

ANTIQUE DEALERS

ADAMS ANTIQUES   ⊖ Chalk Farm
47 Chalk Farm Road, NW1; tel. (071) 267 9241. Open every day 10 a.m.–6 p.m.
While many shops are now offering reproduction pine furniture, this spacious store sells plenty of genuine antique pieces.

ANDREW EDMUNDS   13 L9   ⊖ Piccadilly Circus or Oxford Circus
44 Lexington Street, W1; tel. (071) 437 8594. Open Monday to Friday 10 a.m.–6 p.m.
A delightfully chaotic shop selling 18th- and 19th-century prints, many satirical, by artists such as George Cruikshank and William Hogarth.

68

BUTTON QUEEN   12 J10   ⊖ Bond Street
19 Marylebone Lane, W1; tel. (071) 935 1505. Open Monday to Friday 10 a.m.–6 p.m.; Saturday 10 a.m.–1.30 p.m.
On sale here are billions of buttons, both ancient and modern, in every imaginable style, shape and material. Buckles as well.

CAMERER CUSS   23 L8   ⊖ Green Park
17 Ryder Street, SW1; tel. (071) 930 1941. Open Monday to Friday 9.30 a.m.–5.30 p.m.
Over two centuries' experience in the business lies behind this firm's expertise in selling high-quality antique clocks and watches.

T. CROWTHER & SONS   ⊖ Fulham Broadway
282 North End Road, SW6; tel. (071) 385 1375. Open Monday to Friday 9 a.m.–5.30 p.m.
Lots of fine (and expensive) architectural antiques, including garden statuary and other ornaments. Specializes in fireplaces and wrought ironwork.

DAVID BLACK ORIENTAL CARPETS   ⊖ Holland Park
96 Portland Road, W11; tel. (071) 727 2566. Open Monday to Friday 10 a.m.–6 p.m.; Saturday 11 a.m.–5.30 p.m.

Feast your eyes on the colourful displays of fine rugs here. Owner David Black knows what he's talking about when it comes to Oriental carpets and has written several books on the subject.

DONAY ANTIQUES   ⊖ Angel

35 Camden Passage, N1; tel. (071) 359 1880. Open Tuesday to Saturday 9 a.m.–5 p.m. (Wednesday 7.30 a.m.–5.30 p.m.).

How did people manage before the invention of Monopoly and Trivial Pursuit? Find out by visiting this fascinating antique games shop, which also sells decorative items.

GALLERY OF ANTIQUE COSTUME   **10** F11   ⊖ Edgware Road
AND TEXTILES

2 Church Street, NW8; tel. (071) 723 9981. Open Monday to Saturday 10 a.m.–5.30 p.m.

One of Europe's biggest suppliers of antique clothing, quilts, wall-hangings and fabrics, many of them Victorian and Edwardian. Costumes, however, go up to the 1940s and textiles to the 1920s. An offshoot is the antique cushion shop, Pillows of London, at 48 Church Street, NW8; tel. (071) 723 3171.

HARVEYS ANTIQUES   **22** L8   ⊖ Green Park

5 Old Bond Street, W1; tel. (071) 499 8385. Open Monday to Saturday 10 a.m.–5.30 p.m.

The period 1680 to 1830 is represented by this top-end-of-the-market **69** selection of English furniture and furnishings.

I. & J. L. BROWN ANTIQUES   ⊖ Fulham Broadway

636 King's Road, SW6; tel. (071) 736 4141. Open Monday to Saturday 9 a.m.–5.30 p.m.

One of the few specialists selling 18th- and 19th-century English and French country oak furniture. At the same address, Peter Place Antiques, tel. (071) 736 9945, sell decorative items, including lighting and architectural antiques.

LONDON SILVER VAULTS   **15** P10   ⊖ Chancery Lane

Chancery House, 53 Chancery Lane, WC2; tel. (071) 242 3844. Open Monday to Friday 9 a.m.–5.30 p.m.; Saturday 9 a.m.–12.30 p.m.

Antique and modern silverware and jewellery are sold by a number of dealers with subterranean sales pitches where security is high and window-shopping is not encouraged. There is also one china vault.

NUMBER NINETEEN   ⊖ Angel

19 Camden Passage, N1; tel. (071) 226 1126. Open Tuesday to Saturday 10 a.m.–5 p.m.

The speciality of this intriguing, up-market shop is that it doesn't specialize, but sells a delightful motley of often eccentric antiques.

THE PATCHWORK DOG & THE CALICO CAT ⊖ Camden Town
or Chalk Farm
21 Chalk Farm Road, NW1; tel. (071) 485 1239. Open Monday to Saturday 10 a.m.–6 p.m.
Here you can purchase a fine antique English or American quilt or, if the mood takes you, buy the templates and patterns to make your own.

SPINK & SON   **23** L8   ⊖ Green Park
5–7 King Street, SW1; tel. (071) 930 7888. Open Monday to Friday 9.30 a.m.–5.30 p.m.
Specialists in Oriental art, textiles, English paintings, fine English silver and paperweights, glass, coins and medals.

WHITEWAY & WALDRON   ⊖ Fulham Broadway
or Hammersmith
305 Munster Road, SW6; tel. (071) 381 3195. Open Monday to Friday 10 a.m.–6 p.m.; Saturday 11 a.m.–4 p.m.
Those whose tastes in home décor lean towards the ecclesiastical may well find what they want here—stained glass, church furniture, Gothic pews, panelling, statues and other liturgical paraphernalia.

WILLIAM BEDFORD   ⊖ Angel
70 *The Merchants Hall, 46 Essex Road, N1; tel. (071) 226 9648. Open Monday to Saturday 9.30 a.m.–5.30 p.m.*
An enormous sales area (it's in a disused cinema) packed with English furniture of the 18th and early-19th centuries.

BOOKS ANTIQUARIAN AND SECOND-HAND

 BELL, BOOK AND RADMALL   **23** N9   ⊖ Leicester Square
Cecil Court, WC2; tel. (071) 240 2161. Open Monday to Friday 10 a.m.–5.30 p.m.
First editions of 20th-century English and American literature.

FREW MACKENZIE   **14** M10   ⊖ Tottenham Court Road
106 Great Russell Street, WC1; tel. (071) 580 2311. Open Monday to Friday 10 a.m.–6 p.m.; Saturday 10 a.m.–2 p.m.
Top-of-the-price-range modern first editions, as well as fine and rare antiquarian books on literature and travel. Also sell some illustrated publications.

PLEASURES OF PAST TIMES   **23** N9   ⊖ Leicester Square
11 Cecil Court, WC2; tel. (071) 836 1142. Open Monday to Friday 11 a.m.–2.30 p.m. and 3.30–5.45 p.m.; Saturday by arrangement.
As the name suggests, antiquarian and second-hand books (mainly on the performing arts) are a speciality of this shop, which also sells early children's books and Victorian greetings cards.

SOTHERANS   **23** L8   ⊖ Piccadilly Circus
2–5 Sackville Street, W1; tel. (071) 439 6151. Open Monday to Friday 9.30 a.m.–6 p.m.; Saturday 10 a.m.–4 p.m.
Long-established dealers in rare books, periodicals, maps and prints.

WALDEN BOOKS   ⊖ Camden Town or Chalk Farm
38 Harmood Street, NW1; tel. (071) 267 8146. Open Thursday to Sunday 10.30 a.m.–6.30 p.m.
Stocks a vast quantity of second-hand books on all subjects.

BOOKS NEW

BOOKS ETC   **13** M10   ⊖ Tottenham Court Road
120 Charing Cross Road, WC2; tel. (071) 379 6838. Open Monday to Saturday 9.30 a.m.–8 p.m.
A good, general bookshop with an easily negotiated layout.

71

BOOKS FOR COOKS   ⊖ Ladbroke Grove
4 Blenheim Crescent, W11; tel. (071) 221 1992. Open Monday to Saturday 9.30 a.m.–6 p.m.
Every imaginable type of book dealing with culinary art—British, Continental and American.

COLLET'S INTERNATIONAL   **13** M10   ⊖ Tottenham Court Road
129–131 Charing Cross Road, WC2; tel. (071) 734 0782. Open Monday to Friday 10 a.m.–6.30 p.m.; Saturday 10 a.m.–6 p.m.
Strong on the social sciences and foreign literature. Specializes in Russian and Eastern European books, both in the original language and English translation; also Russian and Eastern European journals and periodicals, records, tapes and CDs.

COMPENDIUM   ⊖ Camden Town
234 Camden High Street, NW1; tel. (071) 485 8944. Open Monday to Saturday 10 a.m.–6 p.m.; Sunday noon–6 p.m.
One of London's leading contemporary bookshops, with titles covering a wide range of subjects, including politics, philosophy, psychology, women's studies, fiction and poetry.

DILLONS **13** M11   ⊖ Goodge Street
82 Gower Street, WC1; tel. (071) 636 1577. Open Monday to Saturday 9 a.m.–5.30 p.m. (Tuesday and Saturday opens at 9.30 a.m.).
Formerly known as Dillons University Bookshop, this large store still stocks an excellent selection of academic and scientific books, as well as masses of publications for the less serious reader. It's well-organized and finding what you want is easy.

FOYLES **13** M10   ⊖ Leicester Square or Tottenham Court Road
119 Charing Cross Road, WC2; tel. (071) 437 5660. Open Monday to Saturday 9 a.m.–6 p.m.(Thursday until 7 p.m.).
This vast, world-famous bookstore sells just about every British book in print, but you need patience to find your way around its cluttered, rather confusing layout.

GRANT & CUTLER **13** L10   ⊖ Oxford Circus
or Tottenham Court Road
55–57 Great Marlborough Street, W1; tel. (071) 734 2012. Open Monday to Friday 9 a.m.–5.30 p.m.; Saturday 9 a.m.–1 p.m.
An excellent choice of new and second-hand foreign-language and literature books—French, German, Italian, Spanish and Portuguese.

72 **HATCHARDS** **23** L8   ⊖ Green Park or Piccadilly Circus
187–188 Piccadilly, W1; tel. (071) 437 3924/439 9921. Open Monday to Friday 9 a.m.–6 p.m.; Saturday 9 a.m.–5 p.m.
This firm has been trading on the same site for almost 300 years and has several branches in other areas of London. Knowledgeable staff sell newly published books in the lower part of the building; fine antiquarian books are upstairs.

HMSO **15** O10   ⊖ Holborn
(HER MAJESTY'S STATIONERY OFFICE)
49 High Holborn, WC1; tel. (071) 873 0011. Open Monday to Friday 8.15 a.m.–6.15 p.m.; Saturday 9 a.m.–1 p.m.
All the government publications you could wish for: thousands of books published annually on every subject, plus White Papers, Bills, Acts and, of course, Hansard.

MURDER ONE **14** M10   ⊖ Tottenham Court Road
23 Denmark Street, WC2; tel. (071) 497 2200. Open Monday to Saturday 10 a.m.–6 p.m. (Thursday until 7 p.m.).
Devoted to the sale of crime and murder mystery books that make your hair stand on end.

PAN BOOKSHOP   **35** E3   ⊖ South Kensington
*158 Fulham Road, SW10; tel. (071) 373 4997. Open Monday to
Saturday 10 a.m.–10 p.m.; Sunday 12–9.30 p.m.*
Not just paperbacks, as the name might suggest, but also an
impressive selection of hardbacks, from a wide range of publishers.

PENGUIN BOOKSHOP   **14** N9   ⊖ Covent Garden
*10 The Market, Covent Garden, WC2; tel. (071) 379 7650. Open
Monday to Saturday 10 a.m.–8 p.m.; Sunday noon–6 p.m.*
Amost every Penguin adult title here, as well as some paper- and
hardbacks from other publishers. Other branches in Camden High
Street, tel. (071) 485 1328, and 157 King's Road, tel. (071) 351 1915
(arts bookshop).

WATERSTONES   **13** M10   ⊖ Tottenham Court Road
*121–125 Charing Cross Road, WC2; tel. (071) 434 4291. Open
Monday and Wednesday to Friday 9.30 a.m.–7.30 p.m.; Tuesday
10 a.m.–7.30 p.m.; Saturday 10.30 a.m.–7 p.m.*
A comprehensive selection of general books efficiently arranged to
enable easy location of any title. Several branches around London.

A. ZWEMMER   **14** M9   ⊖ Leicester Square
*24 Litchfield Street, WC2; tel. (071) 836 4710. Open Monday to
Saturday 9.30 a.m.–6 p.m.*
Lots of good English and foreign-language books on art and architecture. Also a branch at No. 26 dealing in books on photography and
one at 80 Charing Cross Road specializing in works on music.

73

CHINA & GLASS

CHINACRAFT   **11** H9   ⊖ Marble Arch
*499 Oxford Street, W1; tel. (071) 499 9881. Open Monday to Saturday
9 a.m.–6 p.m. (Thursday until 7.30 p.m.).*
Part of a chain selling fine, mainly English, china, figurines and
glassware.

CRAFTSMEN POTTERS SHOP   **13** L9   ⊖ Oxford Circus
*7 Marshall Street, W1; tel. (071) 437 7605. Open Monday to Saturday
10 a.m.–5.30 p.m. (Thursday until 7 p.m.).*
A high standard of handmade pottery, both useful and decorative,
produced by members of the Craftsmen Potters Association.

THE GENERAL TRADING COMPANY   **30** H4   ⊖ Sloane Square
*144 Sloane Street, SW1; tel. (071) 730 0411. Open Monday to Friday
9 a.m.–5.30 p.m. (Wednesday until 7 p.m.); Saturday 9 a.m.–2 p.m.*
A large selection of modern English and Continental china, as well as
kitchenware and other bits and pieces for the home.

GERED WATERFORD WEDGWOOD   **22** L8   ⊖ Green Park
*173 Piccadilly, W1; tel. (071) 629 2614. Open Monday to Friday 9 a.m.–
6 p.m.; Saturday 9 a.m.–4 p.m.*
Probably the best place in London to see displays of traditional English
china, crystal, glass- and earthenware—own brands, as well as others
such as Spode and Royal Doulton. Other branches in Regent Street
and Oxford Circus.

LAWLEYS   **13** L9   ⊖ Oxford Circus or Piccadilly Circus
*154 Regent Street, W1; tel. (071) 734 2621. Open Monday to Saturday
9.30 a.m.–6 p.m. (Thursday until 7 p.m.).*
Well-known makes of china and glass are sold in this popular chain.

REJECT CHINA SHOP   **30** G5   ⊖ Knightsbridge
*33–35 Beauchamp Place, SW3; tel. (071) 581 0737. Open Monday to
Saturday 9 a.m.–6 p.m. (until 7 p.m. on Wednesday).*
China, glass and silverware "seconds" are sold here at bargain
74 prices—and the flaws are often hardly detectable. Perfect goods can
also be purchased at a discount. Also another branch at 183 Brompton
Road, tel. (071) 581 0739.

ROSENTHAL STUDIO HOUSE   **30** G6   ⊖ Knightsbridge
*102 Brompton Road, SW3; tel. (071) 584 0683. Open Monday to
Saturday 9 a.m.–6 p.m. (Wednesday until 7 p.m.).*
An excellent selection of modern china, including the shop's own
brand, plus glassware. Also under the name of Wilson & Gill, 137–141
Regent Street, tel. (071) 734 3076.

THOMAS GOODE   **22** J8   ⊖ Bond Street or Green Park
*19 South Audley Street, W1; tel. (071) 499 2823. Open Monday to
Saturday 9.30 a.m.–5.30 p.m. (Tuesday opens at 10 a.m.).*
A very up-market shop selling fine china, exquisite glass and beautiful
silverware. Also a lighting department offering crystal chandeliers.

VILLEROY & BOCH   **13** L9   ⊖ Oxford Circus or Piccadilly Circus
*155 Regent Street, W1; tel. (071) 434 0249. Open Monday to Saturday
9.30 a.m.–6 p.m. (Thursday until 7 p.m.).*
A wide range of stylish china and glass is available here at more
affordable prices than you might expect at first glance.

FABRICS

ALEXANDER FURNISHINGS 12 J10 ⊖ Bond Street
51–61 Wigmore Street, W1; tel. (071) 935 7806. Open Monday to Friday 9 a.m.–6 p.m.(Thursday until 7 p.m.); Saturday 9 a.m.–1 p.m.
Pick up a bargain here, where furnishing fabric by well-known firms is sold at a discount.

ALLANS 12 J9 ⊖ Bond Street
56–58 Duke Street, W1; tel. (071) 629 3781. Open Monday to Friday 9 a.m.–5.45 p.m.; Saturday 9 a.m.–1 p.m.
Their dressmaking fabrics cover the whole spectrum of prices, including a silk recorded in the *Guinness Book of Records* as the most expensive in the world. The selection for evening and bridal wear is particularly good.

BOROVICK FABRICS 13 L9 ⊖ Oxford Circus
or Tottenham Court Road
16 Berwick Street, W1; tel. (071) 437 2180. Open Monday to Friday 9 a.m.–6 p.m.; Saturday 9 a.m.–1 p.m.
A rich tapestry of colourful dressmaking fabrics from all over the world, popular with television, theatre and film companies. Also bridal **75** material.

BY THE YARD 13 L9 ⊖ Oxford Circus
or Tottenham Court Road
14 Berwick Street, W1; tel. (071) 434 2389. Open Monday to Friday 8.30 a.m.–6 p.m.; Saturday 8.30 a.m.–5 p.m.
As the name suggests, metrification has not yet penetrated this shop. There are fake furs, silks, velvets and glittery fabrics galore, and many bargains to be had.

IAN MANKIN ⊖ Chalk Farm
109 Regent's Park Road, NW1; tel. (071) 722 0997. Open Monday to Friday 10 a.m.–5.30 p.m.; Saturday 10 a.m.–4 p.m.
Reasonably priced, unglazed natural fabrics for upholstery and soft furnishings, such as ticking, muslin, hessian and canvas.

MATERIAL WORLD ⊖ Fulham Broadway
59 New King's Road, SW6; tel. (071) 384 2231. Open Monday to Saturday 9.30 a.m.–6 p.m.
Upholstery and furnishing material at budget prices, including own label.

FASHION

London may not be Paris as far as the fashion scene is concerned, but it does offer a tremendous choice. You can find anything and everything here, from classic raincoats and woollens to the latest trends of today, tomorrow and yesterday!

CLOTHES FOR MEN AND WOMEN

ALLY CAPELLINO   23 M9   ⊖ Piccadilly Circus
95 Wardour Street, W1; tel. (071) 494 0768. Opens noon Tuesday to Saturday; closes 5.30 p.m., except Wednesday and Thursday (7 p.m.).
Beautiful, expensive clothes for both sexes, designed by owner Alison Lloyd.

AQUASCUTUM   23 L9   ⊖ Piccadilly Circus
100 Regent Street, W1; tel. (071) 734 6090. Open Monday to Saturday 9 a.m.–6 p.m. (Thursday until 7 p.m.).
Classic men's and women's raincoats, overcoats, jackets, suits, knitwear and accessories are sold in this world-famous shop. Expensive, but of excellent quality.

ARTÉ   30 H4   ⊖ Sloane Square
55 King's Road, SW3; tel. (071) 730 3607. Open Monday to Saturday 10 a.m.–6 p.m. (Wednesday until 7 p.m.).
Younger fashion enthusiasts will love the daring creations on sale here.

AUSTIN REED   23 L9   ⊖ Piccadilly Circus
103–113 Regent Street, W1; tel. (071) 734 6789. Opens Monday to Saturday 9 a.m. (Tuesday 9.30 a.m.); closes 5.30 p.m. (Thursday 7 p.m.).
A large store with a huge stock of dependable, good-quality menswear. The department known as Cue Shop carries trendier styles for younger men, and women's clothing is sold in the Options section.

BELVILLE SASSOON   30 H6   ⊖ Knightsbridge
73 Pavilion Road, SW1; tel. (071) 235 5801. Open Monday to Friday 9.30 a.m.–5.30 p.m.
A fine collection of ready-to-wear day, cocktail and evening apparel, plus elegant made-to-measure clothes.

BENETTON   **13** K10   ⊖ Oxford Circus
255–259 Regent Street, W1; tel. (071) 493 8600. Open Monday to Saturday 10 a.m.–6.30 p.m. (Thursday until 8 p.m.).
Vividly coloured, unisex separates and knits in young, casual styles that tend to be overpriced. Several branches in other parts of London as well.

BLAZER   **14** N9/10   ⊖ Covent Garden
36 and 117b Long Acre, Covent Garden, WC2; tel. (071) 379 6258/ 0456. Open Monday to Saturday 10 a.m.–6.30 p.m. (Thursday until 8 p.m.).
Good-quality menswear is available at No. 36, while at No. 117b more formal clothing is sold under the Blazer label.

BROWNS   **12** J/K9   ⊖ Bond Street
23–27 South Molton Street, W1; tel. (071) 491 7833. Open Monday to Saturday 10 a.m.–6 p.m. (Thursday until 7 p.m.).
Top British and international designer clothes and accessories are on sale in this exclusive shop. You can bank on high fashion at high prices.

BURBERRYS   **23** M8/9   ⊖ Piccadilly Circus
18–22 Haymarket, SW1; tel. (071) 930 3343. Open Monday to Saturday 9 a.m.–5.30 p.m. (Thursday until 7 p.m.).
Best known for its high-quality raincoats with the distinctive check lining, Burberrys also sells other own-label garments and accessories for men, women and children.

77

C & A   **11** H9   ⊖ Marble Arch
501–519 Oxford Street, W1; tel. (071) 629 7272. Open Monday to Friday 9.30 a.m.–7 p.m. (Thursday until 8 p.m.); Saturday 9 a.m.–6 p.m.
Fashionable clothes at reasonable prices for men, women and children. Good-value ski-wear—the anoraks are ideal for British winters as well as the snow-covered slopes. Other branches throughout the capital.

CAROLINE CHARLES   **30** G5   ⊖ Knightsbridge
56–57 Beauchamp Place, SW3; tel. (071) 589 5850. Open Monday to Friday 9.30 a.m.–5.30 p.m. (Wednesday until 6 p.m.); Saturday 10 a.m.–5.30 p.m.
Exclusive ready-to-wear women's clothes, designed on classic lines using beautiful fabrics and rich colours. A recent move to larger premises has enabled the company to offer a range of menswear, as well.

CECIL GEE **14** N9 ⊖ Covent Garden
47 Long Acre, WC2; tel. (071) 240 1020. Open Monday to Saturday 9.30 a.m.–6.30 p.m. (Friday until 7.30 p.m.).
A full range of menswear and accessories, a little on the expensive side.

DANIEL HECHTER **12** K9 ⊖ Bond Street
105 New Bond Street, W1; tel. (071) 493 1153. Open Monday to Saturday 9.45 a.m.–6.30 p.m. (Thursday until 7 p.m.).
Men's and women's designer clothes that are slow to date.

EDINA RONAY **36** G3 ⊖ Sloane Square
141 King's Road, SW3; tel. (071) 352 1085. Open Monday to Friday 10 a.m.–6 p.m. (Wednesday until 7 p.m.); Saturday 11 a.m.–6 p.m.
Simple, elegant women's wear of excellent quality.

EMPORIO ARMANI **30** G6 ⊖ Knightsbridge
191 Brompton Road, SW3; tel. (071) 823 8818. Open Monday to Saturday 10 a.m.–6 p.m. (Wednesday until 7 p.m.).
Very stylish clothes for men, women and children, by talented Italian designer Giorgio Armani.

FRENCH CONNECTION **14** N9 ⊖ Covent Garden
12 James Street, WC2; tel. (071) 836 0522. Open Monday to Saturday 10.30 a.m.–7 p.m. (Thursday until 8 p.m.); Sunday noon–6 p.m.
Distinctive women's garments made especially for the French Connection label, usually in muted colours. The prices tend to be a little high considering the variable quality of the workmanship. French Connection for Men is at 55–56 Long Acre, WC2; tel. (071) 379 6560.

78

HENNES **11** H9 ⊖ Marble Arch
481 Oxford Street, W1; tel. (071) 493 8557. Open Monday to Friday 10 a.m.–6.30 p.m. (Thursday until 8 p.m.); Saturday 9.30 a.m.–6 p.m.
High-fashion gear for the young and budget-conscious of both sexes.

HYPER-HYPER **19** D6 ⊖ High Street Kensington
26–40 Kensington High Street, W8; tel. (071) 937 6964. Open Monday to Saturday 10 a.m.–6 p.m.
This showcase for the work of young British designers, who are allocated individual units within the store, offers a great selection of avant-garde clothing for women and men.

IN-WEAR **36** G3 ⊖ Sloane Square
150 King's Road, SW3; tel. (071) 351 7474. Open Monday to Saturday 10 a.m.–6 p.m. (Wednesday until 7 p.m.).
Smart women's wear in easy-to-care-for fabrics at middling prices.

JAEGER   **13** L9   ⊖ Oxford Circus
200–206 Regent Street, W1; tel. (071) 734 8211. Open Monday to Saturday 9.30 a.m.–6 p.m. (Thursday until 8 p.m.).
Sophisticated, well-made, classic garments for women and men are sold in this famous shop.

KATHARINE HAMNETT   **30** H6   ⊖ Knightsbridge
20 Sloane Street, SW1; tel. (071) 823 1002. Open Monday to Saturday 9.30 a.m.–6 p.m.; Wednesday 10 a.m.–7 p.m.
Katharine Hamnett's designs range from the outlandish to the simple but stylish (for which she is probably better known).

LAURA ASHLEY   **13** K10   ⊖ Oxford Circus
256–258 Regent Street, W1; tel. (071) 437 9760. Open Monday to Friday 9.30 a.m.–6 p.m. (Thursday until 8 p.m.); Saturday 9 a.m.–6 p.m.
The distinctive Laura Ashley prints are still to be found decorating the women's clothes sold by this chain, though not so prominently as of yore. Attempts to move up-market in recent years have been accompanied by higher prices, which are not always matched by quality.

MARKS & SPENCER   **13** L10   ⊖ Oxford Circus
173 Oxford Street, W1; tel. (071) 437 7722. Opens 9.30 a.m. Monday to Friday; closes 6 p.m. except Wednesday and Friday (7 p.m.); Saturday 9 a.m.–6.30 p.m.
An introduction is scarcely needed to this world-famous chain store that sells reasonably priced, good-quality clothing for all the family. The woollens, shirts and underwear are particularly popular items. Another large branch is to be found further down the road at No. 458; tel. (071) 935 7954.

79

MONSOON   **12** J/K9   ⊖ Bond Street
67 South Molton Street, W1; tel. (071) 499 3987. Open Monday to Saturday 10 a.m.–6 p.m. (Thursday until 7 p.m.).
Glowingly coloured Eastern cottons and silks dominate this women's wear shop. Its attractive and popular party clothes are good value. Other branches throughout London, including one at 23 Covent Garden, tel. (071) 836 9140.

MULBERRY   **12** J10   ⊖ Bond Street
11–12 Gees Court, W1; tel. (071) 493 2546. Open Monday to Saturday 10 a.m.–6 p.m. (Thursday until 7 p.m.).
Sells stylish, well-made belts, bags and accessories at fairly high prices.

NEWPORT   **24** N9   ⊖ Covent Garden

3–7 Southampton Street, WC2; tel. (071) 831 1501. Open Monday to Friday 9.30 a.m.–7 p.m.; Saturday 9.30 a.m.–6.30 p.m.
Comfortable, simple, attractive garments, all in natural fabrics, for women and men. Also clothes with the Marc O'Polo label.

NEXT   **13** L9   ⊖ Oxford Circus

160 Regent Street, W1; tel. (071) 434 2515. Open Monday to Saturday 10 a.m.–6 p.m. (Thursday until 8 p.m.).
The chain that mushroomed during the 1980s, bringing affordable stylish clothes, shoes and accessories to high-street shoppers.

PAUL SMITH   **14** N9   ⊖ Covent Garden

41–44 Floral Street, WC2; tel. (071) 379 7133. Open Monday to Saturday 10 a.m.–6.30 p.m. (Thursday until 7 p.m.).
Own-label, stylish men's clothing, including sportswear.

RED OR DEAD   **14** N10   ⊖ Covent Garden

33 Neal Street, WC2; tel. (071) 379 7571. Open Monday to Saturday 10.30 a.m.–7.30 p.m. (Thursday until 8.30 p.m. and Saturday until 7 p.m.); Sunday 12.30 p.m.–7 p.m.
Trendy, outrageous fashions for both sexes, and a unique line in shoes.

RIVER ISLAND   **28** C6   ⊖ High Street Kensington

80

124 Kensington High Street, W8; tel. (071) 937 0224. Open Monday to Saturday 9 a.m.–6 p.m. (Thursday until 7.30 p.m.).
Very affordable trendy clothes and accessories for younger women, and reasonably priced, but less lively, menswear.

SIMPSON   **23** L8   ⊖ Piccadilly Circus

203 Piccadilly, W1; tel. (071) 734 2002. Open Monday to Saturday 9 a.m.–5.30 p.m. (Thursday until 7 p.m.).
In this large department store, whose own label is DAKS, the emphasis is on high-quality, English clothes for both sexes. British and international designers are also represented.

TOP SHOP/TOP MAN   **13** K10   ⊖ Oxford Circus

214-216 Oxford Street, W1; tel. (071) 636 7700. Open Monday to Saturday 10 a.m.–6.30 p.m. (Thursday until 8 p.m.).
A vast array of inexpensive clothes for the young, plus dearer youthful designer fashions, sold from boutiques within the shop.

WALLIS   **13** L10   ⊖ Oxford Circus

215 Oxford Street, W1; tel. (071) 439 8669. Open Monday to Saturday 9 a.m.–6 p.m. (Thursday 9.30–8 p.m.).
Well-made, tasteful women's clothes at middle-of-the-range prices.

WAREHOUSE   **13** L10   ϴ Oxford Circus
19 Argyll Street, W1; tel. (071) 437 7101. Open Monday to Saturday 9.30 a.m.–6 p.m. (Thursday until 8 p.m.).
Rapidly changing selections of fashionable women's wear at budget prices. Another branch at 27 Duke Street; tel. (071) 486 5270.

WORKERS FOR FREEDOM   **23** L9   ϴ Piccadilly Circus
4 Lower John Street, W1; tel. (071) 734 3767. Open Monday to Saturday 10.30 a.m.–6 p.m.
Innovative men's and women's clothes designed and sold by this highly successful team. The name is misleading—their prices are high.

ZANDRA RHODES   **22** K9   ϴ Green Park
14a Grafton Street, W1; tel. (071) 499 6695. Open Monday to Friday 9.30 a.m.–6 p.m.; Saturday 9.30 a.m.–5 p.m.
Distinctively flamboyant and beautiful women's clothes (especially evening wear) by this colourful British designer who is now something of an institution.

DISCOUNT AND SECOND-HAND CLOTHES   **81**

BROWNS "LABEL FOR LESS"   **12** J/K9   ϴ Bond Street
18 South Molton Street, W1; tel. (071) 493 1230. Open Monday to Saturday 10 a.m.–6 p.m. (Thursday until 7 p.m.).
Garments by top designers, usually just one season old, are sold at up to 70% off retail prices.

DESIGNERS SALE STUDIO   **36** F3   ϴ Sloane Square
241 King's Road, SW3; tel. (071) 351 4171. Open Monday to Friday 10 a.m.–7 p.m.; Saturday 10 a.m.–6 p.m.
Brand-new clothes by leading designers at up to 60% less than the retail price.

DESIGNS   ϴ Hampstead
60 Rosslyn Hill, NW3; tel. (071) 435 0100. Open Monday to Saturday 10 a.m.–5.45 p.m. (Thursday until 7.45 p.m.).
No item is more than two seasons old here, and you could pick up a nearly-new designer garment at a bargain price. Also brand-new clothes at competitive prices.

FLIP ORIGINAL AMERICAN CLOTHING   **14** N9   ⊖ Covent Garden
*125 Long Acre, WC2; tel. (071) 836 7044. Open Monday to Saturday
10 a.m.–7 p.m. (Thursday until 8 p.m.); Sunday noon–7 p.m.*
Two floors packed with a huge selection of second-hand American
clothing from recent decades, including sportswear.

PAMELA'S DRESS AGENCY   **30** G5   ⊖ South Kensington
*93 Walton Street, SW3; tel. (071) 589 6852. Open Monday to Friday
10 a.m.–5 p.m.; Saturday 10 a.m.–1 p.m.*
A selection of top designer labels not more than two years old.

PANDORA   **30** G6   ⊖ Knightsbridge
*16–22 Cheval Place, SW7; tel. (071) 589 5289. Open Monday to
Saturday 10 a.m.–5 p.m.*
An impressive array of second-hand haute couture garments is sold in
this well-known shop. Hats, shoes and bags are also available.

THE DRESSER   **10** F9   ⊖ Paddington or Lancaster Gate
*39–41 Sussex Place, W2; tel. (071) 724 7212. Open Tuesday to
Saturday 11 a.m.–5.30 p.m.*
A range of women's and men's second-hand designer clothes only two
seasons old and in tip-top condition.

THE FROCK EXCHANGE   **34** C1   ⊖ Fulham Broadway
82 *450 Fulham Road, SW6; tel. (071) 381 2937. Open Monday to Saturday
10 a.m.–5.30 p.m.*
Nearly-new clothes ranging from chain-store to designer-label.

HATS

DAVID SHILLING   **11** H11   ⊖ Baker Street
*44 Chiltern Street, W1; tel. (071) 487 3179. Open Monday to Friday
9.30 a.m.–5.30 p.m. (though it's best to make an appointment).*
Everyone must remember the extravagant hats worn by Mrs. Shilling at
Ascot; her son is carrying on the family tradition with his exclusive
millinery models.

HERBERT JOHNSON   **12** K9   ⊖ Bond Street
*30 New Bond Street, W1; tel. (071) 408 1174. Open Monday to Friday
9.45 a.m.–6 p.m.; Saturday 10 a.m.–5 p.m.*
A good range of men's and women's hats is available from this long-
established firm.

SIMONE MIRMAN   **31** H6   ⊖ Knightsbridge
11 West Halkin Street, SW1; tel. (071) 235 2656. Open Monday to
Friday 9 a.m.–5.30 p.m.; Saturday 10 a.m.–2 p.m.
Out-of-the-ordinary hats are created by this exclusive milliner.

THE HAT SHOP   **14** N10   ⊖ Covent Garden
58 Neal Street, WC2; tel. (071) 836 6718. Open Monday to Friday
10 a.m.–6 p.m. (Friday until 7 p.m.); Saturday 10 a.m.–5.30 p.m.
Hats of every description for both sexes from classics to designer
numbers.

KNITWEAR

CAROLYN BRUNN   **30** G5   ⊖ South Kensington
211 Brompton Road, SW3; tel. (071) 584 9065. Open Monday to
Saturday 10 a.m.–6 p.m.
Good-quality knitted dresses, cardigans and jumpers at value-for-
money prices.

JOAN CHATTERLEY   **14** N10   ⊖ Covent Garden
38 Shorts Gardens, WC2; tel. (071) 379 5473. Open Monday to
Saturday 10 a.m.–6 p.m.
Attractive, handmade sweaters and cardigans designed by Joan
Chatterley. Also clothes and accessories.

NATURALLY BRITISH   **24** N9   ⊖ Leicester Square
13 New Row, WC2; tel. (071) 240 0551/2. Open Monday to Saturday
10.30 a.m.–6.30 p.m.
Beautifully made hand-knits in wonderful colours.

SAM FISHER   **14** N10   ⊖ Covent Garden or Tottenham Court Road
72 Neal Street, WC2; tel. (071) 836 2576. Open Monday to Saturday
10.30 a.m.–7 p.m.
As well as the full range of traditional outdoor "country" clothes, you can
buy hand-framed sweaters in lovely colours and patterns.

SCOTTISH MERCHANT   **24** N9   ⊖ Covent Garden
16 New Row, WC2; tel. (071) 836 2207. Open Monday to Friday
10.30 a.m.–6.30 p.m. (Thursday until 7 p.m.); Saturday 10.30 a.m.–
5.30 p.m.
A fine selection of seasonally changing knitted goods from north of the
border.

THE SCOTCH HOUSE   21 H6   ⊖ Knightsbridge
2 Brompton Road, SW1; tel. (071) 581 2151. Open Monday to Saturday 9 a.m.–6 p.m. (Wednesday until 7 p.m.).
A wide choice of traditional Scottish knitwear in Shetland wool, lambswool and cashmere by famous manufacturers. Also Fair Isle and Aran woollens.

WESTAWAY & WESTAWAY   14 M/N10   ⊖ Tottenham Court Road
62–65 & 92 Great Russell Street, WC1; tel. (071) 405 4479 and 636 1718. Open Monday to Saturday 9 a.m.–5.30 p.m.
Reasonably priced knitwear in traditional styles and patterns is sold in this shop, situated close to the British Museum.

SHOES

ANELLO & DAVIDE   14 N10   ⊖ Covent Garden
35 Drury Lane, WC2; tel. (071) 836 1983. Open Monday to Friday 9 a.m.–5.30 p.m.; Saturday 9 a.m.–5 p.m.
Well-known makers of good dance and theatrical shoes at reasonable prices. Also bridal footwear.

84

BERTIE   12 J9   ⊖ Bond Street
409 Oxford Street, W1; tel. (071) 629 5833. Open Monday to Saturday 10 a.m.–6.30 p.m. (Thursday until 8 p.m.).
Imaginative styles in a good range of colours. Prices are higher than those of the average high-street chain but are still within reach.

CHURCH'S   22 K9   ⊖ Bond Street or Green Park
163 New Bond Street, W1; tel. (071) 499 9449. Open Monday to Saturday 9 a.m.–5.30 p.m. (Thursday until 7 p.m.).
Good-quality, good-value-for-money, English men's shoes in classic styles. Their outlet in Brompton Road sells women's shoes as well.

DERBER   18 C6   ⊖ High Street Kensington
80 Kensington High Street, W8; tel. (071) 937 1578. Open Monday to Saturday 9 a.m.–6 p.m.
Affordable trendy shoes for women and men.

IVORY SHOES   12 K9   ⊖ Bond Street
104 New Bond Street, W1; tel. (071) 408 1266. Open Monday to Saturday 10 a.m.–6.30 p.m. (Thursday until 8 p.m.).
Flamboyant women's footwear; quieter styles for men.

LILLEY & SKINNER **12** J10 ⊖ Bond Street
360 Oxford Street, W1; tel. (071) 629 6381. Open Monday to Saturday 9.30 a.m.–6 p.m. (Thursday until 8 p.m.).
A huge shoe store, spread over four floors and catering for most pockets.

MANOLO BLAHNIK **36** F2 ⊖ Sloane Square
49–51 Old Church Street, SW3; tel. (071) 352 8622. Open Monday to Friday 10 a.m.–6 p.m.; Saturday 10.30 a.m.–5 p.m.
Expensive, beautiful, high-fashion footwear in exquisite materials by Manolo Blahnik, who is regarded by many as London's leading designer of women's shoes.

NATURAL SHOE STORE **14** N9 ⊖ Covent Garden
21 Neal Street, WC2; tel. (071) 836 5254. Opens Monday to Saturday 10 a.m.; closes Monday, Tuesday & Saturday 6 p.m.; Wednesday to Friday 7 p.m.
The emphasis here is on healthy and comfortable footwear for men, women and children. Only natural materials are used.

RAVEL **12** K10 ⊖ Oxford Circus
248 Oxford Street, W1; tel. (071) 499 1949. Open Monday to Saturday 9.30 a.m.–6 p.m. (Thursday until 8 p.m.).
This popular high-street chain offers interesting and fashionable styles, but the merchandise is not noted for its hard-wearing qualities.

85

RAYNE **22** L8 ⊖ Green Park
15 Old Bond Street, W1; tel. (071) 493 9077. Open Monday to Friday 9.30 a.m.–6 p.m.; Saturday 9.30 a.m.–5.30 p.m.
At Britain's premier manufacturer of fine-quality footwear, you will find classic and designer styles that are smart and elegant.

RUSSELL & BROMLEY **12** K9 ⊖ Bond Street
24–25 New Bond Street, W1; tel. (071) 629 6903. Open Monday to Saturday 9.30 a.m.–6 p.m. (Thursday 10 a.m.–7 p.m.).
Part of an up-market chain whose shoes, though stylish, tend to be a little overpriced.

TRICKER'S **23** L8 ⊖ Green Park or Piccadilly Circus
67 Jermyn Street, SW1; tel. (071) 930 6395. Open Monday to Friday 9 a.m.–5 p.m.; Saturday 9 a.m.–4.30 p.m.
Sells a wide range of good-quality handmade shoes in traditional styles.

FLORISTS

Modern methods of transport can now bring the fresh blooms of the countryside right into the centre of London, to brighten the dullest day and the plainest interior. In addition to the addresses given below, you'll also see flowers on sale at wayside stalls and barrows at prices that the hardest heart will find difficult to resist.

FELTON & SONS   **30** F/G5   ⊖ South Kensington
                                                        or Knightsbridge
220–224 Brompton Road, SW3; tel. (071) 589 4433. Open Monday to Friday 8.30 a.m.–5.30 p.m.; Saturday 8.30 a.m.–noon.
As old as the century, this business has a high reputation for the freshness of its flowers. It also sells a wide range of good-quality pot plants.

FLOWERS BY CHIVERS   **23** L9   ⊖ Piccadilly Circus
80 Brewer Street, W1; tel. (071) 734 5653/4. Open Monday to Friday 9 a.m.–6 p.m.
A long-established florist selling an excellent range of cut flowers and pot plants.

86

JANE PACKER FLORAL DESIGN   **12** J10   ⊖ Bond Street
56 James Street, W1; tel. (071) 935 2673. Open Monday to Saturday 9 a.m.–6 p.m.
Particularly recommended for bouquets and basket arrangements of both fresh and dried flowers.

MOYSES STEVENS LTD   **22** K9   ⊖ Green Park
6 Bruton Street, W1; tel. (071) 493 8171. Open Monday to Friday 8.30 a.m.–5.30 p.m.; Saturday 8.30 a.m.–1 p.m.
A famous florists noted for their willingness to send almost any type of flower or plant to any destination. Especially good, natural-looking arrangements of seasonal blooms.

THE FLOWERSMITH   **14** N10   ⊖ Covent Garden
34 Shelton Street, WC2; tel. (071) 240 6688. Open Monday to Saturday 10 a.m.–6 p.m.
A most attractive shop selling original combinations of dried flowers, as well as fresh seasonal blooms.

FURNITURE

When it comes to good quality, good-looking furniture, British production is second to none. Whether your tastes run to classic, country-house style or modern designs, you'll find what you want in London, either in the large department stores or at the addresses given below.

ATRIUM **14** M10 ⊖ Tottenham Court Road
22–24 St. Giles High Street, WC2; tel. (071) 379 7288. Open Monday to Friday 9 a.m.–6 p.m.; Saturday 10 a.m.–6 p.m.
Exceptional, stylish modern Continental furniture and lighting is sold here.

CUBESTORE ⊖ Earls Court
58 Pembroke Road, W8; tel. (071) 602 2001. Opens Tuesday to Saturday 10 a.m.; closes 4 p.m. except Thursday (7 p.m.) and Saturday (5 p.m.).
Specializes in self-assembly, space-saving storage and shelving systems that can be formed into endless permutations. The basic unit is a hollow cube.

HABITAT **13** M11 ⊖ Goodge Street
Heal's Building, 196 Tottenham Court Road, W1; tel. (071) 631 3880. **87**
Open Monday 10 a.m.–6 p.m.; Tuesday to Friday 9.30 a.m.–6 p.m; (Thursday until 7.30 p.m.); Saturday 9 a.m.–6 p.m.; Sunday noon– 5 p.m.
Set up by Terence Conran in the 1960s to bring good, contemporary design within the reach of the average householder, Habitat sells furniture, bed linen, furnishing fabrics, wallpapers and accessories, all still at affordable prices.

HEAL'S **13** M11 ⊖ Goodge Street
196 Tottenham Court Road, W1; tel. (071) 636 1666. Open Monday to Friday 9.30 a.m.–6 p.m. (Thursday until 7.30 p.m.); Saturday 9 a.m.– 6 p.m.
Probably London's most well-known furniture store, with a large selection of the best modern British and Continental designs. Superb handmade beds are a speciality.

THE CONRAN SHOP **30** G4 ⊖ South Kensington
Michelin House, 81 Fulham Road, SW3; tel. (071) 589 7401. Open Monday to Saturday 9.30 a.m.–6 p.m. (Tuesday from 10 a.m.).
Nicely housed in the restored former Michelin building are the wares of this pioneering British furniture designer.

TULLEY'S OF CHELSEA LTD   **35** E3   ⊖ Fulham Broadway
or South Kensington

289–291 Fulham Road, SW10; tel. (071) 352 1078. Open Monday to Saturday 9 a.m.–5.30 p.m.
Upholstered furniture is sold here, either uncovered or covered with your own choice of fabric.

ZARACH   **22** J8   ⊖ Hyde Park Corner
or Marble Arch

47 South Audley Street, W1; tel. (071) 491 2706. Open Monday to Friday 9.30 a.m.–6 p.m.
Ultra-modern, somewhat dazzling furniture, light fittings and mirrors in chrome, glass and leather.

GIFTS

88

ALFRED DUNHILL   **23** L8   ⊖ Green Park
30 Duke Street, St. James's, SW1; tel. (071) 499 9566. Open Monday to Friday 9.30 a.m.–6 p.m.; Saturday 9.30 a.m.–5.30 p.m.
Expensive gifts for the dedicated smoker, as well as other luxury gifts for men.

BRITISH MUSEUM SHOP   **14** N10   ⊖ Tottenham Court Road
or Holborn

British Museum, Great Russell Street, WC1; tel. (071) 323 8613. Open Monday to Saturday 10 a.m.–5 p.m.; Sunday 2.30–6 p.m.
Replicas of the sculpture and jewellery on display in the museum, plus a selection of other gifts with museum connections, such as glass, scarves, ties, stationery, posters and prints. Also a separate bookshop, tel. (071) 323 8587, stocking all the museum's own titles, as well as a range of other books of special interest to museum visitors.

CRAFTS COUNCIL SHOP   **29** F5   ⊖ South Kensington
Victoria & Albert Museum, Cromwell Road, SW7; tel. (071) 589 5070. Open Monday to Saturday 10 a.m.–5.30 p.m.; Sunday 2.30–5.30 p.m.
Replicas of the V & A Museum's sculptural ceramics, domestic pottery, glass, textiles, jewellery and metalwork. Also wooden toys and other gifts by contemporary artisans.

KNUTZ   **14** N/O9   ⊖ Covent Garden
1 Russell Street, WC2; tel. (071) 836 3117. Open Monday to Friday
11 a.m.–8 p.m.; Saturday 11.30 a.m.–8.30 p.m.; Sunday noon–
6.30 p.m.
Everything for the practical joker (especially with a dubious sense of
humour), such as plastic dog turds, etc.

LETTS OF LONDON   **22** K8   ⊖ Green Park
3 Shepherd Street, W1; tel. (071) 499 2620. Open Monday to Friday
9.30 a.m.–5.30 p.m.; Saturday 10 a.m.–2 p.m.
The famous diary firm has now opened a shop selling prestige diaries,
stationery, leather goods and travelling luggage.

NEAL STREET EAST   **14** N9   ⊖ Covent Garden
5 Neal Street, WC2; tel. (071) 240 0135. Open Monday to Saturday
10 a.m.–7 p.m. (Friday from 10.30 a.m.).
A fascinating shop with a wide range of mainly Eastern merchandise:
clothes, jewellery, baskets, ceramics and more. Also books, cards and
prints.

OLD CURIOSITY SHOP   **15** O10   ⊖ Holborn
13 Portsmouth Street, WC2; tel. (071) 405 9891. Open April to October
daily 9 a.m.–5.30 p.m. (Saturday and Sunday until 4.30 p.m.); **89**
November to March, daily 9.30 a.m.–5 p.m. (Saturday and Sunday
4 p.m.).
Immortalized by Charles Dickens in *The Old Curiosity Shop*, the picturesque 16th-century shop now sells Victorian bric-à-brac and
mementoes, mainly to tourists. Unfortunately Little Nell is no longer
behind the counter.

PAST TIMES   **30** G6   ⊖ Knightsbridge
146 Brompton Road, SW3; tel. (071) 581 7616. Open Monday to
Saturday 9.30 a.m.–6 p.m.
For a gift with a difference, chose one of Past Times' replicas based on
the history of Britain from the Stone Age to the 20th century. Also sells
books, cards and stationery.

SAVILLE EDELLS   **30** G5   ⊖ Knightsbridge or South Kensington
25 Walton Street, SW3; tel. (071) 584 4398. Open Monday to Saturday
9.30 a.m.–6 p.m.
If you're searching for an unusual present you'll probably find it at this
shop, which has something for every taste and pocket. Specializes in
ornaments and prints.

GOURMET FOOD SHOPS

R. ALLEN & CO   **22** J9   ⊖ Bond Street or Green Park
*117 Mount Street, W1; tel. (071) 499 5831. Open Monday to Friday
4 a.m.–4 p.m.; Saturday 4 a.m.–1 p.m.*
Renowned, long-established **butcher** conducting business from attractive period premises.

BENDICKS   **12** J10   ⊖ Bond Street
*55 Wigmore Street, W1; tel. (071) 935 7272. Open Monday to Friday
9.30 a.m.–5 p.m.*
Best known for their bittermints (the original, and best, after-dinner mints), Bendicks also offers a wide range of succulent **handmade chocolates.**

BIFULCO'S STORES LTD   ⊖ St. John's Wood
*82 St. John's Wood High Street, NW8; tel. (071) 722 8101. Open
Monday to Friday 8 a.m.–5.30 p.m.; Saturday 8 a.m.–1 p.m.*
Continental cuts of **meat**, Dutch veal, grass-reared Scottish beef, free-range chickens and an excellent selection of **ready-prepared meat dishes**, such as kebabs and Kievs.

90

BLAGDEN FISHMONGERS   **12** H11   ⊖ Baker Street
*65 Paddington Street, W1; tel. (071) 935 8321. Open Monday
7.30 a.m.–5 p.m.; Tuesday to Friday 7.30 a.m.–5.30 p.m.; Saturday
7.30 a.m.–1 p.m.*
A wonderful **fishmonger** selling top-quality produce, including **poultry** and **game** when in season.

BOUCHERIE LAMARTINE   **31** J4   ⊖ Victoria or Sloane Square
*229 Ebury Street, SW1; tel. (071) 730 4175. Open Monday to Friday
8 a.m.–7 p.m.; Saturday 8 a.m.–4 p.m.*
Owned by top restaurateurs, the Roux brothers, sells French cuts of **meat**. Also prepared dishes and **pâtisserie** from the Roux brothers' own kitchens, **breads, cheeses** and **vegetables**.

CHARBONNEL ET WALKER   **22** K9   ⊖ Green Park
*28 Old Bond Street, W1; tel. (071) 491 0939. Open Monday to Friday
9 a.m.–5.30 p.m. (Thursday until 6 p.m.); Saturday 9 a.m.–4.30 p.m.*
Don't be fooled by the French-sounding name—this shop sells mouthwatering, handmade **English chocolates** in gloriously extravagant, decorative boxes.

CRANKS   **13** L9   ⊖ Oxford Circus
8 Marshall Street, W1; tel. (071) 437 2915. Open Monday to Friday 8 a.m.–6.30 p.m.; Saturday 9.30 a.m.–5.30 p.m.
Good-quality, **wholefood** sold in the shop adjoining one of the Cranks' restaurants. Really delicious takeaways, too.

DRURY TEA AND COFFEE CO   **24** N9   ⊖ Leicester Square
3 New Row, WC2; tel. (071) 836 1960. Open Monday to Friday 8.30 a.m.–6 p.m.; Saturday 11 a.m.–5 p.m.
A long-established family-run business, selling **coffee** of a consistently high standard and a range of fine **teas**, including own blends.

L. FERN & CO   **13** M10   ⊖ Tottenham Court Road
27 Rathbone Place, W1; tel. (071) 636 2237. Open Monday to Friday 8.30 a.m.–5.30 p.m.; Saturday 9.30 a.m.–1 p.m.
Own-brand **tea** and **coffee** sold by helpful staff in this lovely, old-fashioned shop.

FORTNUM & MASON
See p. 65 for details of these food specialists.

FRATELLI CAMISA   **13** M9   ⊖ Piccadilly Circus or Oxford Circus
1a Berwick Street, W1; tel. (071) 437 7120. Open Monday to Saturday 9 a.m.–6 p.m. (Thursday until 2 p.m.).
A family-run, **Italian food** shop selling wonderful native specialities, such as fresh **pasta, cheeses and wines**.

91

FRY'S OF CHELSEA   **29** F4   ⊖ South Kensington or Sloane Square
14 Cale Street, SW3; tel. (071) 589 0342. Open Monday to Friday 6 a.m.–5 p.m.; Saturday 6 a.m.–1 p.m.
An award-winning **greengrocer** offering really excellent produce.

GERMAN FOOD CENTRE   **21** H7   ⊖ Knightsbridge
44–46 Knightsbridge, SW1; tel. (071) 235 5760. Open Monday to Friday 9 a.m.–5.30 p.m.; Saturday 9 a.m.–5 p.m.
A good selection of **German** sausages, meat, cheeses, breads, cakes, biscuits, beer, wine and liqueurs.

HARRODS
For details of the wonderful food section of this famous department store, see p. 65-6.

HOBBS OF MAYFAIR   **22** J8   ⊖ Bond Street or Green Park
29 South Audley Street, W1; tel. (071) 409 1058. Open Monday to Friday 9 a.m.–8 p.m.; Saturday 9 a.m.–5 p.m.
High-class, **general provisions,** mostly of British origin, sold by attentive staff.

JUSTIN DE BLANK   **30** G5   ⊖ Knightsbridge
HYGIENIC BAKERY   or South Kensington
46 Walton Street, SW3; tel. (071) 589 4734. Open Monday to Friday 7.30 a.m.–6 p.m.; Saturday 7.30 a.m.–1 p.m.
Renowned for its excellent traditional, English **crusty bread** which is baked on the premises. Also an excellent lunch-time source of **ready-made hot** and **cold snacks**, such as pizzas and quiches, sandwiches, etc.

JUSTIN DE BLANK   **31** J5   ⊖ Sloane Square
PROVISIONS   or Victoria
42 Elizabeth Street, SW1; tel. (071) 730 0605. Open Monday to Friday 9 a.m.–7 p.m.; Saturday 9 a.m.–2 p.m.
The **grocery** "arm" of Justin de Blank, sells pâtés, cheeses, bread and cakes, fruit and vegetables, as well as prepared **takeaway dishes**.

LINA STORES   **23** L9   ⊖ Piccadilly Circus
18 Brewer Street, W1; tel. (071) 437 6482. Open Monday to Friday 8 a.m.–6 p.m. (Thursday until 1 p.m.); Saturday 8 a.m.–5 p.m.
An astounding range of **Italian food** is available at this old-style grocers, including superb **fresh pasta**.

92 **MAISON BERTAUX**   **13** M9/10   ⊖ Leicester Square
                or Tottenham Court Road
28 Greek Street, W1; tel. (071) 437 6007. Open Tuesday to Saturday 9 a.m.–8 p.m.; Sunday 9.30 a.m.–1 p.m. and 2–8 p.m.
Everything is baked on the premises at this long-established **pâtisserie**, using only top-quality ingredients.

MARKS & SPENCER   **13** L10   ⊖ Oxford Circus
173 Oxford Street, W1; tel. (071) 437 7722. Opens 9.30 a.m. Monday to Friday; closes 6 p.m. except Wednesday and Friday (7 p.m.); Saturday 9 a.m.–6.30 p.m.
In the food department of this world-famous chain you can rely on the freshness and quality of the produce, though the **fruit** and **vegetables** tend to be expensive.

Particularly recommended for their excellent selection of ready-made meals.

NEAL'S YARD BAKERY CO-OP.   **14** N10   ⊖ Covent Garden
6 Neal's Yard, WC2; tel. (071) 836 5199. Open Monday to Friday 10.30 a.m.–6.30 p.m.; Saturday 10.30 a.m.–4.30 p.m.
A delicious range of **breads** and **wholefood snacks** to take away or eat on the premises.

To market, to market...

Since time immemorial, markets have been held in London, and like many other traditional events in the capital, still take place today. In addition to the antique markets listed on pp. 67-8, the following are some of the places where stall-holders, selling everything from food to furniture, set up their stands:

Bermondsey (New Caledonian Market), SE1—antique and bric-à-brac on Friday from the crack of dawn.

Brixton, SW9—Monday–Saturday (closed Wednesday p.m.) for food, household and second-hand goods.

Camden Lock, NW1—colourful, cosmopolitan market on Thursday, Saturday and Sunday for crafts, bric-à-brac, etc.

Camden Passage, N1—Wednesday and Saturday, mainly antiques.

Jubilee, Covent Garden, WC2—something different every day of the week.

Kensington, W8—Monday to Saturday for fashion.

Leadenhall, EC3—A Victorian masterpiece in iron and glass in action from Monday to Friday for fresh produce and exotic delicacies.

Petticoat Lane, E1—no such lane, but refers to the area between Middlesex and Goulston streets. A rather touristy market, held on Sunday.

Portobello Road, W11—anything and everything on a Saturday.

Shepherds Bush, W12—Monday–Saturday (closed Thursday p.m.) for clothes, ethnic food, cosmetics, etc.

Even if you don't intend to buy, you'll almost certainly enjoy soaking up the atmosphere and listening to the stall-holders' patter. And who knows, you just might walk away with a bargain.

93

NEAL'S YARD DAIRY   **14** N10   ⊖ Covent Garden

9 Neal's Yard, WC2; tel. (071) 379 7646. Open Monday to Saturday 9.30 a.m.–5.30 p.m. (Thursday and Friday until 6 p.m.).

An excellent place to discover the true flavour of **British cheeses** in peak condition.

NEAL'S YARD WHOLEFOOD   **14** N10   ⊖ Covent Garden
WAREHOUSE

21–23 Shorts Gardens, WC2; tel. (071) 836 5151. Open Monday to Saturday 10 a.m.–6.30 p.m. (Thursday until 8 p.m.); Sunday 11 a.m.–5 p.m.

An excellent **health-food supermarket** where you can buy small or bulk quantities. Also organically grown **vegetables**.

PARTRIDGES OF SLOANE STREET　　**30** H5　　⊖ Sloane Square
132–134 Sloane Street, SW1; tel. (071) 730 0651. Open daily 8.30 a.m.–9 p.m.
Luxury foods and the more everyday gastronomic requirements are sold in this **grocery** store, which remains open to a conveniently late hour, every day of the year bar Christmas Day and Boxing Day.

PAXTON & WHITFIELD　　**23** L8　　　⊖ Green Park or Piccadilly
93 Jermyn Street, SW1; tel. (071) 930 0259. Open Monday to Friday 9 a.m.–6 p.m.; Saturday 9 a.m.–4 p.m.
A renowned **cheese** shop whose aroma will tempt you to buy a selection of their hundreds of British and Continental varieties. Home-made **pâtés** and **pies, traditional hams, teas** and **wines** are also sold.

R. PORTWINE　　**14** M/N9　　　　　⊖ Covent Garden
24 Earlham Street, WC2; tel. (071) 836 2353. Opens at 7.30 a.m. Monday to Saturday; closes Monday, Thursday and Saturday 2 p.m.; Tuesday and Wednesday 5 pm.; Friday 5.30 p.m.
Run by the same family for over two centuries, sells **meat** of excellent quality, **game** and superb own-recipe **sausages**.

PRESTAT　　**23** L8　　　　　⊖ Green Park or Piccadilly Circus
14 Princes Arcade, Piccadilly, SW1; tel. (071) 629 4838. Open Monday to Friday 10 a.m.–6 p.m.; Saturday 9.30 a.m.–5.30 p.m.
94 **Chocolate truffles** are Prestat's speciality, but the shop also sells a wonderful selection of other handmade **chocolates**.

R. TWINING & CO　　**15** P9　　　　　　　　⊖ Temple
216 Strand, WC2; tel. (071) 353 3511. Open Monday to Friday 9.30 a.m.–4.30 p.m.
The complete range of this well-known company's **teas** is on sale here, and behind the shop there is a small museum dedicated to the history of tea and Twinings.

SLATER & COOKE, BISNEY & JONES　　**23** L9　⊖ Piccadilly Circus
65–69 Brewer Street, W1; tel. (071) 437 2026/7. Opens at 8 a.m. Monday to Saturday; closes 5 p.m. Monday to Thursday; 5.30 p.m. Friday; Saturday 1.30 p.m.
Exquisitely prepared and dressed **meat** and a huge range of home-made **sausages**.

STEVE HATT　　　　　　　　　　　　　⊖ Angel
88–90 Essex Road, N1; tel. (071) 226 3963. Open Tuesday to Saturday 7.30 a.m.–4.45 p.m. (Thursday closes at 12.45 p.m.).
An impressive selection of **fish** and **seafood** is sold by this family firm. **Game,** too, is available in season.

THORNTONS   **14** N9   ⊖ Covent Garden
2 The Market, Covent Garden Piazza, WC2; tel. (071) 836 2173. Open Monday to Saturday 10 a.m.–7 p.m.
Exiles from the North heaved a sigh of relief when this Yorkshire-based company set up shop in the capital, to tempt those with a sweet tooth with its delicious, chewy **toffee**, "Continental" **chocolates** and other delights, all reasonably priced.

WHITTARD & CO   **30** G4   ⊖ South Kensington
In the Conran Shop, Michelin House, 81 Fulham Road, SW3; tel. (071) 589 4261. Open Monday, Wednesday to Saturday 9.30 a.m.–6 p.m.; Tuesday 10 a.m.–6 p.m.
Specialists in **tea**, of which a wide range is sold, including herb teas. Good selection of **coffees** also available.

WHOLEFOOD   **11** H11   ⊖ Baker Street
24 Paddington Street, W1; tel. (071) 935 3924. Open Monday 8.45 a.m.–6 p.m.; Tuesday to Friday 8.45 a.m.–6.30 p.m.; Saturday 9.30 a.m.–1 p.m.
General provisions for the health-conscious and a fine range of organically grown **fruit** and **vegetables**.

WHOLEFOOD BUTCHER   **11** H11   ⊖ Baker Street
31 Paddington Street, W1; tel. (071) 486 1390. Open Monday to Friday 8:30 a.m.–6 p.m.; Saturday 9 a.m.–1 p.m.
This offshoot of Wholefood, at No. 24 in the same street, sells organically reared **meat**.

95

JEWELLERY

ACSIS   **14** N9   ⊖ Covent Garden
Unit 31, The Market, Covent Garden, WC2; tel. (071) 497 2992. Open Monday to Saturday 10 a.m.–7 p.m.; Sunday noon.–5 p.m.
Fashion and gold and silver jewellery, watches, lighters and gifts, much of which is imported from France and Italy.

ANN BLOOM   **22** K9   ⊖ Bond Street
10a New Bond Street, W1; tel. (071) 491 1213. Open Monday to Saturday 10 a.m.–5.30 p.m.
Reopened recently after a fire, continues to sell Victorian, Edwardian and 20th-century, pre-1950 jewellery, plus beautiful, silver picture frames.

ARMOUR-WINSTON **22** L8   ⊖ Green Park or Piccadilly Circus
43 Burlington Arcade, W1; tel. (071) 493 8937. Open Monday to Friday
9 a.m.–4.30 p.m.
Fine antique and second-hand jewellery. Men's jewellery a speciality.

ASPREY **22** K9   ⊖ Bond Street
165 New Bond Street, W1; tel. (071) 493 6767. Open Monday to Friday
9 a.m.–5.30 p.m.; Saturday 9 a.m.–1 p.m.
Beautiful antique jewellery, and also contemporary items and luxury
gifts.

BENTLEY **12** K9   ⊖ Bond Street
65 New Bond Street, W1; tel. (071) 629 0651. Open Monday to Friday
10 a.m.–5 p.m.
Specialists in antique and period jewellery. Some Russian pieces,
including Fabergé; also antique silver.

BUTLER & WILSON **29** F4   ⊖ South Kensington
189 Fulham Road, SW3; tel. (071) 352 3045. Open Monday to Saturday
10 a.m.–6 p.m.
Bright, fashionable costume jewellery, attractively displayed.

CARTIER **22** K9   ⊖ Bond Street
175 New Bond Street, W1; tel. (071) 493 6962. Open Monday to Friday
96 *10 a.m.–6 p.m.; Saturday 10 a.m.–5 p.m.*
This world-famous jewellers counts royalty among its clients and its
merchandise is, not surprisingly, of the highest quality with prices to
match.

COBRA & BELLAMY **30** H4   ⊖ Sloane Square
149 Sloane Square, SW1; tel. (071) 730 2823. Open Monday to
Saturday 10.30 a.m.–6 p.m.
Best known for their beautiful silver and costume jewellery dating from
the 1920s to the 1950s; also modern designer pieces in precious
metals.

ELECTRUM **12** J/K9   ⊖ Bond Street
21 South Molton Street, W1; tel. (071) 629 6325. Open Monday to
Friday 10 a.m.–6 p.m.; Saturday 10 a.m.–1 p.m.
Unusual high-fashion designer jewellery is displayed and sold here.

JESS JAMES **13** L9   ⊖ Oxford Circus
3 Newburgh Street, W1; tel. (071) 437 0199. Open Monday to Friday
11 a.m.–6.30 p.m. (Thursday until 7 p.m.); Saturday 11 a.m.–6 p.m.
A stylish shop selling modern designer jewellery and also a few antique
pieces.

KEN LANE   **30** G5   ⊖ Knightsbridge
50 Beauchamp Place, SW3; tel. (071) 584 5299. Open Monday to Saturday 9.30 a.m.–5.30 p.m.
Unusual costume jewellery of the kind beloved of glossy magazine fashion stylists.

KUTCHINSKY   **30** G6   ⊖ Knightsbridge
73 Brompton Road, SW3; tel. (071) 584 9311. Open Monday to Friday 10 a.m.–5.30 p.m.; Saturday 10.30 a.m.–5 p.m.
Swiss watches and fine jewellery of superb quality.

PHILIP ANTROBUS   **22** K9   ⊖ Bond Street
11 New Bond Street, W1; tel. (071) 493 4557. Open Monday to Friday 10 a.m.–5 p.m.
Exquisite antique and modern gold jewellery and pieces set with precious stones.

TESSIERS   **12** K9   ⊖ Bond Street
26 New Bond Street, W1; tel. (071) 629 0458. Open Monday to Friday 9.30 a.m.–5 p.m.
Dealers in fine antique jewellery and silver, who have been in business for well over a hundred years. Also sell reproduction silver, jewellery and objets d'art.

97

KITCHEN EQUIPMENT

DAVID MELLOR   **30** H4   ⊖ Sloane Square
4 Sloane Square, SW1; tel. (071) 730 4259. Open Monday to Saturday 9.30 a.m.–5.30 p.m.
High-quality kitchen equipment with prices to match.

DIVERTIMENTI   **29** F4   ⊖ South Kensington
139–141 Fulham Road, SW3; tel. (071) 581 8065. Open Monday to Friday 9.30 a.m.–6 p.m.; Saturday 10 a.m.–6 p.m.
Kitchen- and tableware of every description, including good-quality, Continental cooking utensils.

ELIZABETH DAVID COOKSHOP   **14** N9   ⊖ Covent Garden
3 North Row, The Market, Covent Garden, WC2; tel. (071) 836 9167. Open Monday to Saturday 10 a.m.–8 p.m.; Sunday noon–5.30 p.m.
An excellent range of kitchenware, from the most basic items to specialist tools for the dedicated cook.

PERFUMES & TOILETRIES

THE BODY SHOP   **13** L9   ⊖ Oxford Circus
*32–34 Great Marlborough Street, W1; tel. (071) 437 5137. Opens at
9.30 a.m. Monday to Saturday (Tuesday 10 a.m.); closes 6 p.m. except
Thursday (7.30 p.m.) and Friday (7 p.m.).*
One of an attractive chain of stores with "green" aims, offering a wide
range of reasonably priced toiletries, mainly made from natural
ingredients and not tested on animals. Products for men and women.

CRABTREE & EVELYN   **18** C6   ⊖ High Street Kensington
*6 Kensington Church Street, W8; tel. (071) 937 9335. Open Monday to
Saturday 9.30 a.m.–6 p.m. (Tuesday from 10 a.m.; Thursday until
7 p.m.).*
A relatively new company, despite its "olde Englishe" name, selling
luxuriously packaged toiletries not tested on animals, which make ideal
gifts.

CULPEPER HERBALISTS   **14** N9   ⊖ Covent Garden
*8 The Market, Covent Garden Piazza, WC2; tel. (071) 379 6698. Open
Monday to Saturday 10 a.m.–8 p.m.; Sunday 11 a.m.–6 p.m.*
You will be lured into this shop by the wonderful aroma of herbs, also
used in the manufacture of the company's toiletries and cosmetics.

98

FLORIS   **23** L8   ⊖ Piccadilly Circus
*89 Jermyn Street, SW1; tel. (071) 930 2885. Open Monday to Friday
9.30 a.m.–5.30 p.m.; Saturday 9.30 a.m.–4 p.m.*
Visit this long-established perfumer simply for the experience of seeing
a beautifully fitted, period shop. While you are there, treat yourself to
one of the exclusive English flower perfumes or matching toiletries.

MARY CHESS   **22** K8   ⊖ Green Park
*7 Shepherd Market, W1; tel. (071) 629 5152. Open Monday to Friday
9.30 a.m.–5.30 p.m.*
Located in the heart of Mayfair, this delightful shop sells traditional
perfumes and toilet preparations with an English theme, none of which
is tested on animals.

MOLTON BROWN   **12** J/K9   ⊖ Bond Street
*58 South Molton Street, W1; tel. (071) 629 1872. Open Monday to
Friday 10 a.m.–5.30 p.m.; Saturday 9 a.m.–4.30 p.m.*
One of London's top hairdressers, this firm also sells an excellent range
of herb-based hair and beauty products.

PENHALIGON'S   14 O9   ⊖ Covent Garden
*41 Wellington Street, WC2; tel. (071) 836 2150. Open Monday to Friday
10 a.m.–6 p.m.; Saturday 10 a.m.–5.30 p.m.*
Traditional English perfumes and toilet preparations for both sexes.

PHOTOGRAPHIC EQUIPMENT

DIXONS   13 M10   ⊖ Tottenham Court Road
*88 Oxford Street, W1; tel. (071) 636 8511. Open Monday to Saturday
9.30 a.m.–6 p.m. (Wednesday from 10 a.m; Thursday until 7 p.m.).*
Part of a chain selling new photographic and audio-visual equipment,
as well as computers.

FOX TALBOT   24 N8   ⊖ Charing Cross
*443 Strand, WC2; tel. (071) 379 6522. Open Monday to Friday 9 a.m.–
5.30 p.m.; Saturday 9 a.m.–5 p.m.*
Specialists in new and second-hand cameras by top manufacturers.

KEITH JOHNSON & PELLING   13 L10   ⊖ Oxford Circus
Ramillies House, 1–2 Ramillies Street, W1; tel. (071) 439 8811. Open
Monday to Friday 9 a.m.–5.30 p.m. **99**
These stockists of most big-name cameras offer attentive service to
both professional and amateur photographers.

KINGSLEY PHOTOGRAPHIC   13 L11   ⊖ Goodge Street
Warren Street
*93 Tottenham Court Road, W1; tel. (071) 387 6500. Open Monday to
Friday 9 a.m.–5.30 p.m.; Saturday 10 a.m.–4 p.m.*
A wide range of new and second-hand cameras sold by helpful staff.

R. G. LEWIS   14 N/O10   ⊖ Holborn
*217 High Holborn, WC1; tel. (071) 242 2916. Open Monday to Friday
8.30 a.m.–6 p.m.; Saturday 9.30 a.m.–4 p.m.*
Both new and second-hand stock sold by this century-old firm. The
staff are knowledgeable and the standard of service high.

STRAND USED CAMERA EXCHANGE   24 O9   ⊖ Charing Cross
*146 Strand, WC2; tel. (071) 836 1693. Open Monday to Friday
8.30 a.m.–5.30 p.m.; Saturday 9 a.m.–3.15 p.m.*
Competitively priced, second-hand cameras and new photographic
accessories.

YORK CAMERAS (LONDON)   **14** N10   ⊖ Holborn
1 Victoria Colonnade, Southampton Row, WC1; tel. (071) 242 7182.
Open Monday to Friday 9.30 a.m.–5.30 p.m.; Saturday 10 a.m.–3 p.m.
The best-quality, second-hand photographic equipment is sold here.

RECORDS, TAPES, CDs

ALTO   **32** K5   ⊖ Victoria
18 Victoria Place, Victoria Street, SW1; tel. (071) 821 5526. Open
Monday to Friday 9 a.m.–8 p.m.; Saturday 9 a.m.–6 p.m.; Sunday
11 a.m.–6 p.m.
All types of music on cassette and CD, but particularly outstanding in
classical CDs.

CASSETTES PLUS   **23** M/N9   ⊖ Leicester Square
9 St. Martin's Court, WC2; tel. (071) 836 8514. Open Monday to
Saturday 10 a.m.–6 p.m.
A specialist cassette and CD shop covering every type of music, as
well as the spoken word.

100
CHEAPO CHEAPO RECORDS   **13** M9   ⊖ Piccadilly Circus
53 Rupert Street, W1; tel. (071) 437 8272. Open Monday to Saturday
11 a.m.–10 p.m.
Second-hand pop, rock, blues, jazz and classical records, tapes and
CDs, all at competitive prices.

DADDY KOOL MUSIC   **13** L9   ⊖ Piccadilly Circus
9 Berwick Street, W1; tel. (071) 437 3535. Open Monday to Saturday 10
a.m.–6.30 p.m.
The place in the West End to get your reggae and ska, in which the shop
excels.

DOBELLS   **14** M/N9   ⊖ Leicester Square
21 Tower Street, WC2; tel. (071) 240 1354. Open Monday to Saturday
10 a.m.–7 p.m. (jazz shop), 10 a.m.–6 p.m. (folk shop).
Two shops packed with lots of recorded jazz, blues and folk music.

HAROLD MOORE'S RECORDS   **13** L10   ⊖ Oxford Circus
2 Great Marlborough Street, W1; tel. (071) 437 1576. Open Monday to
Saturday 10 a.m.–6.30 p.m.; Sunday noon–6.30 p.m.
Specializing in classical music, has probably the largest selection of
second-hand and out-of-print LPs in Europe. Current CDs also
available.

JAMES ASMAN'S RECORD CENTRE 24 N9 ⊖ Leicester Square
*23a New Row, WC2; tel. (071) 240 1380. Open Monday to Saturday
10 a.m.–6 p.m.*
All kinds of jazz and nostalgia records are sold in this tiny shop, which
offers many second-hand bargains.

MUSIC DISCOUNT CENTRE 13 M10   ⊖ Tottenham Court Road
*29 Rathbone Place, W1; tel. (071) 637 4700. Open Monday to Friday
10 a.m.–6 p.m.; Saturday 9.30 a.m.–5.30 p.m.*
Classical music on cassette and CD only is sold here. There are also
two other branches, one at 437 Strand, WC2, tel. (071) 240 2157, and
another at 1 Creed Lane, St. Paul's, EC4, tel. (071) 489 8077.

OUR PRICE RECORDS 13 M10   ⊖ Tottenham Court Road
*12 Tottenham Court Road, W1; tel. (071) 636 4631. Open Monday to
Saturday 10 a.m.–7 p.m.*
Part of a chain offering reasonably priced pop and rock records.

TOWER RECORDS 23 L9   ⊖ Piccadilly Circus
*1 Piccadilly, W1; tel. (071) 439 2500. Open Monday to Saturday 9 a.m.–
midnight.*
In this megastore, every kind of recorded music is available, including **101**
an impressive array of U.S. imports.

Visitors to London used to reckon that it was difficult to get a good meal at any price. Now the complaint is more likely to concern the difficulty of choosing from the wealth of possibilities. Whatever your budget, you can dine as well in London as in any major city.

The improvement of recent years has primarily been the result of domestic demand: English palates have come a long way from the overcooked meat and two veg. that formerly passed for good food. More and more Britons are travelling abroad, and when they come back they seek food of the quality and variety they had in France or Italy.

The top end of the restaurant scene is dominated by **French cuisine**, sometimes (but not always) cooked by Gallic chefs who have crossed the Channel. **Italian** food usually means pizza houses or *trattoria*-style places serving the inevitable pasta, both catering for the budget-conscious rather than gourmets. Even **American** food has made its mark, both in restaurants featuring Californian-style cooking and in steak and burger houses offering simpler fare at reasonable prices. Then there's the **ethnic** influence, diverse and all-pervasive. Almost every street seems to have an Indian restaurant, and Chinese food is immensely popular at every level. Thai became a major presence in the nineties, and Vietnamese is also gaining ground.

Booking is always advisable, and sometimes essential, especially for the top-class establishments, where there may be a waiting list of several weeks. But remember that some "ethnic" restaurants do not accept reservations—or take a casual attitude towards the practice.

103

Prices quoted below are for a basic meal for one person. Where the service is à la carte, the figure given is based on the average cost of a three-course meal (or selection of typical dishes). Drinks are not included. In an expensive restaurant you will probably need to spend £12–15 for a bottle of basic wine; in a more modest establishment as little as £6–7. In Chinese and Indian restaurants you may prefer beer or tea.

Please note that many establishments are closed on public holidays, especially at Christmas, when those that do open serve a sumptuous meal and tables are booked up weeks in advance.

Credit cards are accepted by most restaurants, but not all. If this is a potential problem, ring the restaurant to check.

Presto! The roast is revealed in a traditional London carvery .

WORLD-CLASS COOKING

CAPITAL **30** H6 ⊖ Knightsbridge
22–24 Basil Street, SW3; tel. (071) 589 5171. Service 12.30–2.30 p.m. and 7–11 p.m.
A small, awkwardly shaped, fussy dining room, where Philip Britten, trained under Mosimann and former right-hand man of Nico Ladenis, serves a short, regularly changing menu of full-flavoured, artistic, rich and innovative food. Rather old-fashioned service and stiff atmosphere. Lunch from £18.50; à la carte from £45, including wine.

CHEZ NICO **13** L10 ⊖ Oxford Circus
35 Great Portland Street, W1; tel. (071) 436 8846. Service noon–2 p.m. and 7–11 p.m.; closed Saturday and Sunday.
London's middle-aged *enfant terrible*, Nico Ladenis, irritates many by his exacting attitude, but no one can deny that he is one of the most talented chefs in the world. His dedication to perfection is legendary and his total lack of training belies his extraordinarily delicious food. Best value is the two-course set lunch at £25, otherwise from £50 a head without wine.

CONNAUGHT HOTEL GRILL ROOM **22** J9 ⊖ Green Park
Carlos Place, W1; tel. (071) 499 7070. Service: grill room: 6–10.30 p.m.; closed weekends and public holidays; restaurant: 12.30–2.30 p.m. and 6.30–10.15 p.m.
Michel Bourdin, the French chef at this bastion of the Establishment, presides over what many regard as London's finest grill room. It's pricey, but the game is served with exemplary, traditional accompaniments, the beef and lamb are properly reared and hung and even the rice pudding is perfection. Also bourgeois French cooking and a top-price wine list. Set lunch £20, otherwise from £50 a head without wine.

FOUR SEASONS, INN ON THE PARK **22** J7 ⊖ Green Park
or Hyde Park Corner
Hamilton Place, Park Lane, W1; tel. (071) 499 0888. Service noon–3 p.m. and 7–11 p.m.
Bruno Loubet's cooking shows the influence of his old boss and mentor, Raymond Blanc (of Le Manoir aux Quat' Saisons, Oxford) and is modern *haute cuisine*. Recent, unusual and mouth-watering dishes have included sea bass with an aubergine and sweet-pepper purée and a gâteau of chicken with wild mushrooms and foie gras, so complex in its composition that it would take a page just to describe it.

104

Like M. Blanc, Loubet produces gourmet food that is elegant, innovative, elaborate and stunningly presented. The restaurant is grandiose and oppressive. Count around £40 per head.

HARVEY'S
⇄ Wandsworth Common

2 Bellevue Road, SW17; tel. (081) 672 0114. Service 12.30–2.15 p.m. and 7.30–11 p.m.; closed Sunday.

Marco Pierre White is the remarkable, outrageous, young chef here. Having worked his way round the kitchens of all the top chefs in the country, he has developed his own style of eclectic, modern French cooking. Try his oysters with tagliatelle, his foie gras with a Sauternes sauce, his Bresse pigeon with lentils and truffles and his heavenly lemon tart, coated with a wafer-thin layer of caramel. Everything is cooked to order and service can be slow. Set lunch at £20, dinner £35.

L'ARLEQUIN
⇄ Queenstown Road

123 Queenstown Road, SW8; tel. (071) 622 0555. Service 12.30–2 p.m. and 7.30–10 p.m.; Closed Saturday, Sunday and public holidays.

Understatement is the name of the game at this calm, elegant restaurant, where Christian Delteil cooks superb, modern French food. Fresh, distinct flavours, marvellous vegetables and an excellent value set lunch (under £20). A la carte from £35.

LA TANTE CLAIRE   36 H3
⊖ Sloane Square

68 Royal Hospital Road, SW3; tel. (071) 352 6045. Service 12.30–2 p.m. and 7–11 p.m.; closed Saturday, Sunday and public holidays.

105

A delightful, pale primrose-yellow dining room with attractive modern art and pleasing atmosphere. The chef and patron is Pierre Koffmann, whose hallmark dish is a boned pig's trotter stuffed with morels—a lot tastier than it sounds. Koffman places more emphasis on rustic food (he comes from the Basque region) than other top chefs and he imports his own fresh ingredients from France. Set lunch is a bargain £19.50, à la carte minimum is £40.

LE GAVROCHE   21 H9
⊖ Marble Arch

43 Upper Brook Street, W1; tel. (071) 408 0881. Service noon–2 p.m. and 7–11 p.m.; closed Saturday and Sunday.

London's most highly rated restaurant, where Albert Roux and his son Michel serve exquisite, classic French food. There is perfection, too, in the service, though the sombre décor is more subjective. Marvellous attention to detail right through from the *amuse-gueules* to the coffee and delicate petits fours. The set lunch is a remarkable bargain at £24 (beware, though, of the wine list), otherwise from £50 a head.

HIGHLY RECOMMENDED

192
⊖ Ladbroke Grove

192 Kensington Park Road, W11; tel. (071) 229 0482. Service Monday to Saturday 12.30–3.30 p.m. and 7.30–11.30 p.m.; Sunday 1–3 p.m. and 7.30–10.30 p.m.

Popular with West London's literary crowd, 192 has an upstairs wine bar serving food and downstairs the restaurant, initially made famous when Alastair Little (see below) was in charge of the kitchen. Chefs come and go but the food remains fashionable, often with a Mediterranean bias; the wine list is excellent and great value. Around £15 a head but no minimum charge.

ALASTAIR LITTLE   13 M9
⊖ Leicester Square

49 Frith Street, W1; tel. (071) 734 5183. Service Monday to Friday 12.30–2.30 p.m. and 7.30–11.30 p.m.; Saturday 7.30–11.30 p.m.; closed Sunday and public holidays.

Alastair Little's cooking is born out of constant experimentation and a zealot's preoccupation with food. He is entirely self-taught, with the unlikely background of a Cambridge degree in archaeology. His daily menu relies on the finest seasonal ingredients and is best described as eclectic—a term he himself hates. Marvellous *sashimi* and *carpaccio*, simple but sophisticated soups, superb pasta and interesting use of all the fashionable ingredients. The décor, too, is unusual, verging on the austere, but with an aggressive taste in paintings. From £20 a head. Downstairs, a shorter bar menu is available.

106

BIBENDUM   30 G4
⊖ South Kensington

Michelin House, 81 Fulham Road, SW3; tel. (071) 581 5817. Service Monday to Saturday 12.30–2.30 p.m.; Sunday noon–3 p.m. and 7–10.30 p.m.

Sir Terence Conran spent a packet restoring this imposing building to house his publishing concern, shop and Bibendum. Chef, and partner, is Simon Hopkinson, whose fine cooking is based on his philosophy of getting the best out of good ingredients. Flavour is everything and the daily-changing menu shows many influences: truffle omelette, grilled aubergine with *pesto* and cod with saffron potatoes, but roast beef and Yorkshire pudding and roast chicken, too. Similarly, succulent desserts include a sublime lemon tart, chocolate Pithiviers and individual steamed fruit pudding. Stylish but comfortable, the restaurant is chic without being self-conscious. The only drawback is the cost: set lunch £20 but à la carte £40 a head and an up-market wine list.

BLUEPRINT CAFÉ ⊖ Tower Hill
Design Museum, Butlers Wharf, SE1; tel. (071) 378 7031. Service noon–3.30 p.m. and 7–10.45 p.m.; closed Sunday and Monday evenings.

A Mediterranean menu cooked by a young American chef. Great views across the Thames, a few *al fresco* tables and chic, modern mood. It's busy at lunch time, and the weekend brunch is especially good. From £20, but no minimum charge.

BURT'S **13** M9 ⊖ Piccadilly Circus or Leicester Square
42 Dean Street, W1; tel. (071) 734 3339. Service Monday to Friday 12.30–2.30 p.m. and 5.30–11.30 p.m.; Saturday 5.30–11.30 p.m.; closed Sunday and public holidays.

A gourmet vegetarian restaurant whose menu, *From the Earth*, is inspired by meat equivalents of other top chefs. There is also a seafood menu, *From the Sea*, plus a few meat dishes. The atmosphere is theatrical, and the colour scheme a symphony of greys with black and white photos for decoration. Set lunch and early dinner under £20, otherwise from £25.

CHEZ MAX ⊖ Kew Gardens
291 Sandycombe Road, Kew, Richmond; tel. (081) 940 3590. Service Tuesday to Saturday 12.30–2 p.m. and 7.30–10.15 p.m.; Sunday 7.30–9 p.m.; closed public holidays.

This authentic replica of a Left Bank bistro is run by two francophile **107** twins, Max (who greets) and Marc (who cooks). Marvellous, robust food with rich sauces, plentiful portions and thoroughly bourgeois recipes. Lunch is less hectic. Set menu: lunch around £22–25, dinner and Sunday lunch £27.50, but lots of supplements.

CHRISTIAN'S ⇌ Cheswick
1 Station Parade, Burlington Lane, W4; tel. (081) 995 0382. Service 12.30–2 p.m. and 7.30–10.45 p.m. Tuesday to Saturday and Sunday lunch.

The epitome of the perfect local restaurant—delicious smells from the open kitchen, a short but imaginative menu, fair prices and a pleasant, relaxed and informal ambiance.

Christian Gustin cooks wholesome, unfussy French food; great cheese and other soufflés, salmon quenelles with hollandaise sauce and occasionally more inventive combinations such as roast wild pigeon with pepper sauce and pears. English cheese board and especially good fruit tarts. From £18 a head.

CLARKE'S   18 C7   ⊖ High Street Kensington or Notting Hill Gate
124 Kensington Church Street, W8; tel. (071) 221 9225. Service Monday to Friday 12.30–2 p.m. and 7–10 p.m. Closed Saturday and Sunday.

Sally Clarke's elegant, pretty and summery restaurant (book a table downstairs if you enjoy watching the cooks at work) produces a daily three-course, no-choice dinner menu and a small-choice lunch. Her food is much influenced by her spell cooking in California and she is always first off the mark with new ingredients. Marvellous pizzas, effective use of the charcoal grill, delicate, interesting salads and unusual vegetable dishes. English and Irish cheeseboard. Next door, *& Clarke's*, a small food shop, sells the restaurant's home-made breads, cheeses, wines, teas and coffees. Set lunch from £16, dinner from £28.

GAVVERS   31 H4   ⊖ Sloane Square
61–63 Lower Sloane Street, SW1; tel. (071) 730 5983. Service Monday to Friday noon–2.30 p.m. and 5.30–11.30 p.m.; Saturday 5.30–11.30 p.m.; closed Sunday and public holidays.

The original site of Le Gavroche (see p. 105), now run by the Roux brothers as a *prix-fixe* restaurant. Great value for fine, if somewhat unimaginative, modern French cooking, but rather stuffy, smart restaurant that lacks atmosphere. Two-course set lunch £12.25, dinner, with aperitif, half a bottle of wine, coffee and petits fours, £27.

KENSINGTON PLACE   18 C8   ⊖ Notting Hill Gate
201–205 Kensington Church Street, W8; tel. (071) 727 3184. Service Monday to Saturday noon–3.15 p.m. and 6.30–11.45 p.m.; Sunday noon–4 p.m. and 6.30 p.m.–12.30 a.m.

Fashionable, stylish and huge brasserie, owned by a dynamic duo who have worked in all London's trendiest restaurants, the kitchens presided over by a Roux-trained chef. The combination is irresistible and ensures the place is always packed and noisy. Frequently changing menu and daily specials, but expect stylish Mediterranean food, full-flavoured and pretty on the plate. Short, keenly priced wine list. From £20 a head.

L'ESCARGOT   13 M9/10   ⊖ Leicester Square
48 Greek Street, W1; tel. (071) 437 2679. Service: restaurant 12.30–3 p.m. and 6.30–11.15 p.m.; brasserie noon–3 p.m. and 5.30–11.15 p.m.; both closed Saturday lunch, Sunday and public holidays.

Enormous, gracious and elegant old Soho building now revitalized and run as a brasserie/wine bar (on the ground floor) and restaurant presided over by one of London's most charming manageresses. The brasserie menu is less ambitious than the restaurant's and both rely on seasonal ingredients to provide stylish, interesting, modern French cooking. Exceptional wine list. Brasserie from £10, restaurant from £30.

LA CROISETTE   **34** D3   ⊖ Earl's Court
168 Ifield Road, SW10; tel. (071) 373 3694. Service noon–3 p.m. and 7.30–11.30 p.m.; closed all day Monday and Tuesday lunch.
An authentic touch of the South of France. Go here and pretend you've crossed the Channel while munching through their enormous *plateau de fruits de mer* that seems to contain every known edible mollusc and crustacean. Follow with plainly but exquisitely cooked fish, while turning a blind eye to the dull vegetables. The all-in £25 set meal also includes salad, Stilton and dessert. Modestly priced wine list.

LE CAFÉ DU MARCHE   **16** R11   ⊖ Barbican
22 Charterhouse Square, Charterhouse Mews, EC1; tel. (071) 608 1609. Service noon–2.30 p.m. and 6–10 p.m.; closed Saturday lunch and Sunday.
Loft-style warehouse conversion with a live pianist every night. Low-priced set, no-choice menu (£11) and one with a choice of six dishes per course at £17.50. Good, everyday, French food; fish soup, *sole bonne femme*, *daube de bœuf* and *crème caramel*. Pleasant, low-key atmosphere, it's good for post-Barbican outings.

LE CAPRICE   **22** L8   ⊖ Green Park
Arlington House, Arlington Street, SW1; tel. (071) 629 2239. Service noon–3 p.m. and 6–12 p.m.
Stylish haunt of media and theatrical world. French, but internationally **109** influenced menu, constantly being updated. A few dishes, however, such as eggs Benedict, salmon fishcakes with sorrel sauce and veal sausages with mash, are never dropped. Similarly well-chosen wine list. From £20 a head.

LOU PESCADOU   **28** D5   ⊖ Earls Court
241 Old Brompton Road, SW5; tel. (071) 370 1057. Service noon–3 p.m. and 7–12 p.m.
There's a no-bookings policy at this French seafood café which is modelled on its South of France equivalent. It's relatively informal, has a bar, serves great pizzas, as well as oysters and all seafoods in season, cooked simply and well. From £15.

MANZI'S   **23** M9   ⊖ Leicester Square
1–2 Leicester Street, WC2; tel. (071) 734 0224. Service noon–2.30 p.m. and 5.30–11.30 p.m.
Old-fashioned but delightful Italian fish restaurant and part of a family-run hotel. Has terrific waiters who know all their regulars (it's a popular

lunch spot for publishers and media folk) and a great menu of seasonal fish, steamed, grilled, poached, deep-fried or mornay. Excellent smoked cod's roe, oysters and prawn cocktail followed by plaice or haddock with the best chips in London. Forget the puddings. Italian wines. From £15 a head.

MUSEUM STREET CAFÉ   **14** N10   ⊖ Tottenham Court Road
47 Museum Street,WC1; tel. (071) 405 3211. Service 12.30–2.45 p.m. and 7.30–9 p.m.; closed Saturday and Sunday.
A tiny, modest restaurant run on a shoe-string by young chefs, Gail Koerber and Mark Nathan (late of the River Café and Clarke's). Throughout the day they serve home-made breads, cakes and other delights, at lunch, a small, daily menu of Mediterranean food and in the evening a *prix-fixe* menu. Three-course set lunch around £12 a head, and dinner £17.50. Credit cards are not accepted.

ORSO   **14** O9   ⊖ Covent Garden
27 Wellington Street, WC2; tel. (071) 240 5269. Service daily noon– midnight.
Like its neighbour, Joe Allen, this is a famous media and stage hang-out that is popular for post-production first-night parties. Delicious menu of rustic Italian food; great little pizzas, simple, charcoal-grilled fish and meat dishes, as well as interesting ways with vegetables. Italian wine list. From £20 a head.

110

RIVER CAFÉ, THE   ⊖ Hammersmith
Thames Wharf, Rainville Road,W6; tel. (071) 385 3344. Service 12.30– 2.30 p.m. and 7.30–9.15 p.m.; closed Monday and public holidays.
Housed on the ground floor of architect Richard Roger's warehouse-empire with great views across the Thames. Italian country cooking with great emphasis on seasonal produce that is cooked simply. Potato gnocchi, mozzarella salad with sun-dried tomatoes and garlic toast, pheasant braised with cabbage and terrific charcoal-grilled fish and meats. Italian wine list. From £25 a head.

ROTISSERIE   ⊖ Shepherd's Bush Green
56 Uxbridge Road, Shepherd's Bush Green, W12; tel. (081) 743 3028. Service noon–3 p.m. and 6.30–11.30 p.m.; closed Saturday lunch and all day Sunday.
Has a deceptive frontage hiding a large, café-style restaurant, in a plainly but pleasantly decorated room dominated by the rotisserie grill. A compact menu of salads, charcoal-grilled meat, fowl and fish, cheeses or a small choice of desserts to finish. Well-run, and useful in a gastronomic desert. Reasonably priced wine list. From £12 a head.

ST. QUENTIN   30 G4   ⊖ Knightsbridge or South Kensington
243 Brompton Road, SW3; tel. (071) 589 8005. Service Monday to Saturday noon–3.30 p.m. and 7 p.m.–midnight; Sunday noon–4 p.m. and 7–11.30 p.m.
A smart, Parisian-style restaurant where you expect to see rouged ladies with white poodles amongst the customers. Inconsistent food but has so much else going for it. Great cheeseboard and desserts. Set meals from £12 but à la carte from £25.

SUTHERLANDS   13 L9   ⊖ Oxford Circus or Piccadilly Circus
45 Lexington Street,W1; tel. (071) 434 3401. Service 12.15–2.15 p.m. and 6.15–11.15 p.m.; closed Saturday lunch, Sunday and public holidays.
Sian Sutherland-Dodd is a charming, sophisticated hostess while her chef, Gary Hollihead, has made a name for himself with his artistic-looking but well-flavoured, sophisticated French food. The restaurant provides a modern but elegant backdrop for the food, and the place attracts a smart set, especially at lunch time. Portions verge on the small. From £25 at lunch, from £35 for dinner.

THE IVY   14 M9   ⊖ Leicester Square
1 West Street, WC2; tel. (071) 836 4751. Service daily noon–3.30 p.m. and 6 p.m.–midnight.
A long-established, theatrical restaurant recently rekindled. Stylish, understated and comfortable with a somewhat ambitious menu of internationally flavoured, modern French food. From £20 a head but flexible menu. **111**

TINY TIM   ⊖ Camden Town
7 Plender Street, NW1; tel. (071) 388 0402. Service Tuesday to Friday noon–2 p.m.; Tuesday to Saturday 7–11 p.m.; Sunday 12.30–3 p.m.
A small, but perfectly designed French bistro offering a choice of five dishes per course plus daily specials. Interesting, well-flavoured rustic food, such as *carré d'agneau* with mustard, lemon *creme brûlée* and exceptional vegetables. Modest wine list. From £15 a head.

TURNER'S   30 G5   ⊖ Knightsbridge or South Kensington
87–89 Walton Street, SW3; tel. (071) 584 6711. Service 12.30–2.30 p.m. and 7.30–11 p.m.; closed Saturday lunch and public holidays.
A delightful and very pretty blue-and-white restaurant, with etched glass screens and a marvellous menu of top-notch French and, occasionally, classic British, fare. Lunch is a bargain at £15.50; set dinner from £20.

VERY SIMPLY NICO   32 L5   ⊖ Pimlico or Victoria
48a Rochester Row, SW1; tel. (071) 630 8061. Service noon–2 p.m. and 7–11 p.m.; closed Saturday lunch and all day Sunday.
This is Nico Ladenis' brasserie, where Tony Tobin presents a set-price menu with dishes such as garlic mushrooms, smoked mackerel pâté, salmon steak, grilled steaks, great chips and other vegetables. Somewhat characterless and doggedly brightly lit, but the food is perfect. Appropriate lower-price-range wine list. Set meals from £20.

THE BEST OF BRITISH

GREEN'S RESTAURANT & OYSTER BAR   23 L8   ⊖ Green Park
36 Duke Street, St. James's, SW1; tel. (071) 930 4566. Service Monday to Saturday 12.30–3 p.m. and 6–11 p.m.; Sunday brunch noon–3.30 p.m..
A rather clubby, frightfully genteel atmosphere. Oysters top a menu of classic but dolled-up British food as delicate as asparagus with hollandaise sauce, as hearty as bangers (sausages) and mash. From £30 a head.

HYATT CARLTON RIB ROOM   30 H6   ⊖ Knightsbridge
Cadogan Place, SW1; tel. (071) 235 5411. Service Monday to Saturday 12.30–2.45 p.m. and 7–11 p.m. Sunday 12.30–2.30 p.m. and 7–11 p.m.
The hotel itself has changed name several times since its origin as the Carlton Tower, but the Rib Room's succulent beef has stayed consistently admirable. Pleasantly appointed restaurant with service to match. Piano bar's sophisticated melodies unobtrusively brighten the atmosphere. Set lunch £23.50, otherwise count £32 and up.

112

PORTERS   24 N9   ⊖ Covent Garden
17 Henrietta Street, WC2; tel. (071) 836 6466. Service noon–11.30 p.m. (10.30 p.m. on Sunday).
One of the few places in Covent Garden that serves decent, reasonably priced food and can generally offer a table. Soundly British: pies, roasts, etc. and good puddings. From £10 a head.

RITZ   22 K/L8   ⊖ Green Park
Piccadilly, W1; tel. (071) 493 8181. Service Monday to Saturday 7–10.30 a.m., 12.30–2.30 p.m. and 6–11.30 p.m.; Sunday and public holidays 8–10.30 a.m., 12.30–3 p.m. and 6.30–10.30 p.m.
No London restaurant round-up would be complete without the Ritz. Its inimitability owes less to gastronomic promise, (classic English and

very expensive) than to architectural beauty and atmosphere. Tea is served in the Palm Court, while lunch and dinner are taken in the Louis Quinze restaurant. Set lunch £25, set dinner £40.

RULES 24 N9 ⊖ Covent Garden
35 Maiden Lane, WC2; tel. (071) 836 5314. Service Monday to Saturday noon–midnight.
Distinguished, historic home of tasteful, traditional fare—Aberdeen Angus beef, steak and kidney pie, and game in season. Celebrities, both royal and showbiz, gravitate here, but mere mortals with big budgets can be served if they book in advance.

SIMPSON'S IN THE STRAND 24 O9 ⊖ Charing Cross
GRAND DIVAN TAVERN
100 Strand, WC2; tel. (071) 836 9112. Service Monday to Saturday noon–3 p.m. and 6–10 p.m.
Roast beef at its best since time immemorial. The joints here are beef and lamb, on the trolley, generously sliced to your taste. If the appetite can take it, round off your meal with one of the calorific English "puddings". Classy atmosphere precludes jeans.

SWEETINGS 17 S9 ⊖ Bank or Mansion House
39 Queen Victoria Street, EC4; tel. (071) 248 3062. Service 11.30 a.m.– 3 p.m.; closed Saturday and Sunday.
A favourite City lunch spot, justly famous for its oysters and menu of superior British fish dishes. Go early and grab a place at one of the bars, drink draught Guinness and close your ears to the braying City gents. Also good bar sandwiches. From £12.

113

TATE GALLERY RESTAURANT 33 N4 ⊖ Pimlico
Millbank, SW1; tel. (071) 834 6754. Service Monday to Saturday noon– 3 p.m.
Although you'd never expect to find fine food in a museum, Londoners in the know go arty for authentic English cuisine at lunch-time. The Tate's chef deals in old masters of classic cuisine, plus his own variations. Noted for wines, too. A splendid mural adds to the cheery atmosphere. From £15.

TIDDY DOLS 22 K8 ⊖ Green Park
55 Shepherd Market, W1; tel. (071) 499 235. Service daily 6 p.m.– 1 a.m.
In an 18th-century house in Shepherd's Market, tourists sample dishes as authentic as cock-a-leekie soup and Welsh rarebit, accompanied by music ranging from Madrigals to music-hall. Tiddy Dol gingerbread is the trademark. Average around £20.

ETHNIC

As in most large cities, London has collected its fair share of incomers, and the restaurant scene reflects their influence.

African

BLUE NILE   ⊖ Westbourne Park
341a Harrow Road, W9; tel. (071) 286 5129. Service daily 7–11.30 p.m.
Go here for Ethiopian food and be surprised by its variety, spiciness and flavour. Much is vegetarian, and can be either hot (*berbere* dishes, flavoured with a mixture of fresh ginger, garlic and chilli pepper), or, for the more conservative, mild (*alecha*). Food is scooped up with a pancake-like bread made from fermented millet, called *ingera*. Set menus or à la carte, from around £12.

CALABASH   **14** N9   ⊖ Covent Garden
The Africa Centre, 38 King Street, WC2; tel. (071) 836 1976. Service 12.30–3 p.m. and 6–11 p.m.; closed all day Sunday.
The menu changes frequently at this restaurant in the depths of the Africa Centre and features popular dishes from different parts of Africa. Good atmosphere, often live music and rum cocktails. From £15 a head.

114

CHEZ LILINE   ⊖ Finsbury Park
101 Stroud Green Road, N4; tel. (071) 263 6550. Service noon–3 p.m. and 6.30–11.30 p.m.; closed public holidays.
Eccentric and informal French/Mauritian fish restaurant, where the food is cooked to order, so a meal can take an age but it's worth it. *Bouillabaisse, moules marinière,* scallops with mushrooms and less familiar, slightly exotic flavours. Modestly priced wine list. From £15 a head.

LAURENT   ⊖ Golders Green
428 Finchley Road, NW2; tel. (071) 794 3603. Service noon–2 p.m. and 6–11 p.m.; closed Sunday and public holidays.
A neighbourhood café, run by a Tunisian family and specializing in *couscous*. Start with *brik à l'œuf*, an interesting, deep-fried triangle of filo pastry stuffed with egg, chopped onion and parsley. Follow with a hearty dish of steamed meat and vegetables on *couscous*, with a side dish of fiery-hot *harissa* sauce. Drink Moroccan wine. From £12 a head.

European and Mediterranean

ANNA'S PLACE   ⊖ Angel, then 73 bus
90 Mildmay Park, N1; tel. (071) 249 9379. Service 12.15–2.30 p.m. and 7.15–10.45 p.m.; closed Sunday and Monday.
A popular Swedish wine bar/restaurant run with idiosyncratic energy by Anna Hegarty and a team of young, friendly staff. Blackboard menu includes Jansson's Temptation, meatballs with cranberry sauce, new potatoes and cucumber salad, grilled *gravad lax* and memorable home-made ice cream. Drink wine or Swedish beer with a Schnapps chaser. Attractive garden. From £15 a head.

GAY HUSSAR   13 M10   ⊖ Tottenham Court Road
2 Greek Street, W1; tel. (071) 437 0973. Service 12.30–2.30 p.m. and 5.30–10.45 p.m.; closed Sunday and public holidays.
A long-established Hungarian restaurant that is particularly popular at lunch time with London's literary set and left-wing politicians. Homely and old-fashioned, with terrific waiters and a long menu of comforting food, such as bean soup, *borsch*, Serbian chicken and duck. Also, try their scrumptious apple strudel, cherry soup or stuffed pancakes. Excellent wine list. Set lunch £12, otherwise from £20.

KALAMARAS   19 D9   ⊖ Bayswater or Queensway
76–78 Inverness Mews, W2; tel. (071) 727 9122. Service 7 p.m.– midnight; closed Sunday and public holidays.
London's best Greek restaurant, where the menu is in Greek. Décor is native with colourful rugs on the whitewashed walls, ladder-back chairs and the odd cow bell. *Tiropitas*, hot pastries stuffed with feta cheese, oregano and mint, simply grilled, fresh sardines and sweetbreads cooked with courgettes are particularly good, but this is proper Greek home-cooking and not a kebab house. Greek wines. From £15 a head.

115

LEMONIA   ⊖ Camden Town
154 Regent's Park Road, NW1; tel. (071) 586 7454. Service Monday to Saturday 6–11.30 p.m.; closed Sunday.
A delightful, popular Greek-Cypriot restaurant, with a good *meze* menu and dishes not often found in this country. *Trahana* is an unusual wheat and milk soup, aubergines are grilled with chopped onion, oil and aromatic herbs, and *spinakopitta* is that delicious spinach and feta filo pastry pie.
   Good atmosphere and a sliding roof that is opened in the summer. From £15 a head.

OGNISKO POLSKIE   **29** F6   ⊖ South Kensington

55 Prince's Gate, Exhibition Road, SW7; tel. (071) 589 4635. Service 12.30–3 p.m. and 6.30–11 p.m.

The Polish Club's restaurant, open to the public, is tasteful elegance in pale yellow with pillars, oil paintings and views of their garden. The menu changes daily, but invariably offers standards such as tender meat dumplings, boiled beef with horseradish and cold beetroot salad, or the national game stew called *bigos*. Don't miss the potato fritters. Round off the meal with cream-cheese pancakes. From £12 a head.

PHOENICIA   ⊖ High Street Kensington

11–13 Abingdon Road, W8; tel (071) 937 0120. Service daily noon–midnight.

Unintimidating, family-run Lebanese restaurant decorated in comfortable, classless style. The most interesting feature of the menu is a long list of meat and vegetable *meze* and the idea is to choose a selection to share. Only the very hungry go on to the kebab-style main dishes. Spicy, delicious dips such as *moutabel*, made with baked aubergine, yoghurt and garlic and *hummus*, served with a sesame sauce and called *falafel*; *tabbouleh*, a chopped parsley, tomato and buckwheat salad and garlicky chicken livers. Buffet lunch £8, otherwise £15 and over.

116 REBATO'S   ⊖ Stockwell or Vauxhall

169 South Lambeth Road, SW8; tel. (071) 735 6388. Service noon–3 p.m. and 7–11 p.m.; closed Saturday lunch and public holidays.

London's first and, some say, most authentic *tapas* bar in London. It's certainly noisy, hectic and its selection of little hot and cold Spanish appetizers that make up the menu are very good indeed. The bar adjoins a full-scale Spanish restaurant. Drink San Miguel beer, or Spanish wines and sherries.

WODKA   **28** D6   ⊖ High Street Kensington

12 St. Albans Grove, W8; tel. (071) 937 6513. Service 12.30–2.30 p.m. and 7.30–11 p.m.; closed Saturday and Sunday lunch.

A tiny, busy Polish restaurant with an enticing menu of *blinis*, soups, substantial salads and interesting game dishes. The short menu changes frequently and the restaurant is fashionable and trendy. As you might expect, their hallmark is a great list of superb flavoured vodkas.

Far Eastern

AJIMURA **14** N9 ⊖ Covent Garden
51–53 Shelton Street, WC2; tel. (071) 240 9424. Service Monday to Friday noon–3 p.m., Monday to Saturday 6–11 p.m., Sunday 6–10.30 p.m.; closed public holidays.
A delightful, informal Japanese restaurant and *sushi* bar with a well-explained and reasonably priced menu that includes *tempura*, *sashimi*, noodle- and rice-based dishes. Set meals centre around popular dishes such as *sukiyaki*, *shabu-shabu* etc. and there is a lengthy à la carte menu. Drink sake or Japanese beer. About £15 a head.

BEDLINGTON CAFÉ ⊖ Chiswick Park
or Turnham Green, then any bus
24 Fauconberg Road, W4; tel. (081) 994 1965. Service noon–2 p.m. and 6–10 p.m.; closed Sunday.
By day a greasy-spoon British café and by night one of London's best Thai café/restaurants. Run by a delightful Thai family, the food is always fresh, usually cooked to order and booking is vital. Count from £10 a head.

BLUE ELEPHANT **34** C1 ⊖ Fulham Broadway
4–6 Fulham Broadway, SW6; tel. (071) 385 6595. Service noon–3 p.m. and 7 p.m.–12.30 a.m.; closed Saturday lunch and Sunday evening.
An exotic, romantic Thai restaurant, decorated with a profusion of plants and flowers to simulate a Thai village. By night it's candlelit, the staff wear traditional dress and are gracious and charming. The food is good but expensive. Best dishes include their *satay*, chicken salad and prawn curry. Set menu around £23.

117

BUSAN ⊖ Highbury & Islington
43 Holloway Road, N7; tel. (071) 607 8264. Service noon–3 p.m. and 6–11 p.m.; closed Sunday lunch.
A tiny, family-run, Korean restaurant where the chef is a *sashimi* expert and offers an exceedingly reasonably priced platter. Otherwise expect a combination of Chinese, Thai and Japanese cooking, with the Oriental rule of five flavours (salt, sweet, sour, spicy-hot and bitter). *Kimchee*, pickled cabbage, is eaten with everything and the most famous dish is *bulgogi*, in which beef is first marinated, then cooked at the table and rolled in lettuce. Also good is a stuffed pancake called *bindae duk*. Drink sake. From £12 a head.

DALAT ⊖ Kilburn

11 Willesden Lane, NW6; tel. (071) 624 8521. Service daily 6–11 p.m.
An informal, but professionally run Vietnamese restaurant, owned by
genuine boat people. Explicit menu whose spring rolls, soups and do-
it-yourself pancakes stuffed with salad, mint, prawns or meat are
delicious. Friendly and helpful staff and a reasonable wine list. From
£10 a head.

DRAGON INN ⊖ Woodford

*63 Westbourne Grove, W2; tel. (071) 229 8806. Service noon–mid-
night.*
A stylish, modern Cantonese restaurant where the lunch-time *dim sum*
is excellent. Good also for one-dish meals. Their branch in Soho—12
Gerrard Street, W1; tel. (071) 494 0870—is always full by 12.15 p.m.

GOLDEN DUCK   **35** D3   ⊖ South Kensington, then 14 bus

*6 Hollywood Road, SW10; tel. (071) 352 3500. Service Monday to
Friday 7 p.m.–midnight; Saturday and Sunday noon–3 p.m.*
One of London's most consistently good and fashionable Chinese
restaurants, where the menu keeps pace with the changing fashions in
Chinese food. Great leave-it-to-us feasts, but do try their griddle-fried
dumplings and whole, steamed sea bass. The décor is smart and
elegant behind a stunning Yin-Yang motif painted on the window.
Sophisticated wine list. From £15 a head.

HUNG TOA   **19** D9   ⊖ Bayswater or Queensway

54 Queensway, W2; tel. (071) 727 6017. Service noon–11 p.m.
Crispy-skinned, barbecued meats are the speciality of this Cantonese
dining-room. Choose duck or pork, which will be deftly chopped into
chunks and served with rice and eaten lukewarm. Also good soup and
fried noodle dishes. Most people drink Chinese tea. From £10 a head.

IKKYU   **13** L/M11   ⊖ Goodge Street

*67 Tottenham Court Road, W1; tel. (071) 636 9280. Service Monday to
Friday 12.30–2.10 p.m. and 6–10.30 p.m.; Sunday 6.30–10.30 p.m.*
Informal, simply decorated, basement Japanese restaurant, where the
portions are plentiful and the food tasty and freshly made. Great value
set lunches. From £10 a head.

ZEN W3 ⊖ Hampstead

*83 Hampstead High Street, NW3; tel. (071) 794 7863. Service daily
noon–3 p.m. and 7 p.m.–midnight.*
A trendy Chinese restaurant, serving a menu of regional food enlivened
by the use of fashionable ingredients. Hence quail rather than chicken,
asparagus and other fancy foods. Popular with Hampstead's smart,
young set. An appropriately sophisticated wine list. From £20 a head.

Indian and Pakistani

BABA BHEL POORI HOUSE ⊖ Queensway or Royal Oak
29–31 Porchester Road, W2; tel. (071) 221 7502. Service noon–3 p.m. and 6–10.45 p.m.; closed Monday.
A highly unusual, but superb, Indian vegetarian restaurant where the food is delicately spiced. Try their *thali, aloo papri chat* and *masalai dosai*, a particularly good stuffed pancake. Drink the yoghurt-based *lassi* or choose from the short wine list. From £10 a head.

BOMBAY BRASSERIE **28** D5 ⊖ Gloucester Road
Courtfield Close, Courtfield Road/Gloucester Road, SW7; tel. (071) 370 4040. Service 12.30–2.30 p.m. and 7.30–midnight.
London's most successful attempt at recreating colonial India. The large, elegant room is decorated with Indian antiques and lit by reproduction old lamps. The cooking is regional and, though not always as good as it might be, everything else about the place is a compensation. At lunch their buffet is a bargain at £11.50, choosing à la carte will be from £15.

JAMDANI **13** L11 ⊖ Goodge Street or Warren Street
34 Charlotte Street, W1; tel. (071) 636 1178. Service noon–2.45 p.m. and 6–11.30 p.m.; closed Sunday.
Simply, but strikingly, decorated in natural finishes with slate floor, textured terracotta walls and colour provided by lengths of fabric (*jamdani* is a gossamer-fine weave, used for wedding saris in Bangladesh). Elegant, lightly spiced and sophisticated Indian fare, with the emphasis on healthy, wholesome food well presented. Sophisticated wine list too, featuring Californian wines. From £20.

119

RAJ DOOT ⊖ Ravens Court Park
291 King Street, W6; tel. (081) 748 7345. Service 6 p.m.–midnight.
An exceptional Indian restaurant, where the food is of a consistently high standard. Outstanding prawn *bhoona* with *poori* (the bread that puffs up like a ball), chicken *tikka masala*, Bombay *aloo* (potatoes) and *tarka dal*. Drink Kingfisher lager. Décor is the style of Moghlai print, off-white walls, comfy chairs and banks of fake greenery. From £10 a head.

SALLOOS **21** H6 ⊖ Knightsbridge
62–64 Kinnerton Street, SW1; tel. (071) 235 4444. Service noon–2.30 p.m. and 7–11 p.m.; closed Sunday and public holidays.
A smart and expensive Pakistani restaurant, where the action takes place upstairs and the décor has mosque-like overtones. It's preferable to go at lunch time, as in the evening it attracts noisy high-

flyers. Try *tandoori* lamb chops, *alu zeera*—a version of Bombay *aloo*—and chicken *taimuri*, which is a speciality of this restaurant. Pricey wine list. From £20 a head.

SURUCHI ⊖ Angel

18 Theberton Street, Islington, N1; tel. (071) 359 8033. Service daily noon–2.30 p.m. and 6–10.30 p.m.

A bright and breezy Indian vegetarian *bhel poori* house. Short and explicit menu, quick service and pleasant, relaxed atmosphere. From £10 a head.

ON A BUDGET

CAFÉ FLO ⊖ Belsize Park

205 Haverstock Hill, NW3; tel. (071) 435 6744. Service noon–5 p.m. 6–11 p.m.

An authentic French café/bistro with an espresso machine on the bar, a short regional menu and terrific-value set meals. Best are *L'Idée Flo*, a soup or salad followed by steak and *frites*, or vegetable moussaka at £6.50 or *The Special*, offering greater choice and coffee, at £8.50.

DIANA'S DINER 14 N10 ⊖ Covent Garden

39 Endell Street, WC2; tel. (071) 240 0272. Service Monday to Saturday 7 a.m.–7 p.m.; Sunday 8 a.m.–2 p.m.

An unlicensed café/restaurant famous for its hefty portions of cosmopolitan Italian food, casseroles, meat pies, vegetarian dish of the day, braised sausages and mash and fry-ups. From £5.

JOE ALLEN 24 N9 ⊖ Covent Garden

13 Exeter Street, WC2; tel. (071) 836 0651. Service daily noon–12.45 a.m. (11.45 p.m. on Sunday).

A famous, but discreetly located, restaurant serving a blackboard menu of American food. Popular with media and advertizing folk (at lunch time) and for pre- and post-theatre dinners. Salads are served in big wooden bowls, burgers are available, though not on the menu, and there are good soups and chips. No minimum charge.

LE CASINO 31 H4 ⊖ Sloane Square

77 Lower Sloane Street, SW1; tel. (071) 730 3313. Service Monday to Saturday noon–3 p.m. and 6 p.m.–1 p.m.; Sunday noon–11.30 p.m.

A lively, informal restaurant, part of a small but eccentric chain. All starters £1.95 and main dishes £4.65. Food is Frenchified international, such as duck *en croûte* and lamb marinated with garlic and honey.

MÉLANGE   **14** N10   ⊖ Covent Garden
59 Endell Street, WC2; tel. (071) 240 8077. Service Monday to Friday noon–midnight; Saturday 6 p.m.–midnight; closed Sunday.
This place looks as if it's run by art students and for some years has provided cheap, interesting, varied food. It's the sort of place you'll either love or hate; the music is loud but good and a visit is an experience. From £15 a head.

MILDRED'S   **13** M9/10   ⊖ Tottenham Court Road
58 Greek Street, W1; tel. (071) 494 1634. Service daily noon–10 p.m.
A small, functional, but style-conscious vegetarian café/restaurant run by a group of women. Interesting food with stir-fry as the mainstay, but also good soups, home-made breads and puddings. Also fish and vegan dishes. Take your own wine. From £8 a head.

NEW SERPENTINE   **20** F7   ⊖ South Kensington or Knightsbridge
Hyde Park, W2; tel. (071) 402 1142. Service daily 10 a.m.–10.30 p.m.
Looking like a triple ice-cream cone, this "temporary" restaurant, next to the Lido, overlooks the Serpentine and provides anything from a cup of tea or coffee to a full-blown, three-course meal. High standards and modest prices for wholesome, home cooking. Short, good wine list; dinner or lunch about £15 per head.

PARSONS   **35** E3   ⊖ South Kensington, then no. 14 bus
311 Fulham Road, SW10; tel. (071) 352 0651. Service daily noon– 12.30 a.m.; last orders at midnight on Sunday.
A noisy, lively diner-style restaurant that specializes in spaghetti. Second helpings of certain toppings are free. Otherwise burgers, Tex-Mex and US sandwiches and salads. From £10.

121

QUALITY CHOP HOUSE   **15** Q11   ⊖ Farringdon
94 Farringdon Road, EC1; tel. (071) 837 5093. Service Monday to Friday 7–9.30 a.m., noon–3 p.m and 6.30–11.30 p.m.; Saturday 6.30–11.30 p.m.; Sunday brunch noon–3 p.m.
A Victorian working-man's café, given a new lease of life by Charles Fontaine, who used to be the chef at Le Caprice. He cooks everything to order and his menu is seasonal, down-to-earth, French or British food. Breakfast, bangers (sausages) and mash, steak and chips, good salads and charcoal-grilled meats, etc. Short, but well-chosen, wine list. Table-sharing is inevitable but turnover is fast. From £10 a head.

SPAGHETTI HOUSE   **13** L11   ⊖ Goodge Street
15–17 Goodge Street, W1; tel. (071) 636 6582. Service noon–11 p.m.
Offers an unfashionable, but extremely good, unambitious menu of Italian pasta dishes. Lasagne, spaghetti bolognaise, cannelloni etc. Cheerful, fast, no-frills service. From £10.

CASUAL

ED'S EASY DINER   **13** M9

⊖ Leicester Square
or Tottenham Court Road

12 Moor Street, W1; tel. (071) 439 1955. Service Sunday to Thursday 11.30 a.m.–midnight; Friday and Saturday 11.30 a.m.–1 a.m.
An authentic replica of a 50s American diner, complete with bar stools, jukebox and a menu of well-prepared, American fast food: burgers, hot dogs, French fries and sandwiches. From £5 a head.

ICA CAFÉ   **23** M8

⊖ Piccadilly Circus
or Charing Cross

The Mall, SW1; tel. (071) 930 8535. Service noon–9 p.m. (bar open until 11 p.m.); closed public holidays.
You're safe in the hands of the Institute of Contemporary Arts' catering division; there's a good, daily-changing menu of fresh, wholesome and reasonably priced food. The drawback is the cavernous location. Also pub licence and bar food.

MITCHELL & O'BRIEN   **13** M10

⊖ Tottenham Court Road

2 St. Anne's Court, W1; tel. (071) 434 9941. Service Monday to Friday noon–3.30 p.m.; bar service only Saturday 6.30–11 p.m.
Fashionable, modern and tasteful American diner with Art Déco overtones to its bar-dominated design. Good pastrami on rye, US sandwiches, bagels, etc. Good beers, cocktails and espresso coffee.

122

PIZZA EXPRESS   **14** N10

⊖ Holborn
or Tottenham Court Road

30 Coptic Street, WC1; tel. (071) 636 3232. Service daily noon–midnight.
The most idiosyncratic of a London-wide chain of excellent, Italian pizza restaurants, where the chefs can be watched at work. Distinctive décor, with black-and-white chequered floor, black-painted chairs and marble-topped tables. From £5 for pizza and drink.

STOCKPOT   **23** M9

⊖ Piccadilly Circus

40 Panton Street, SW1; tel. (071) 839 5142. Service Monday to Saturday 8 a.m.–11.30 p.m.; Sunday noon–9.45 p.m.
Reasonably priced, generous portions of international food: lasagne, spaghetti bolognaise, cannelloni, casseroles and kidneys in red wine with rice or chips. Friendly, low-key and efficient. From £10 a head.

A SNACK OR A CUP OF TEA

CAFÉ PELICAN   **24** N9   ⊖ Leicester Square
45 St. Martin's Lane, WC2; tel. (071) 379 0309. Service daily 11 a.m.–1 a.m.
A Parisian-style brasserie with outside tables, bar food, informal dining area and restaurant. Flexible menu include *croque-monsieur*, soups, *prix-fixe* menu and wine bar licence.

CHELSEA BUN DINER   **35** E2   Bus no. 11, 19 or 31
9a Limerstone Street, SW10; tel. (071) 352 3635. Service Monday to Saturday 7 a.m.–11.30 p.m.; Sunday 11 a.m.–11.30 p.m.
An attractive British diner with a health-conscious slant to a sensible menu that embraces omelettes, toasted sandwiches and old stalwarts like liver and bacon. Outside tables and good espresso coffee.

FIELDS   **23** N8   ⊖ Charing Cross
St. Martin-in-the-Fields Church, Duncannon Street, WC2; tel. (071) 839 4342. Service Monday to Saturday 10 a.m.–9 p.m.; Sunday noon–6 p.m.
An excellent, informally run 180-seater café/restaurant in the crypt of a church. Good value home cooking but also home-made breads, cakes and pastries, served in the morning and at tea time.

JUSTIN DE BLANK   **30** H4   ⊖ Sloane Square
In the General Trading Co., 141 Sloane Street, SW1; tel. (071) 730 6400. Service Monday to Friday 9 a.m.–5.15 p.m. and 6–10.15 p.m.; Saturday 9 a.m.–1.45 p.m.; closed Sunday.
A useful bolt hole in the basement of the Sloane Rangers' favourite shop, which also has a large patio. Queue for a table and enjoy the wholesome food and home cooking.

123

MUFFIN MAN   **28** C6   ⊖ High Street Kensington
12 Wrights Lane, W8; tel. (071) 937 6652. Service 8.15 a.m.–5.45 p.m.; closed Sunday.
A quaintly old-fashioned English tearoom serving top-quality sandwiches, home-made cakes, breakfasts and high tea. Always busy.

PATISSERIE VALERIE   **13** M9   ⊖ Tottenham Court Road
44 Old Compton Street, W1; tel. (071) 437 3466. Service Monday to Friday 8 a.m.–8.30 p.m.; Saturday 8 a.m.–7 p.m.; Sunday 10 a.m.–5.30 p.m.
A Soho landmark now fashionable with the Soho set. Functional, busy and serving a wide range of authentic French patisserie for eat-in or takeaway. Choose from the well-stocked window display.

PRIMROSE PATISSERIE   ⊖ Chalk Farm

136 Regent's Park Road, NW1; tel. (071) 722 7848. Open 8.30 a.m.– 10 p.m.

Small and delightful homely tearoom handy for Regent's Park. Filled croissants, Polish fruit fritters, wonderful sandwiches and savoury pastries. Very busy mid-morning, tea time and early evening.

FISH & CHIPS

GEALES   18 C8   ⊖ Notting Hill Gate

2 Farmer Street, W8; tel. (071) 727 7969. Service Tuesday to Saturday noon–3 p.m. and 6–11 p.m.; closed Sunday and Monday.

West London's favourite fish and chip restaurant that looks more like an olde worlde teashoppe. Blackboard menu of the day's catch, which often runs out, two sizes of fish portions and great chips. Fast turnover and queueing normal. From £8 a head.

GRAHAME'S SEAFARE   13 L9/10   ⊖ Oxford Circus

38 Poland Street, W1; tel. (071) 437 3788. Service Monday to Saturday noon–2.45 p.m.; Monday to Thursday 5.30–9 p.m.; Friday and Saturday 5.30–8 p.m.; closed Sunday, Jewish and public holidays.

A Soho institution that is consistently popular for its kosher fish menu. Gefilte fish, smoked salmon and all seasonal fish served poached, steamed, pan- or deep-fried. This last is the favourite here and you can choose batter made with matzo meal which gives a nutty crunch. Great potato *latkes* and chips, with cream cheese *blintzes* to finish. Drink lemon tea at lunch, wine at dinner. From £12 a head.

NORTH SEA FISH RESTAURANT   7 N12   ⊖ King's Cross

7–8 Leigh Street, WC1; tel. (071) 387 5892. Service Monday to Saturday noon–2.30 p.m. and 5.30–10.30 p.m.; closed Sunday and public holidays.

A charming, pleasantly clean and fresh sit-down or takeaway chippie, much favoured by cabbies. Matzo-meal batter is available but, unusually for such a restaurant, fish is also served poached and potatoes boiled (if required!). From £5 a head.

SEASHELL FISH RESTAURANT   11 G11   ⊖ Marylebone

49 Lisson Grove, NW1; tel. (071) 723 8703. Service Monday to Friday noon–2 p.m. and 5–10.30 p.m.; Saturday noon–10.30 p.m.

London's most famous fish and chip restaurant and takeaway. Great, crisp batter and good chips, queueing inevitable and everything cooked to order. Set lunch £6.50, otherwise from £10 a head.

PUBS

London may not have many cafés, European style, but it does have pubs. Many of them date from the 17th century, when they sold coffee and port and acted as meeting places for lawyers, insurers and merchants. Today, their role is still mainly social, and a visit can be a great way of getting to know the British way of life and the people.

Food is available in most pubs. Often fairly basic, it's casual and reasonably priced, and usually typically British, like fish and chips or a ploughman's lunch. But don't expect to be waited on—order both food and drinks at the bar. Below, we have indicated which pubs sell above-average food.

Premises that are licensed (that is, licensed to serve alcoholic drinks) are legally allowed to open from 11 a.m. to 11 p.m. from Monday to Saturday, and on Sundays from noon to 3 p.m., and 7 p.m. to 10.30 p.m. But please note that some pubs in the centre of London are closed on Saturday and/or Sunday, and many pub-owners call "Time" in the late afternoon.

Youngsters under 14 are not allowed on licensed premises, although some pubs get round this law by setting aside a room for families, and of course there's nothing to stop them using the garden (except the British weather). Also, alcohol can only be served to adults aged 18 and over—those under age be warned!

ALBERT, THE **32** L6 ⊖ St. James's Park **125**
52 Victoria Street, SW1; tel. (071) 222 5577.
A grand Victorian public house, the Albert opens at 8 a.m. on weekdays to serve breakfast, and keeps normal pub hours as well. There's a carvery restaurant on the first floor and snack food available in the bar.

AUDLEY **22** J9 ⊖ Bond Street
or Marble Arch
41 Mount Street, W1; tel. (071) 499 1843.
A large Victorian pub gleaming with mirrors and etched glass windows, close to the American Embassy. Good food in the pub, as well as in the restaurant upstairs (closed Saturday lunch time)—it's advisable to reserve a table.

AUSTRALIAN, THE **30** G5 ⊖ Sloane Square
29 Milner Street, SW3; tel. (071) 589 3114.
The Australian customers seem to have moved out, leaving a typical English Sloane crowd. Food is available Monday to Friday.

BLACK FRIAR, THE   16 Q9   ⊖ Blackfriars
174 Queen Victoria Street, EC4; tel. (071) 236 5650.
Admire the unusual Art Nouveau marble and bronze interior of this pub, except on Saturday and Sunday, when it's closed.

BRITANNIA   28 C6   ⊖ High Street Kensington
1 Allen Street, W8; tel. (071) 937 1864.
A large, popular pub with conservatory, three bars, good food (hot at lunch time, cold in the evening) and, first things first, excellent beer.

BUNCH OF GRAPES   22 K8   ⊖ Green Park
16 Shepherd Market, W1; tel. (071) 629 4989.
An old, old pub that has a village-inn atmosphere.

CHELSEA POTTER   36 G3   ⊖ Sloane Square
119 King's Road, SW3; tel. (071) 352 9479.
Small and full of character, with a loud jukebox, young crowd and food available during the day (except Sunday).

CHESHIRE CHEESE   15 P9   ⊖ Temple
5 Little Essex Street, WC2; tel. (071) 836 2347.
Push your way through the lawyers and business people for excellent beer and reasonable food. A good, old-fashioned atmosphere, perhaps because it's supposed to be haunted. Closed Saturday and Sunday.

CITTIE OF YORK   15 P10/11   ⊖ Holborn
22–23 High Holborn, WC1; tel. (071) 242 7670.
Dating from late 17th century, it boasts one of the longest bars in London. Closed on Sunday.

DOGGETT'S COAT AND BADGE   25 Q9   ⊖ Blackfriars
1 Blackfriars Bridge, SE1; tel. (071) 633 9081.
Large, with lovely views over the Thames. Pub food in the bar and a restaurant, which is usually closed on Saturday and Sunday evenings.

FLASK   ⊖ Highway
77 Highgate West Hill, N6; tel. (081) 340 7260.
One of North London's most famous—and oldest—pubs, open 7 days a week. Dick Turpin and William Hogarth drank here, though not at the same time. Sit outside on warm days and enjoy some excellent food.

FOX AND GRAPES   ⊖ Wimbledon
Camp Road, Wimbledon Common; SW19; tel. (071) 946 5599.
A very busy 300-year-old pub on the edge of Wimbledon Common, which serves some jolly good food (roasts at Sunday lunch time) every day except Sunday evening.

FRENCH HOUSE, THE   **13** M9   ⊖ Leicester Square or Piccadilly Circus

49 Dean Street, W1; tel. (071) 437 2799.
Claims many eccentric, former customers, including Brendan Behan and Dylan Thomas. It was the meeting place for de Gaulle's Free French during the Second World War. French atmosphere and French wines.

GILBERT & SULLIVAN   **14** O9   ⊖ Covent Garden
23 Wellington Street, WC2; tel. (071) 836 6930.
A café-bar lined with Gilbert & Sullivan memorabilia, designed to pack in the crowds, with a wine bar upstairs. Food Monday to Friday; closed Sunday evenings.

GRENADIER, THE   **21** J6   ⊖ Hyde Park Corner
18 Wilton Row, SW1; tel. (071) 235 3074.
A small Belgravia pub, which is supposed to be haunted, perhaps by the old soldier himself.

GREYHOUND, THE   ⊖ Kew Gardens
82 Kew Green, Kew; tel. (081) 940 0071.
Laze on Kew Green outside this mock-Tudor pub and watch the traditional English summer pastime—cricket. You can get standard pub food, except on Sunday evenings.

HOLLY BUSH, THE   ⊖ Hampstead **127**
22 Holly Mount, off Heath Street, NW3; tel. (071) 435 2892.
The present building is 160 years old, but there has been an inn of some description here for about 400 years. Bar food is available (not on Sunday evenings or Monday).

ISLAND QUEEN   ⊖ Angel
87 Noel Road, N1; tel. (071) 226 5507.
An eccentric and wildly popular local, the bar dominated by theatrical puppets. The upstairs restaurant, tel. (071) 226 0307, provides imaginative food at lunch time from Monday to Saturday, and is open Friday and Saturday evenings, and Sunday for lunch.

JACK STRAW'S CASTLE   ⊖ Hampstead
Northend Way, Hampstead, NW3; tel. (071) 435 8885.
A well-loved, weatherboard building named after one of the leaders of the Peasants Revolt of 1381 and built on the site of an old coaching inn. The bar is downstairs and a carvery restaurant (open daily) upstairs. Great views of Hampstead Heath.

JAMAICA WINE HOUSE   17 T9   ⊖ Bank
St. Michael's Alley, Cornhill, EC3; tel. (071) 626 9496.
London's first coffee house (the predecessor of the public house) was rebuilt by Sir Christopher Wren after the Great Fire of 1666, and has been restored several times since. Food available at lunch times; closed Saturday and Sundays.

KING'S HEAD & EIGHT BELLS   36 G2   ⊖ Sloane Square
50 Cheyne Walk, SW3; tel. (071) 352 1820.
Good food in an old favourite haunt of artists and writers.

LAMB AND FLAG   14 N9   ⊖ Covent Garden
33 Rose Street, WC2; tel. (071) 408 0132.
Had a reputation for being rough, but has cleaned up its act in the last couple of centuries. A small, traditional pub, hidden away in a Covent Garden side street. Closed on Sunday.

MINOGUE'S   ⊖ Angel
80 Liverpool Road, N1; tel. (071) 354 4440.
It's worth making the trip to Islington to visit this lively Dublin-pub lookalike, with Guinness on tap. An upmarket, noisy Irish bar with a highly rated restaurant attached, where you'll need to reserve your table in advance. The restaurant is closed on Sunday evening and at lunch time, except on Sunday.

MITRE   10 E9   ⊖ Lancaster Gate
24 Craven Terrace, W2; tel. (071) 262 5240.
128 The archetypal English pub, over 200 years old, the Mitre is large and popular. Food is sold daily.

MUSEUM TAVERN   14 N10   ⊖ Tottenham Court Road
49 Great Russell Street, WC1; tel. (071) 242 8987.
Opposite the British Museum, it's a pub Karl Marx used to frequent, and one that remains popular today.

NAG'S HEAD, THE   21 H6   ⊖ Knightsbridge
53 Kinerton Street, SW1; tel. (071) 235 1135.
Well away from the main Knightsbridge bustle, the Nag's Head is a dark and interesting little pub, well known for its good food and beer.

ORDNANCE ARMS   ⊖ St. John's Wood
29 Ordnance Hill, NW8; tel. (071) 722 0278.
Could be known as the "Cricketers' Arms", since it attracts some of the game's stars after a day spent in the field at Lords. It's small, 300 years old and welcoming, with a conservatory and garden. Hot food is on offer during the week, snacks only on Saturday and Sunday.

QUEEN'S ELM   **35** F3   ⊖ South Kensington
241 Fulham Road, SW3; tel. (071) 352 9157.
An out-of-the-ordinary pub, frequented by writers. Food is available.

RED LION, THE   **23** L8   ⊖ Piccadilly Circus
2 Duke of York Street, SW1; tel. (071) 930 2030.
A large, old Mayfair pub with a reputation for good food. Closed on Sundays.

SILVER CROSS, THE   **23** N8   ⊖ Charing Cross
33 Whitehall, SW1; tel. (071) 930 8350.
One of Westminster's most popular watering holes, the Silver Cross has an olde-worlde atmosphere. Food is available daily.

SMITHFIELD TAVERN   **16** Q11   ⊖ Barbican
105 Charterhouse Street, EC1; tel. (071) 253 5153.
A famous pub beside Smithfield Meat Market which opens at 5 a.m. to serve hearty breakfasts and copious glasses of bitter to market and night-workers until 9 a.m. It re-opens again 11 a.m.–3 p.m. Closed on Saturdays and Sundays.

SPANIARDS INN   ⊖ Hampstead
Spaniards Road, NW3; tel. (081) 455 3276.
A famous pub on Hampstead Heath, which Dick Whittington is supposed to have popped into on his way to London.

SUN IN SPLENDOUR   **18** B9   ⊖ Notting Hill Gate
7 Portobello Road, W11; tel. (071) 727 6345.

129

At the edge of Portobello Market, the Sun in Splendour is a bohemian pub which attracts a regular crowd of rock musicians, fashion slaves and local people. Food is served daily (except Sunday evenings) and it's reckoned they serve the best pint of Guinness in London.

WARWICK CASTLE   ⊖ Warwick Avenue
6 Warwick Place, W9; tel. (071) 286 6868.
A small family house with a pleasant atmosphere in scenic Little Venice, with a roaring fire in winter, a good selection of beers and food available twice a day.

The extraordinary thing about the entertainment in London is its sheer quality and variety. Some of the very best theatrical productions can be seen in the National Theatre, at the Barbican Centre and on the West End stage. Classical music and opera programmes feature many of world's finest musicians. From innovative contemporary dance companies to experimental film, noisy nightclubs and late-night restaurants, London is a city of entertainment.

Theatre performances usually start between 7.30 and 8 p.m., while the cinemas have screenings from around midday to 9 or 10 p.m. The nightclubs don't come to life until 10 or 11 p.m., about the time the pubs are starting to close. Many Londoners spend the early evenings in the pubs before going on to restaurants or the theatre.

The West End is reasonably safe to walk around at night, but, as at any time, keep to the well-lit areas where there are crowds. Some of the rock music and cabaret clubs included in this section are in slightly out-of-the-way places. When in doubt, take a taxi.

For details of what's on and where, check one of the listings magazines, *Time Out, City Limits* or *What's On;* they also include information on advance reservations for coming events.

CLASSICAL MUSIC

The European capital of classical music, London is renowned for the excellence and range of performances on offer. World-class London orchestras include the London Symphony Orchestra, the Philharmonia, the Royal Philharmonic, the English Chamber Orchestra, the BBC Symphony Orchestra and the Academy of St. Martin-in-the-Fields. There are three major concert halls within the South Bank Centre and one at the Barbican, plus a superb venue for recitals at the Wigmore Hall. Lunchtime recitals in churches is a long-standing tradition. These concerts are usually free, but a donation is appreciated.

Long-stemmed English talent adorns a nightclub stage.

BARBICAN   17 S11   ⊖ Barbican
                                                             or Moorgate
The Barbican Centre, Silk Street, EC2; tel. box office (071) 638 8891; enquiries (071) 628 2295; recorded information (071) 628 9760. Box office open daily 9 a.m.–8 p.m.
Belying its rather drab appearance, the Barbican Centre has much to offer music lovers. Resident companies are the London Symphony Orchestra and the English Chamber Orchestra, and guest companies and soloists frequently appear.

FENTON HOUSE   ⊖ Hampstead
Hampstead Grove, NW3; tel. (071) 435 3471.
In this elegant Queen Anne House, summer concerts are held, using their fine collection of early keyboard instruments. Also annual open-air Shakespearian productions.

KENWOOD HOUSE   ⊖ Archway
                                                             or Golders Green
Hampstead Lane, NW3; tel. (071) 379 4444. Telephone bookings 24 hours daily.
A classic London summer outing—Saturday evening spent picnicking while an orchestra or opera company performs classical music in the concert bowl on the other side of the lake. Deck chairs are available, or you can sit on the grass. It is quite a distance from the underground stations; take a 210 bus from Archway or Golders Green station.

ROYAL ALBERT HALL   20 E6   ⊖ Knightsbridge
Kensington Gore, SW7; tel. (071) 589 8212. Box office open daily 10 a.m.–6 p.m., closed Sunday if no performance.
Orchestral and choral concerts throughout the year by the Royal Philharmonic Orchestra and international artists. However, the high point is the annual BBC Henry Wood Promenade Concerts, better known as "The Proms". Held from July to September, they are an essentially British institution, where the audience is as much part of the spectacle as the music. Try to go on the last night, which always concludes with an audience-participation rendering of *Land of Hope and Glory.*

ST. BRIDE'S CHURCH   15 Q9/10   ⊖ St. Paul's
Fleet Street, EC4; tel. (071) 353 1301.
Three lunchtime concerts a week are held in this old Wren church, at 1.15 p.m. on Tuesday, Wednesday (always an organ recital) and Friday.

ST. JAMES'S CHURCH, PICCADILLY 23 L8 ⊖ Piccadilly Circus
Piccadilly, W1; tel. (071) 734 4511. Tickets available one hour before performance.
Lunchtime concerts by younger musicians are presented during the week, and sponsored festivals featuring leading players from all over the world are also sometimes held in the summer. Worth a visit for its architecture alone.

ST. JOHN'S 33 N5 ⊖ Westminster
Smith Square, SW1; tel. (071) 222 1061. Bookings Monday–Friday 10 a.m.–5 p.m., and one hour before concert starts.
Right in London's political heartland, this 18th-century church is used for chamber and solo recitals. There are lunchtime concerts sponsored and broadcast by the BBC, and occasional evening concerts in addition.

ST. MARTIN-IN-THE-FIELDS 23 N8 ⊖ Charing Cross
Trafalgar Square, WC2; tel. (071) 839 1930.
Weekly lunchtime and evening concerts in this famous church on Trafalgar Square (Monday, Tuesday and Friday at 1.05 p.m.).

SOUTH BANK ARTS CENTRE 24 O8 ⊖ Waterloo
or Embankment
South Bank, SE1; tel. box office (071) 928 8800; general information (071) 928 3002; recorded information (071) 633 0932. Box office open 10 a.m.–9 p.m. daily.
This major arts centre boasts three concert halls. The largest, the Royal Festival Hall, features orchestral concerts (by the resident **133** Royal Philharmonic as well as guest orchestras) and recitals by eminent soloists; there are also occasional films, jazz and band concerts.
   Both the smaller Queen Elizabeth Hall and intimate Purcell Room usually present solo or chamber music recitals, often with young artists.

WIGMORE HALL 12 J10 ⊖ Bond Street
36 Wigmore Street, W1; tel. (071) 935 2141. Box office open Monday to Saturday 10 a.m.–8.30 p.m.; from 45 minutes prior to Sunday performance.
A lovely old hall built for solo and small chamber recitals. It's famous for its acoustics and its song recitals featuring many top international singers (book 4–6 weeks in advance). Also Sunday morning "coffee" concerts at 11.30 a.m. (book 1 week in advance).

OPERA AND DANCE

The two major opera companies are the Royal Opera Company and the English National Opera; the former is based at the famous Royal Opera House in Covent Garden, the latter, which uses only British singers and performs everything in English, is at the Coliseum. The Royal Ballet Company shares the Covent Garden Royal Opera House. All these companies hold back about 50 tickets to sell on the day of the performance (10 a.m. onwards)—a real bargain if you don't mind queueing.

The modern dance scene is centred around the excellent Ballet Rambert and the London Contemporary Dance Theatre, with many visiting foreign companies as well.

HOLLAND PARK THEATRE   **18** B6   ⊖ Kensington High Street
Holland Park, Kensington High Street, W8; tel. (071) 603 1123.
A 600-seat open-air theatre in Holland Park, covered by a canopy. The dance programme features contemporary companies, as well as classical. The Royal Ballet School performs in mid-summer every year (book 6–8 weeks in advance). There are also opera and drama productions.

THE COLISEUM   **24** N9   ⊖ Charing Cross
St. Martin's Lane, WC2; tel. box office (071) 836 3161; credit cards (071) 240 5258; recorded information (0836) 430 909. Box office open Monday to Saturday 10 a.m.–9 p.m.
Home of the English National Opera, which performs classic opera in English translation. High-quality productions, often freely adapted in terms of setting and period. Also some appearances by guest companies.

THE PLACE THEATRE   **7** M12   ⊖ Euston or Kings Cross
17 Duke's Road, WC1; tel. (071) 387 0161. Box office open Monday to Saturday 12 noon–8.30 p.m. (until 6 p.m. on days without performance).
Home of the London Contemporary Dance Theatre and the London School of Contemporary Dance, it features innovative British dance as well as international modern dance by visiting companies.

ROYAL OPERA HOUSE   **14** N9   ⊖ Covent Garden
Bow Street, WC2; tel. box office (071) 240 1066; credit cards
(071) 240 1911; recorded information (0836) 430 911. Box office open
Monday to Saturday 10 a.m.–8 p.m.
Forget the official name: everyone calls it "Covent Garden". A world-
class house for opera and ballet, with tickets in the same high price
bracket as those in Vienna or New York.

   Opened in 1732, today it is home to the Royal Opera and Royal
Ballet, and can draw on the cream of international performers and
conductors.

SADLER'S WELLS THEATRE   **9** Q13   ⊖ Angel
Rosebery Avenue, EC1; tel. box office (071) 278 8916; general
information (071) 278 5450; recorded information (0836) 430 941. Box
office open Monday to Saturday 10.30 a.m.–7.30 p.m.
The emphasis is on dance—the Ballet Rambert, the London
Contemporary Dance and the London City Ballet perform here
regularly, as well as the resident New Sadler's Ballet and Sadler's Wells
Royal Ballet companies. Also wide-ranging world dance and music
programme. Book 2–4 weeks in advance.

JAZZ MUSIC

The place to hear the best visiting musicians is Ronnie Scott's, which **135**
has a wonderful 50s' bohemian air about it. For years, this and the 100
Club were the only places to hear jazz in London. But recently a number
of smaller venues have opened, notably the Bass Clef and the Jazz
Café. And the more clubs that open, the more crowded they all get.
London is turning into Jazz City.

BASS CLEF   ⊖ Old Street
35 Coronet Street, off Hoxton Square, N1; tel. (071) 729 2440/2476.
Open Monday to Saturday 7.30 p.m.–2 a.m.; Sunday 1–3 p.m. and 7.30
p.m.–midnight.
Jazz, African and Latin American music every week, plus live jam
sessions (Tuesdays) and DJ. Features some interesting international
musicians. Restaurant (closed Mondays) and bar.

BRAHMS & LISZT   14 N/O9   ⊖ Covent Garden
19 Russell Street, WC2; tel. (071) 240 3661. Open Monday to Saturday 10 p.m.–1 a.m.; Sunday 7.30 –11 p.m.
Underneath a busy Covent Garden wine bar, a variety of jazz (modern and traditional), some 60s' soul, rhythm & blues. Tapas and bar.

JAZZ CAFÉ   ⊖ Highbury & Islington
56 Newington Green, N16; tel. (071) 359 4936. Open Monday to Sunday 7 p.m.–midnight; Saturday and Sunday noon–3 p.m.
A small café serving a mixed menu of contemporary jazz, world music and vegetarian food. A 12-minute walk from underground station, or take a 73, 141 or 171 bus from the West End.

100 CLUB   13 L10   ⊖ Tottenham Court Road
100 Oxford Street, W1; tel. (071) 636 0933. Open Monday to Saturday 7.45 p.m.–1 a.m.; Sunday until 11.30 p.m.
Swing bands, blues, African, traditional and modern jazz in this long-established basement club.

PALOOKAVILLE   14 N9   ⊖ Covent Garden
13a James Street, WC2; tel. (071) 240 5857. Music every day until midnight or 1 a.m.
Modern and traditional jazz—particularly British and European—in a downstairs wine bar and restaurant.

PIZZA EXPRESS   13 M10   ⊖ Tottenham Court Road
10 Dean Street, W1; tel. (071) 437 9595. Music daily from 9.30 p.m.
A pizzeria of jazz with restaurant upstairs. All types of jazz are on the menu. You can order food and alcohol together (no alcohol without food). Reserve table. Also outposts in Ealing and Golders Green.

136

PIZZA ON THE PARK   21 J7   ⊖ Hyde Park Corner
11 Knightsbridge, Hyde Park Corner, SW1; tel. (071) 235 5550. Music Monday to Saturday from 9.15 p.m.
A lively mixture of traditional and modern jazz, blues, and the occasional cabaret. Full menu and bar service. Book in advance.

RONNIE SCOTT'S   13 M9/10   ⊖ Leicester Square
                                             or Piccadilly Circus
47 Frith Street, W1; tel. (071) 439 0747. Open Monday to Saturday 8.30 p.m.–3 a.m.
The jazz club this side of the Atlantic. Virtually every major jazz musician has played here. There are two sessions each night, at 10 p.m. and 1 a.m. Essential to book a table in advance.

ROCK, POP AND FOLK MUSIC

Since the 60s, London has been the mecca of all forms of rock, pop and folk music, with close to 1,000 bands playing in the city every week. This is where to see some of the rawest and most interesting new talents along with the famous, the currently trendy and a few old ravers. Venues range from the enormous concert arena-cum-football field, Wembley Stadium, to back rooms in pubs where you can watch bands for free. We have listed the major venues (which are often seating-only former cinemas or theatres), as well as some of the legendary music clubs; others are listed under NIGHTCLUBS & DISCOTHEQUES (See pp. 143-4). It's essential to book well in advance for major stars.

ASTORIA 13 M10 ⊖ Tottenham Court Road
157 Charing Cross Road, WC2; tel. (071) 434 0403/9592. Bookings Monday to Friday 10.30 a.m.–5.30 p.m.; Saturday 10.30 a.m.–5 p.m.
Although somewhat faded after a glittering period in the late 70s, the Astoria is regaining its reputation. Live music, including heavy rock; large auditorium with large dance floor.

BRIXTON ACADEMY ⊖ Brixton
211 Stockwell Road, SW9; tel. (071) 326 1022. Box office open Monday to Saturday 10 a.m.–8 p.m.
The atmosphere is charged in this large converted theatre, which features some of the more adventurous musical events, holds 4,000 and has a sloping floor.

CAMDEN PALACE ⊖ Camden Town or Mornington Crescent
1a Camden Road, NW1; tel. (071) 387 0428. Open daily except Sunday 9 p.m.–2.30 a.m.

137

Dance the night away in this three-floor nightclub offering a variety of disco and live music, ranging from 50s' and 60s' favourites to the latest in modern trends. Some big-name stars.

DOMINION 13 M10 ⊖ Tottenham Court Road
Tottenham Court Road, W1; tel. (071) 580 9562. Box office open Monday to Saturday 10 a.m.–8 p.m.
A large former cinema featuring many well-known rock, country and western and soul acts. Seating only.

HAMMERSMITH ODEON ⊖ Hammersmith
Queen Caroline Street, W6; tel. (081) 748 4081. Box office open Monday to Friday 11 a.m.–8 p.m.
The latest in big names and heavy-metal bands appear in this 3,500-seat theatre. No bopping—the security guards see you stay seated.

LONDON ARENA
DLR Crossharbour

4 Limeharbour, Isle of Dogs, E14; tel. (071) 538 1212. Bookings Monday to Friday 10 a.m.–8 p.m.; Saturday 10 a.m.–4.30 p.m.

This newly built stadium in the Docklands is ideal for pop idols, from David Bowie to Kylie Minogue. Docklands Light Railway to Crossharbour from Tower Hill or Stratford tube station.

MARQUEE   14 M10
⊖ Leicester Square
or Tottenham Court Road

105 Charing Cross Road, WC2; tel. (071) 437 6601/3. Bookings (members only, otherwise buy at door before performance) Monday to Friday 11 a.m.–6 p.m.; Saturday noon to 6 p.m.

The legendary Marquee, a haunt of the Rolling Stones, has been relocated several blocks away from the original, but is complete with black paint, dankness and heavy rock.

POWERHAUS
⊖ Angel

The Pied Bull, 1 Liverpool Road, N1; tel. (071) 837 3218. Bookings Monday to Friday 11 a.m.–7 p.m.; Saturday noon–5 p.m.

Folk, country and rock acts thrive in the small-scale venue (450 capacity) with a lively atmosphere.

ROCK GARDEN   14 N9
⊖ Covent Garden

6–7 The Piazza, corner of James and King streets, WC2; tel. (071) 240 3961. Tickets available at door.

Famous for being famous in the late 70s, the Rock Garden has become a tourist attraction without much to offer.

TOWN & COUNTRY CLUB
⊖ Kentish Town

9–17 Highgate Road, NW5; tel. (071) 284 0303. Bookings Monday to Friday 11 a.m.–8 p.m.; Saturday 11 a.m.–4 p.m.

The place to see major international musicians of all breeds. Town & Country 2—Highbury Corner, N5; tel. (071) 700 5716—is smaller and gentler.

138

WEMBLEY ARENA AND STADIUM
⊖ Wembley Park
or Wembley Central

Empire Way, Wembley, Middlesex; tel. (081) 900 1234. Bookings Monday to Saturday 9 a.m.–9 p.m.; Sunday 10 a.m.–6 p.m.

Two large-scale venues which attract the big names and the big crowds. The Arena, London's largest indoor venue, is not renowned for its sound system, its sightlines or its comfort. The Stadium is the enormous outdoor sports field seen by billions around the world via the televised Band Aid and Mandela concerts. Beware the souvenir sellers and ticket touts.

CINEMA

There are more film shows in London every week than almost anywhere else in the world. As well as new releases, there are a number of repertory cinemas—most notably the National Film Theatre—which show films from every era and every part of the world.

The West End cinemas usually show first-run movies at high prices. Many of these films are then shown on the regional cinema circuit. Repertory theatres often have a membership system—usually available when you buy your ticket and often only a nominal amount.

Here, we have listed only the National Film Theatre and several of the more interesting cinemas with repertory programmes or experimental films.

EVERYMAN ⊖ Hampstead
Hollybush Vale, NW3; tel. (071) 435 1525.
One of the best repertory cinemas, which generally shows two or three different films per day, with old and new works from all over the world.

INSTITUTE 23 M8 ⊖ Charing Cross
OF CONTEMPORARY ARTS (ICA)
Nash House, The Mall, SW1; tel. (071) 930 3647. Box office open daily noon–9 p.m.
Two cinemas: the ICA Cinema which shows international films, and the ICA Cinemathèque featuring experimental works.

LONDON FILM MAKERS CO-OP ⊖ Camden Town
42 Gloucester Avenue, NW1; tel. (071) 586 8516.
A low-budget centre for experimental films where you can see avant-garde and rare international films.

139

NATIONAL FILM THEATRE 24 O8 ⊖ Waterloo or Embankment
South Bank, SE1; tel. box office (071) 928 3232; recorded information (071) 633 0274..
Intelligently programmed seasons, often focussing round a director, a country or a genre, are the hallmarks of the National Film Theatre. There are two cinemas within the building—part of the South Bank Arts Centre.

SCALA 8 N13 ⊖ King's Cross
275–277 Pentonville Road, N1; tel. (071) 278 0051.
An eccentric fleapit with a repertory programme concentrating on the obscure, horror and science fiction. All-night sessions on Saturday.

THEATRE

The quality of British theatre is second to none. The excellence of the great companies is legend, as is the range and sheer professionalism of the commercial theatre based in the West End.

London also has a thriving "fringe" theatre scene of small theatres producing new plays, drama by neglected foreign playwrights, polemic works and experimental theatre. We have listed only the most interesting of these theatres, along with the three publicly subsidized companies.

West End theatre encompasses everything from Shakespeare and the classics to bedroom farces, romantic comedies and spectacular musicals. For information on how to get tickets, see p. 141.

ALMEIDA
⊖ Angel
Almeida Street, N1; tel. (071) 359 4404. Box office open Monday to Saturday 10 a.m.–6 p.m.
A small theatre renowned for daring productions of often obscure plays, serious drama and European writers. Also hosts an international festival of theatre, music, dance and opera in July.

BUSH THEATRE
⊖ Goldhawk Road or Shepherd's Bush
The Bush, Shepherd's Bush Green, W12; tel. (081) 743 3388. Box office open 10 a.m.–10 p.m. daily.
A small theatre club above a pub, with a reputation for discovering new talent, the Bush concentrates on work by new writers.

GATE THEATRE CLUB   18 B8
⊖ Notting Hill Gate
The Prince Albert, 11 Pembridge Road, W11; tel. (071) 229 0706. Box office open Monday to Friday 11 a.m.–6 p.m.; Saturday 2–6 p.m.
An above-pub theatre club dedicated to world theatre, particularly neglected classics. Also "Late at the Gate", an improvisational cabaret, 10 p.m., Thursday and Fridays.

140

HAMPSTEAD THEATRE
⊖ Swiss Cottage
Swiss Cottage Centre, Avenue Road, NW3; tel. (071) 722 9301. Box office open Monday to Saturday 10 a.m.–8 p.m.; telephone bookings 10.30 a.m.–7.30 p.m.
All new work, often by famous playwrights and famous actors in a very small, but firmly established theatre. Saturday matinée.

INSTITUTE   23 M8
OF CONTEMPORARY ARTS (ICA)
⊖ Charing Cross
The Mall, SW1; tel. (071) 930 3647. Box office open daily noon–9 p.m.
Experimental works, as well as poetry readings.

WEST END THEATRE TICKETS

Ticket prices to the West End theatres vary from around £5 to £35. The most difficult to get are those for the long-running musicals. Avoid buying from ticket touts outside the theatre; it's better to contact the box office directly (many will accept telephoned bookings and credit card payment), or go through one of the reputable agents listed below. *Always* determine the amount of commission: 15 –20% is the norm, but you can pay through the nose.

First Call (071) 240 7200/836 3464
Keith Prowse (071) 741 9999
London Theatre Bookings (071) 434 1811/439 3371
Premier (071) 240 0771/240 2245/379 7622
Ticketmaster (071) 379 4444

The price of matinée tickets is lower than that for the evening performance. Most West End theatres have matinées on Wednesday and Saturday, although the stars do not always appear.

Discount tickets can be bought on the day of the performance at the Society of West End Theatres (SWET) ticket booth in Leicester Square; phone (071) 836 0971 for information. Tickets for matinée performances are on sale Monday to Saturday from noon, and tickets for evening performances from 2.30 to 6.30 p.m. You may have to queue for 30 to 60 minutes.

KING'S HEAD THEATRE CLUB   ⊖ Angel
115 Upper Street, N1; tel. (071) 226 1916. Box office open Monday to Saturday 10 a.m.–6 p.m.; Sunday 10 a.m.–4 p.m.
One of the first pub-theatres, it continues innovative tradition with interesting new plays. Matinée and evening shows. Meals available one hour before the performance starts (book in advance).

141

LILIAN BAYLIS   9 P/Q13   ⊖ Angel
Sadler's Wells Theatre, Arlington Way, N1; tel. (071) 278 8916. Box office open Monday to Saturday 10.30 a.m.–7.30 p.m.
Small community theatre (part of Sadler's Wells, see p. 135) offering a varied programme of theatre, music and dance for small-scale productions, often experimental work. Book 1–6 weeks in advance.

NATIONAL THEATRE   25 P8   ⊖ Waterloo
South Bank, SE1; tel. (071) 928 2252. Box office open Monday to Saturday 10 a.m.–8 p.m.
Part of the South Bank Arts complex, the home of the National Theatre Company comprising three theatres: the Olivier, largest and most prestigious; the Lyttelton, a conventional theatre, and the Cottesloe, for smaller-scale, often experimental work. Book 1–6 weeks in advance.

OLD VIC   **25** P7   ⊖ Waterloo
Waterloo Road, SE1; tel. box office (071) 928 7616; rec. information (0836) 430 930. Box office open Monday to Saturday 10 a.m.–8 p.m.
One of the most important London theatres giving intellectual productions, and famous for its avant-garde interpretations of Shakespeare, Ibsen, Corneille, and the like. Book 2–6 weeks ahead.

OPEN AIR THEATRE   **5** H12   ⊖ Baker Street or Regent's Park
Regent's Park, NW1; tel. box office (071) 486 2431; rec. information (0836) 430 931. Box office open Monday to Saturday 10 a.m.–8 p.m.
Outdoor summer productions in a stone amphitheatre (matinee and evening). Plays by Shakespeare and often works by Bernard Shaw. Late May to early September; no performances on Sunday. Book 2–4 weeks in advance.

RIVERSIDE STUDIOS   ⊖ Hammersmith
Crisp Road, W6; tel. (081) 748 3354. Box office open Monday to Saturday 10 a.m.–8 p.m.; Sunday noon–8.30 p.m.
International companies present experimental theatre and focus on British work. Book 1–4 weeks in advance.

ROYAL COURT   **31** H4   ⊖ Sloane Square
Sloane Square, SW1; tel. box office (071) 730 1745; credit card bookings (071) 836 2428; rec. information (0836) 430 939. Box office open Monday to Saturday 10 a.m.–8 p.m.; telephone bookings until 6 p.m.
The Royal Court has a long-standing policy of producing new works, many of them polemical. Also the studio Theatre Upstairs.

142 **THE BARBICAN**   **17** S11   ⊖ Barbican or Moorgate
The Barbican Centre, EC2; tel. box office (071) 638 8891; 24-hour information (071) 628 2295; recorded information (0836) 430 906/7. Box office open daily 9 a.m.–8 p.m.
The Royal Shakespeare Company's London home, specialising in the works of Britain's most celebrated playwright. Also has a small studio theatre, The Pit. Book 4 weeks in advance.

TRICYCLE THEATRE   ⊖ Kilburn
269 Kilburn High Road, NW6; tel. (071) 328 1000. Box office open Monday to Saturday 10 a.m.–8 p.m.
Broad-ranging programme of small-scale works, sometimes with Irish or Anglo-Caribbean themes.

YOUNG VIC
See CHILDREN p. 165.

NIGHTCLUBS AND DISCOTHEQUES

Nightclubs in London are hectic and ever-changing. A club is likely to have a different type of music every night, so checking beforehand is essential.

Dress is the key to gaining admittance to many clubs, and bouncers may turn away anyone they don't like the look of. Basically, the rule is to dress the part—respectable for the more conventional up-market clubs, trendy for the more casual ones catering for a younger clientele. Some of the best-known London clubs, such as Annabel's and Tramps, because they have a very restricted members-only policy, are not included here.

Because they are licensed to sell alcohol, nightclubs will not admit anyone under 18.

BUSBY'S 13 M10 ⊖ Tottenham Court Road
157 Charing Cross Road, WC2; tel. (071) 734 6963. Open Monday to Saturday 10.30 p.m.–3.30 a.m.; Sunday 8.30 p.m.–midnight.
This Deco-style disco has a large dance floor, and throbs to all the latest music trends.

CAFÉ DE PARIS 23 M9 ⊖ Piccadilly Circus
3 Coventry Street, W1; tel. (071) 437 2036. Open Monday and Thursday 7.30 p.m.–1 a.m.; Friday and Saturday 7.30 p.m.–3 a.m.; Sunday 7.30 p.m.–midnight.
An old-fashioned club for old-fashioned folk who like to get up and dance waltzes and tangos to middle-of-the-road music (Mondays, Thursdays and Sundays). On Fridays and Saturdays, the mood changes to disco and the crowd gets younger. Regular tea dances with ballroom dancing (Wednesday to Sunday except Friday).

143

THE FRIDGE ⊖ Brixton
Town Hall Parade, Brixton Hill, SW2; tel. (071) 326 5100. Open Monday to Saturday 10 a.m.–2 p.m.; Sunday times vary.
This famous club with its large screens has always set the trends in music and décor. Different styles every night and lots of the very latest live music. A successful gay night on Tuesday, and the biggest women-only night in Europe on the first Wednesday in every month. Capacity 1,500. Restaurant.

GOSSIPS 13 M9 ⊖ Piccadilly Circus
69 Dean Street, W1; tel. (071) 434 4480. Open Monday to Saturday 10 p.m.–3.30 a.m.
A good music club, with live music of all types. It's in a dingy but very lively basement.

HEAVEN   **24** N8   ⊖ Charing Cross or Embankment

Under the Arches, Villiers Street, WC2; tel. (071) 839 3852. Open Monday to Friday 10 p.m.–3.30 a.m.; Saturday 10.30 p.m.–4 a.m.

A large, trendsetting club. DJs typically play the latest style of music, and share time with bands. "Theme" nights are a speciality, and there are three dance floors, a food counter and bars.

     Entrance may be restricted to members only or to gay men or women—ring first to check.

HIPPODROME   **14** M9   ⊖ Leicester Square

Hippodrome Corner, Leicester Square, WC2; tel. (071) 437 4311. Open Monday to Thursday 9 p.m.–3.30 a.m.; Friday and Saturday 8.30 p.m.–3.30 a.m.

Different styles on different nights—disco, 60s, 70s and 80s and heavy metal are regular features of this large fashionable ex-theatre, with the big attraction being heavy rock on Wednesdays. Also boasts a restaurant.

LEGENDS   **22** L9   ⊖ Green Park or Oxford Circus

29 Old Burlington Street, W1; tel. (071) 437 9933. Open Friday and Saturday 10 p.m.–3.30 a.m. and some weekdays.

In this below-stairs disco, the music is generally house, the décor strictly 80s' post-Modern, and the crowd fashionable.

LIMELIGHT   **14** M9   ⊖ Leicester Square

136 Shaftesbury Avenue, WC2; tel. (071) 434 0572. Open Monday to Saturday 10.30 p.m.–3 a.m.

Fashionable dancing spot for the young and not so young with designer disco, live music and serious hip-shaking. Dress—fairly smart (i.e. no trainers or tracksuits and jeans must be smart).

144

STRINGFELLOWS   **14** N9   ⊖ Leicester Square

16–19 Upper St. Martin's Lane, WC2; tel. (071) 240 5534. Open Monday to Saturday 8 p.m.–3 a.m.

Stringfellows attracts a more sophisticated crowd than most, including the famous. It's glitzy with lots of commercial pop music, live and DJ. Restaurant. You'll only get in if your clothes are smart.

WAG CLUB   **23** M9   ⊖ Piccadilly Circus or Leicester Square

35 Wardour Street, W1; tel. (071) 437 5534. Open Monday to Thursday 10.30 p.m.–3.30 a.m.; Friday and Saturday until 6 a.m.

A very fashionable venue offering two floors of varied music—DJs and occasional live music of the very latest trend. Dress—strictly casual.

CABARET AND VARIETY

London cabaret has undergone something of a renewal in the last decade or so. Although there are still one or two traditional variety shows complete with high-kicking dancers and crooners or old-fashioned music hall acts, the accent is on "alternative" cabaret, which includes pointed political comment, sophisticated variety acts, and musical satire. These shows are very popular and often do not accept reservations—you may have to queue at the door for 30 to 60 minutes to be sure of getting in.

BANANA'S UPSTAIRS $\ominus$ Balham
The Bedford Theatre, Bedford Hill, SW12; tel. (081) 673 8904.
Shows Tuesday to Sunday in a circular domed room. There's an imaginative programme, including cabaret, improvised comedy and comic plays.

CANAL CAFÉ THEATRE $\ominus$ Warwick Avenue
The Bridge House, Delamere Terrace, Little Venice, W2; tel. (071) 289 6054.
Two shows, an innovative drama, usually at 8 p.m., and a popular satirical review at 10 p.m., Thursday to Sunday.

COCKNEY CABARET & MUSIC HALL   6 L12 $\ominus$ Warren Street
161 Tottenham Court Road, W1; tel. (071) 408 1001. Open daily 7.45-11.30 p.m.
Traditional turn-of-the-century music hall entertainment, with 4-course Cockney supper and dancing. Essential to book in advance.

COMEDY STORE   23 M9 $\ominus$ Leicester Square **145**
28a Leicester Square, WC2; tel. (071) 839 6665.
The home of alternative cabaret, famous for stand-up comics and variety entertainers. No booking—box office opens one hour before the show; minimum age 18.

HACKNEY EMPIRE $\rightleftharpoons$ Hackney Central or Hackney Downs
291 Mare Street, E8; tel. (081) 985 2424.
This old variety theatre has been given a new lease of life with a lively programme of comedy and music. Entertainment for all the family.

JONGLEURS $\rightleftharpoons$ Clapham Junction
The Cornet, 49 Lavender Gardens, SW11; tel. (081) 780 1151. Telephone bookings Monday to Friday noon–3 p.m.
Some of the best cabaret acts appear here regularly. Shows on Friday, Saturday, and sometimes Sunday. It's essential to book.

NEW VARIETY PERFORMERS   ⊖ Brixton
The Old White Horse, 261 Brixton Road, SW9; tel. (071) 487 3440.
Every Friday at the White Horse, and at various other venues round
London. Each programme is made up of two or three comedians, a
speciality act and perhaps some live music. Telephone reservation
through the Hackney Empire box office (081) 985 2424.

RED ROSE CLUB   ⊖ Finsbury Park or Holloway Road
129 Seven Sisters Road, N7; tel. (071) 263 7265.
Fast and funny shows by a mixed bag of comedians, magicians and so
on. Friday and Saturday.

TALK OF LONDON   **14** N10   ⊖ Holborn or Covent Garden
*Parker Street, WC2; tel. (071) 408 1001. Bookings Monday to Friday
9 a.m.–8 p.m.; Saturday 10 a.m.–8 p.m.; Sunday 11 a.m.–7 p.m.*
An old-fashioned cabaret evening in this high-class venue, with singers
and dancers, dinner and some dancing. Reservation essential.

LATE-NIGHT LONDON

Late-night London can be rather limited. Virtually the only bars open
after midnight are in jazz clubs, music venues or nightclubs where you
have to pay entrance charges. However, a few restaurants—mainly
foreign ones—stay open late. Public transport is restricted to night
buses (see p. 205); taxis are the best way to get around.

ANGELO'S   ⊖ Bayswater or Notting Hill Gate
146 *78 Westbourne Grove, W2; tel. (071) 221 8843. Open Monday to
Saturday, licensed until 3 a.m.*
A lively Greek restaurant and club where it's hard to avoid a spot of
dancing.

BAR ITALIA   **13** M9/10   ⊖ Leicester Square
*22 Frith Street, W1; tel. (071) 437 4520. Open daily 7 a.m.–2 a.m.,
sometimes later at weekends.*
An excellent espresso café (no alcohol), the Bar Italia also offers pizza
and panini, and has a large TV screen for all the major sports events.
Conveniently opposite Ronnie Scott's (see p. 136).

BILL STICKERS   **13** M9/10   ⊖ Tottenham Court Road
*18 Greek Street, W1; tel. (071) 437 0582. Open Monday to Saturday,
licensed until 3 a.m.; Sunday until 11 p.m.*
Late bar and restaurant. Mexican food served until 2 a.m. (11 p.m. on
Sunday).

CAFÉ PELICAN   **24** N9   ⊖ Charing Cross
                                               or Leicester Square
45 St. Martin's Lane, WC2; tel. (071) 379 0309. Open Monday to Saturday until 1 a.m.; Sunday until 11.30 p.m.
A good, French-style brasserie right in the middle of the West End, with live jazz music.

COSTA DORADA   **13** M10   ⊖ Tottenham Court Road
47-55 Hanway Street, W1; tel. (071) 636 7139. Open Monday, Tuesday, Thursday to Saturday, licensed until 3 a.m.; Sunday until midnight.
Twice-nightly flamenco shows (10.30 and 12.30 p.m.) with lots of Spanish food—tapas and paella.

DOVER STREET   **22** K8   ⊖ Green Park
WINE BAR/RESTAURANT
8–9 Dover Street, W1; tel. (071) 491 7509/629 9813. Open Monday to Thursday noon–3 p.m. and 5.30 p.m.–3 a.m.; Friday and Saturday 8 p.m.–3 a.m.
A basement wine bar better known for its wine and live jazz than its food.

HARRY'S   **13** L9   ⊖ Oxford Circus
19 Kingly Street, W1; tel. (071) 434 0309. Open Monday to Saturday 5.30 p.m.–6 a.m.
If you need an English breakfast in the middle of the night, this is the place to find it. The bar closes at midnight but meals are served from 10 p.m. all through the night.

LOS LOCOS   **14** N/O9   ⊖ Covent Garden **147**
24–26 Russell Street, WC2; tel. (071) 379 0220. Open Monday to Saturday, licensed until 3 a.m.
Wash down TexMex food with a Los Locos cocktail. Disco.

REY CAMINO   **36** G3   ⊖ Sloane Square
152 King's Road, SW3; tel. (071) 351 3084. Open Monday to Saturday, licensed until 2 a.m.; Sunday 7 p.m.–10.30 p.m.
A tapas bar with a good selection of Spanish wines, beers and liqueurs. Live music some evenings.

TIBERIO   **22** K8   ⊖ Green Park
22 Queen Street, W1; tel. (071) 629 3561. Open Monday to Saturday, licensed until 2 a.m.
A reliable and popular Italian restaurant in Mayfair with live music and dancing.

London's superb luxury hotels enjoy world-wide reputations, and the capital's medium-range establishments meet international standards for their class. There are, also, comfortable, country-house hotels that are small and intimate, and typically English. Down the price scale, though, London is short of good, inexpensive accommodation similar to the dependable *pensions* of continental Europe.

The London Tourist Board provides information about accommodation and also runs an efficient hotel booking service, for either same-day or advance reservations, and will handle applications in person, in writing or by telephone (see p. 153). Its guide *Where to Stay in London* and brochures on budget accommodation are available from the board's office at 26 Grosvenor Gardens, SW1; tel. (071) 730 3488; open Monday to Friday 9 a.m.–6 p.m.

Hotels are inspected and categorized according to the facilities they offer. The grades go up from "listed" to 1 crown, 2 crowns, etc., peaking at 5 crowns and, in rare cases, 5 gold crowns. Grades are usually displayed next to the front door.

The hotels listed here are grouped according to the cost of a double room for one night.

ECONOMY

ANNE ELIZABETH HOUSE   28 D4   ⊖ Earl's Court
30 Collingham Place, SW5; tel. (071) 370 4821.
One of the least expensive hostels in London, with a good location, basic facilities, a bed in a five-person room for £8 per night, and a single room at £14.75 (charges include Continental breakfast).

At a top London hotel, a top-hatted doorman greets the guests.

CURZON HOUSE HOTEL   28 D4   ⊖ Gloucester Road
58 Courtfield Gardens, SW5; tel. (071) 373 6745.
The lowest-priced beds here are in dormitories (from £11 per night);
single and double rooms are also available (from £20 and £28
respectively). Charges include Continental breakfast.

KENT HOUSE   ⊖ Manor House
325 Green Lanes, N4; tel. (081) 802 0800/9070.
One of a number of economical hotels in this part of north London, the
Kent is fairly basic, low-priced (£9 per person per night when sharing
a four-person room; £14 for a single room) and (with a few exceptions)
restricted to those aged between 16 and 45. Group reductions.

UP TO £50

AMSTERDAM HOTEL   28 C4   ⊖ Earl's Court
7 Trebovir Road, SW5; tel. (071) 370 2814; fax (071) 244 7608.
A small bed-and-breakfast hotel, which has 20 rooms, all with private
facilities. Single £37, double £48, Continental breakfast included.

APOLLO   28 C5   ⊖ Earl's Court or Gloucester Road
*18–22 Lexham Gardens, W8; tel. (071) 835 1133; telex 264 189;
fax (071) 370 4853.*
60 rooms, most with private facilities. Single £28–40, double £50; triple
£60, breakfast included. A reasonably priced hotel offering good
amenities and friendly service.

150 **ATLAS**   28 C5   ⊖ Earl's Court
*24–30 Lexham Gardens, W8; tel. (071) 835 1155; shares telex and fax
with the Apollo Hotel above.*
A modernized Victorian building with 60 rooms, most with bath or
shower and toilet. Single £28–40, double £50, Continental breakfast
included.

GOWER HOTEL   10 E9   ⊖ Paddington
129 Sussex Gardens, W2; tel. (071) 262 2262; fax (071) 262 2006.
21 rooms, 19 with bath or shower and toilet. Single £22–30, double
£34–40, triple £18 per person, English breakfast included. A
convenient, family-run hotel, close to Hyde Park and the shops and
restaurants of Notting Hill.

EDWARD LEAR   **11** H10   ⊖ Marble Arch
30 Seymour Street, W1; tel. (071) 402 5401; fax (071) 706 3766.
Named after the author of the nonsense poem, *The Owl and the Pussy-cat,* this comfortable hotel in a converted Georgian house has 31 rooms, 12 with private facilities. Single £37.50–55, double £49.50–59.50, English breakfast included. Conveniently situated in the West End.

ELIZABETH   **32** K4   ⊖ Victoria
37 Eccleston Square, SW1; tel. (071) 828 6812.
27 rooms, some with bath or shower and toilet. Single from £30, double £46–66, English breakfast included. Situated in a quiet square, the Elizabeth has recently been redecorated.

HOTEL IBIS (EUSTON)   **6** L12   ⊖ Euston or Euston Square
3 Cardington Street, NW1; tel. (071) 388 7777; telex 221 15; fax (071) 388 0001.
300 rooms, all with private facilities. Single £49, double £54, triple £64; breakfast: Continental £4, English £6.25. Part of a reliable French chain, the Ibis offers comfort rather than luxury, and good amenities.

HOTEL LA PLACE   **12** J11   ⊖ Baker Street
17 Nottingham Place, W1; tel. (071) 486 2323; fax (071) 486 4335.
24 rooms, all with bath or shower and toilet. Single from £50, double £60–70, family suite from £70, English breakfast included. A small hotel, with friendly and efficient service. Restaurant and bar.

HOSTELS

For obvious reasons, youth hostels are very popular, so it is advisable to book well in advance in the high season.

151

YHA. You must be a member to benefit from the YHA's reasonably priced, basic accommodation (dormitories). Every hostel has a cafeteria. Staff at the headquarters at 14 Southampton Street, WC2, tel. (071) 836 1036, can direct you to one of the hostels it runs in and around London, you can phone (0727) 40211 for information on membership, or you can contact one of the following addresses:
Holland House, Holland Walk, Kensington, W8; tel. (071) 937 0748
Carter Lane, EC4;   tel. (071) 236 2965
Earl's Court Hostel, 38 Bolton Gardens, SW5;   tel. (071) 373 7083
Hampstead Hostel, 4 Wellgarth Road, NW11;   tel. (081) 458 9054
Highgate Hostels, 84 Highgate West Hill, N6;   tel. (081) 340 1831.

LONDON CONTINENTAL   11 H11   ⊖ Baker Street
88 Gloucester Place, W1; tel. (071) 486 8670; fax (071) 252 8687.
26 rooms, all with bath or shower and toilet. Single £35–40, double £55–60, triple £20–25 per person, English breakfast included. Popular with business people as well as tourists, and close to Oxford Street.

NAYLAND   10 F9   ⊖ Paddington
132–134 Sussex Gardens, W2; tel. (071) 723 4615; fax (071) 402 3292.
41 rooms, all with shower and toilet. Single from £44, double from £52, family suite £22 per person, English breakfast included. Recently renovated, the rooms have good facilities, including video movies.

PARKWOOD   11 G9   ⊖ Marble Arch
4 Stanhope Place, W2; tel. (071) 402 2241; fax (071) 402 1574.
18 rooms, 12 with private facilities. Single £38.50–53.50, double £52.50–63.50, English breakfast included. A homely atmosphere, good amenities and a convenient location.

SANDRINGHAM   ⊖ Hampstead
3 Holford Road, NW3; tel. (071) 435 1569; fax (071) 431 5932.
19 rooms, some with bath or shower and toilet. Single £30–40, double £50–56, triple and family from £59, English breakfast included. A family-run bed-and-breakfast hotel, high on the hills in Hampstead, which makes you feel you're staying in someone's home.

SLAVIA   18 C9   ⊖ Notting Hill Gate
2 Pembridge Square, W2; tel. (071) 727 1316; telex 917 458; fax (071) 229 0803.
31 rooms, all with private facilities. Single £33–38, double £44–52, English breakfast included. Situated in a quiet garden square, the Slavia is a modernized, family-run hotel.

152 SOUTH KENSINGTON   29 E4   ⊖ South Kensington
GUEST HOUSE
13 Cranley Place, SW7; tel. (071) 589 0021.
14 rooms, some of which have private facilities. Single £25–35, double £60–69, triple £60, breakfast included. Clean and convenient, near the South Kensington museums.

TERRY'S/PREMIER WEST HOTEL   ⊖ Hammersmith
28–34 Glenthorne Road, W6; tel. (081) 748 6181; telex 932 515 (shared); fax (081) 748 2195.
A bed-and-breakfast hotel near the Riverside Studios, a short Underground journey from the West End. 49 rooms, 41 with private facilities. Single from £45, double from £55, triple from £75, English breakfast included.

WINDERMERE HOTEL   **31** K4   ⊖ Victoria
*142–144   Warwick   Way,   SW1;   tel. (071) 834 5163/834 5480;
telex 940 17 182; fax (071) 630 8831.*
24 rooms, 20 with bath or shower and toilet. Single £40–45, double
£48–74, 3- or 4-bedded room £75–85, English breakfast included.
Well-placed near Victoria Station, the hotel offers comfortable rooms
and friendly service.

YORK   **19** D9   ⊖ Queensway or Bayswater
*30–34 Queensborough Terrace, W2; tel. (071) 229 9511; telex 298 392;
fax (071) 221 9594.*
A hundred rooms, some of which are currently being refurbished, all
with private facilities and other amenities. Single room £43, double or
twin £65 and triple £75, Continental breakfast included. A pleasant
hotel close to Hyde Park, with a friendly atmosphere.

Booking a Room

The London Tourist Board runs an efficient hotel booking service for
either same-day or advance reservations and will deal with
applications in writing, by telephone or in person. Please note that
the opening hours given may vary according to the season.
TABS—Access and Visa cardholders may make **telephone** bookings for the same day or up to six weeks in advance by ringing
(071) 824 8844.

Advance bookings may be made **in writing** to Derek Williams, London
Tourist Board, 26 Grosvenor Gardens, London SW1 1W0DU.

Personal callers can contact the Information Centres at the following
locations:

Liverpool Street Station, EC2; open Monday to Friday 9.30 a.m.–6.30
p.m., Saturday 8.30 a.m.–6-30 p.m., Sunday 8.30 a.m.–3.30 p.m.

Harrods (Basement Booking Hall) Brompton Road, SW1; open during
normal store hours

Heathrow Airport; open daily 8 a.m.–6.30 p.m.

Selfridges (basement), Oxford Street, W1; open during normal store
hours

Tower of London, West Gate, Tower Hill, EC3; open (Easter to
November) Monday to Saturday 9.30 a.m.–6 p.m., Sunday 10 a.m.–
6 p.m.

Victoria Station (forecourt), SW1; open Monday to Saturday 8 a.m.–
7 p.m., Sunday 8 a.m.–5 p.m.

UP TO £100

ABCONE HOTEL **28** D5 ⊖ Gloucester Road
10 Ashburn Gardens, SW7; tel. (071) 370 3383; fax (071) 373 3082.
35 rooms, many with private facilities. Single £35–49, double £48–78,
English breakfast included. A comfortable hotel in a spot very
convenient to the South Kensington museums, shops and restaurants.

DURRANTS **12** J10 ⊖ Marble Arch
George Street, W1; tel. (071) 935 8131; fax (071) 487 3510.
100 rooms, most with bath or shower and toilet. Single from £55, double
from £94, family suite £140, suite £185; breakfast: Continental £5.25,
English £8. A good base between Oxford Street and Regent's Park,
which offers traditional service and well-equipped, quiet bedrooms.

EBURY COURT **31** K6 ⊖ Victoria
26 Ebury Street, SW1; tel. (071) 730 8147; fax (071) 823 5966.
46 rooms, many with private facilities. Single £50–55, double £75–95,
luxury and family rooms £130–160, English breakfast included.
Recently refurbished and family-run, this is one of the best of the small
hotels in this group, with an inviting country feel and friendly service.

FIELDING **14** N9/10 ⊖ Covent Garden
4 Broad Court, Bow Street, WC2; tel. (071) 836 8305; fax (071) 497 0064.
26 rooms, 24 with private facilities. Single £36–59, double £59–80.50,
triple £87.75, suite £80.50; breakfast: Continental £2.50, English £4.
A no-nonsense, comfortable and friendly place.

HAZLITT'S **13** M9 ⊖ Leicester Square
6 Frith Street, W1; tel. (071) 434 1771; fax (071) 439 1524.
23 rooms, all with en suite bath/shower and toilet. Single £88.55, double
£99, suite £156; Continental breakfast £4.85. Light and airy rooms, lots
of wood panelling, and a unique location in the middle of Soho.

HOTEL NUMBER SIXTEEN **29** F4 ⊖ South Kensington
16 Sumner Place, SW7; tel. (071) 589 5232; fax (071) 584 8615.
36 rooms, almost all with private facilities. Single £60–95,
double £105–155, Continental breakfast included. Light rooms,
efficient service and a garden combine to keep guests coming back
time and time again.

KNIGHTSBRIDGE **30** G6 ⊖ Knightsbridge
10 Beaufort Gardens, SW3; tel. (071) 589 9271; fax (071) 823 9692.

20 rooms, a few with bath or shower and toilet. Single £38.50–52.50, double £60–85, family suite from £72, Continental breakfast included. Moderately priced and small-scale, this hotel is well situated in a quiet corner of Knightsbridge.

KNIGHTSBRIDGE GREEN   **20** G6   ⊖ Knightsbridge
159 Knightsbridge, SW1; tel. (071) 584 6274; fax (071) 225 1635.
24 rooms, all with private facilities. Single £85, double £100, suite £115; breakfast: Continental £6, English £8. Newly decorated, with the emphasis on suites.

NEW BARBICAN   ⊖ Old Street
120 Central Street, EC1; tel. (071) 251 1565; fax (071) 253 1005.
Nearly 500 rooms, all with private facilities. Single from £66.50, double from £79.50, suite from £145; breakfast: Continental £4.95, English £7.25. One of the few hotels in the City, this is friendly and comfortable.

NOVOTEL LONDON   ⊖ Hammersmith
1 Shortlands, W6; tel. (081) 741 1555; fax (081) 748 8061.
640 rooms, all with private facilities. Single £77, double £84, suite £150; breakfast £7.50. A good place to stay—in Hammersmith—if you need to get to Heathrow early but want a night out on the town first.

SWISS COTTAGE   ⊖ Swiss Cottage
4 Adamson Road, NW3; tel. (071) 722 2281; fax (071) 483 4588.
81 rooms, most with private facilities, and also some apartments. Single £39–115, double £68–115, suite £115, apartment £420 per week (£14 per extra person), English breakfast included. Tucked away among large Victorian villas, the hotel has just been renovated and offers attractive rooms and furnishings, as well as a bar, restaurant and conference room.

WILBRAHAM   **30** H5   ⊖ Sloane Square **155**
1 Wilbraham Place, SW1; tel. (071) 730 8296; fax (071) 730 6815.
50 rooms, most with bath or shower and toilet. Single £59.25, double £71.30–92; breakfast: Continental £3.50, English £5.50. A solid Victorian house, which offers a good location and smallish but comfortable rooms.

WILLETT   **31** H4   ⊖ Sloane Square
32 Sloane Gardens, SW1; tel. (071) 824 8415; fax (071) 824 8415.
19 rooms, most with private facilities. Single £63.20–68, double £68.95–80.40, family suite from £126.32, English breakfast included. Recommended more for its location than its service, the Willett does have large rooms.

UP TO £150

ABBEY COURT   18 C8   ⊖ Notting Hill Gate
20 Pembridge Gardens, W2; tel. (071) 221 7518; fax (071) 792 0858.
22 rooms with en suite facilities. Single £75, double £110–145;
Continental breakfast £7. An extremely pleasant, cosy feel to this hotel
close to Portobello antiques market. Notable for its breakfasts.

ALEXANDER   29 F4   ⊖ South Kensington
9 Sumner Place, SW7; tel. (071) 581 1591; fax (071) 581 0824.
36 rooms, all with private facilities. Single £80.50, double £92–149.50,
suite £189.75, English breakfast included. A beautifully kept hotel,
offering comfort, good service, a homely atmosphere and a garden.

BASIL STREET   21 H6   ⊖ Knightsbridge
8 Basil Street, SW3; tel. (071) 581 3311; fax (071 581 3693.
100 rooms, a large number of which have bath or shower and toilet.
Single £49.50–93.50; double £76–121; suite £188; breakfast:
Continental £4.50, English £9. Discreetly elegant and full of
good-looking furniture, the Basil Street Hotel is popular because of
its charming small sitting rooms and its position right behind Harrods.

CLAVERLY   30 G6   ⊖ Knightsbridge
13–14 Beaufort Gardens, SW3; tel. (071) 589 8541; fax (071) 584 3410.
32 rooms, most with private facilities. Single £55–70, double £65–120,
family suite £100, English breakfast included. Regarded as one of
the best bed-and-breakfasts in London, the Claverley can be
recommended for its good service and inviting rooms. Quietly and
conveniently situated in Knightsbridge.

KENILWORTH   14 M10   ⊖ Tottenham Court Road

156 *97 Great Russell Street, WC1; tel. (071) 636 3283/637 3477; telex 258 42; fax (071) 631 3133.*
192 rooms, all with bath or shower and toilet. Single £99, double £135,
suite £145–175; breakfast: Continental £7, English £9. Smallish rooms,
but is centrally situated and the service is above average

L'HOTEL   21 H6   ⊖ Knightsbridge
*28 Basil Street, SW3; tel. (071) 589 6286; telex 919 042;
fax (071) 225 0011(marked: Attention l'Hôtel).*
12 rooms, all with private facilities. Double £110, suite £145;
Continental breakfast included. Small and perfectly appointed, L'Hôtel
has a rustic décor, impeccable service and an excellent location
behind Harrods.

RAMADA HOTEL   **13** L10   Θ Tottenham Court Road
Berners Street, W1; tel. (071) 636 1629; telex 257 59; fax (071) 580 3972.
235 rooms, all with private facilities. Single £92–130, double £150, suite £230–299; breakfast: Continental £7, English £9. Expensive-looking and comfortable, the Ramada is part of a world-wide hotel chain.

REGENT CREST   **6** K11   Θ Great Portland Street
Carburton Street, W1; tel. (071) 388 2300; telex 224 53; fax (071) 387 2806.
320 rooms with private facilities. Single £110–125, double £125–145, suite £220–320, jacuzzi room £195; breakfast: Continental £6.95, English £9.95. One of the few London hotels that offers special facilities for women travellers. Men are welcome, too.

RUSSELL HOTEL   **7** N11   Θ Russell Square
Russell Square, WC1; tel. (071) 837 6470; telex 246 15; fax (071) 837 2857.
326 rooms, all with private facilities. Single £107, double £130, suite £148–198; breakfast: Continental £7.95, English breakfast £9.85. A handsome old turn-of-the-century hotel, the Russell has recently undergone a much-needed face-lift and is back among the recommended places to stay.

STRAND PALACE   **24** O9   Θ Charing Cross
Strand, WC2; tel. (071) 836 8080; telex 242 08; fax (071) 836 2077.
Over 750 rooms, all with bath or shower and toilet. Single £85–95, double £100–110, triple £114–124; breakfast: Continental £6.50, English £8.50. A large, comfortable hotel near Charing Cross with spacious rooms, good facilities and efficient service.

THE PORTOBELLO   Θ Notting Hill Gate
22 Stanley Gardens, W11; tel. (071) 727 2777; telex 268 349; **157**
fax (071) 792 9641.
25 rooms, all with private facilities. Single £59.80–63.25, double £95.45–139.15, suite £150.65, Continental breakfast included. A small, eccentric hotel in a six-floor mansion, in the centre of Notting Hill.

TOWER THISTLE HOTEL   Θ Tower Hill
St. Katharine's Way, E1; tel. (071) 481 2575; fax (071) 488 4106.
826 rooms, all with bath or shower and toilet. Single £109–132, double £128–145, suite £210; breakfast: Continental £6.25, English £8.95. The views overlooking the River Thames are magnificent, the position on the edge of the City is good for business travellers and tourists alike, and the standards of comfort and service are high.

UP TO £280

All hotels in this and the following category (GRAND) have private facilities in every room.

ATHENAEUM   **22** K7   ⊖ Green Park or Hyde Park Corner
116 Piccadilly, W1; tel. (071) 499 3464; telex 261 589; fax (071) 493 1860.
Over 100 rooms and suites. Also, 30 apartments. Single £160, double £173–188, suite £230–270, apartment £190–220 (£975–1,200 per week); breakfast: Continental £9, English £11.50. Conveniently situated opposite Green Park, the Athenaeum is quietly comfortable in an expensive, homely way. The staff are exceptionally courteous.

BEAUFORT   **30** G6   ⊖ Knightsbridge
33 Beaufort Gardens, SW3; tel. (071) 584 5252; telex 929 200; fax (071) 589 2834.
28 quiet and comfortable rooms, with many extras. Single £150, double £160–250, breakfast included. 24-hour complimentary bar and food service, and membership of health club are among the attractions of this luxury hotel. The Beaufort's staff are outstandingly helpful.

BLAKES   **29** E4   ⊖ South Kensington or Gloucester Road
33 Roland Gardens, SW7; tel. (071) 370 6701; fax (071) 373 0442.
52 rooms and suites. Single £120–150, double £170–270, suite £220–600; breakfast from £7.50. Eclectic décor, this is the closest London comes to the stylishness of some of New York's top hotels. Best described as "80s pop romanticism", the style is all black and mirrored, or frills and flounces. De luxe rooms and good basement restaurant.

BROWN'S   **22** K8   ⊖ Green Park
Albemarle Street, W1; tel. (071) 493 6020; telex 286 86; fax (071) 493 9381.
175 rooms and suites. Single £150, double £190, suite £330–390; breakfast: Continental £10.25, English £11.75. Brown's has been the hotel for the more discerning of the English county set for close on 150 years now. The atmosphere is all leather and old wood, the service is discreet and the bedrooms very comfortable.

CAPITAL   **30** H6   ⊖ Knightsbridge
22–24 Basil Street, SW3; tel. (071) 589 5171; telex 919 042; fax (071) 225 0011.
48 rooms. Single £150, double £175–200, suite £265; breakfast: Continental £7.50, English £10.50. A sophisticated and charming Ralph Lauren-style interior oozes country-house comfort.

158

DUKE'S   **22** L7   ⊖ Piccadilly Circus or Green Park
35 St. James's Place, SW1; tel. (071) 491 4840; telex 282 83; fax (071) 493 1264.
62 rooms and suites. Single from £165, double from £194, suite from £380; breakfast: Continental £8.25, English £10.50. The club atmosphere of the public rooms hints at the homely comfort of the bedrooms. The service is excellent, and the restaurant well worth trying.

FORTY-SEVEN PARK STREET   **21** J9   ⊖ Marble Arch
47 Park Street, W1; tel. (071) 491 7282; telex 221 16; fax (071) 491 7281.
52 suites. Studio from £258.75, 1-bedroom suite £287.50–419.75, 2-bedroom £454.25–494.50, 2 connecting 1-bedroom suites £615.25; breakfast: Continental £10.95, English £14.40. A small hotel of suites in a quiet pocket of Mayfair near the American Embassy. It is conveniently situated next to the Roux brothers' La Gavroche restaurant.

HOLIDAY INN MAYFAIR   **22** K8   ⊖ Green Park
3 Berkeley Street, W1; tel. (071) 493 8282; telex 245 61; fax (071) 629 2827.
186 rooms and suites. Single £140–160, double £170–185, suite £290–550; breakfast: Continental £8.75, English £10.75. Luxury service and facilities and a good location in the West End compensate for the rather boring modern building.

INN ON THE PARK   **22** J7   ⊖ Hyde Park Corner
Hamilton Place, Park Lane, W1; tel. (071) 499 0888; telex 227 71; fax (071) 493 1895.
Over 200 rooms and suites. Single £211.25, double £247.25, suite £299–£1,006.25; breakfast: Continental £8.75, English £11.50. Notable for the consistency of service, the high standard of comfort and the conservatories incorporated into the suites, the Inn on the Park also has one of London's best restaurants, the Four Seasons (see p. 104).

159

STAFFORD   **22** L8   ⊖ Green Park
16–18 St. James's Place, SW1; tel. (071) 493 0111; telex 286 02; fax (071) 493 7121.
62 rooms—single £170, double £185–205, suite £245–400; breakfast: Continental £8.50, English £11.50. Small and elegant, the Stafford is one of that gentle breed of English hotels that is all old-world service and traditions.

THE FENJA   **30** H4   ⊖ Sloane Square
69 Cadogan Gardens, SW3; tel. (071) 589 7333; telex 934 272; fax (071) 581 4958.
13 rooms. Single £90, double £120–180; breakfast: Continental £6, English £9. Generously sized, en suite rooms in the trendy Sloane Square area.

THE GORING   **31** K6   ⊖ Victoria
15 Beeston Place, Grosvenor Gardens, SW1; tel. (071) 834 8211; telex 919 166; fax (071) 834 4393.
90 rooms. Single £105, double £155, suite £180–190; breakfast: Continental £6.50, English £9.50. This is one of London's secrets—a splendid, very English hotel, a stone's throw from Victoria Station, with traditional standards of comfort and service—and a good restaurant.

GRAND

CLARIDGE'S   **12** K9   ⊖ Bond Street
Brook Street, W1; tel. (071) 629 8860; telex 218 72; fax (071) 499 2210.
190 rooms and suites. Single £185–215, double £235–280, suite £430; breakfast: Continental £9.50, English £13.50. One of the great London hotels, where the Art Déco interior is wonderful, the service is impeccable, the facilities are perfect and regular guests include royalty, heads of state and film stars.

CONNAUGHT   **22** J9   ⊖ Bond Street
Carlos Place, W1; tel. (071) 499 7070; fax (071) 499 7070.
120 rooms and suites. Room rates vary from £150 to £400 plus 15% service charge; details on application. The Connaught is small and select, filled with antiques and fresh flowers, and is often booked up months in advance. The restaurant is outstanding.

160

THE RITZ   **22** K/L8   ⊖ Green Park
Piccadilly, W1; tel. (071) 493 8181; telex 267 200; fax (071) 493 2687.
Over 100 rooms and suites. Single £175, double £205–245, suite £465–595; breakfast: Continental £7.75, English £11.75. Marble and gilt splendour dazzles even the most sophisticated guests. Some of the bedrooms have magnificent views over Green Park. Tea in the Palm Court is a wonderful experience (see p. 112).

THE SAVOY 24 O9 ⊖ Charing Cross
Strand, WC2; tel. (071) 836 4343; telex 242 34; fax (071) 240 6040.
Over 200 rooms and suites. Single £155, double £180–240, suite £260–550; breakfast: Continental £9.50, English £14. Now over a hundred years old, the Savoy has undergone something of a renaissance in recent years and once again offers the type of service and comfort that made it the favourite hotel of the Establishment.

SELF-CATERING APARTMENTS

ASHBURN GARDEN APARTMENTS 28 D5 ⊖ Gloucester Road
3 Ashburn Gardens, South Kensington, SW7; tel. (071) 370 2663; telex 940 163 18; fax (071) 370 6743.
25 apartments—studios, one- and two-bedrooms—at £420–700 per week. This family-run apartment agency offers a sensible alternative to hotel accommodation. Reserve well in advance for the summer season.

CHANCEWELL LONDON 12 J10 ⊖ Bond Street
23 Greengarden House, St. Christopher's Place, W1; tel. (071) 935 9191; fax (071) 935 8858.
24 flats, 16 one-bedroom at around £842 per week, and eight two-bedroom at about £1,100. A block away from Oxford Street shopping area, the apartments are privately owned. Single-night lets are possible, according to availability. There are also several de luxe apartments.

EMPEROR'S GATE APARTMENTS 28 C5 ⊖ Earl's Court
8 Knaresborough Place, SW5; tel. (071) 244 8409; fax (071) 373 6455.
12 studio and one-bedroom apartments from £55–115 per night, for up to four persons (a fifth bed costs about £20 extra). Daily maid service, laundry room and parking by arrangement. Also six apartments at 5 Emperor's Gate (Gloucester Road underground).

HUNTINGDON HOUSE LIMITED 28 C/D5 ⊖ Earl's Court
200–222 Cromwell Road, SW5; tel. (071) 373 4525; telex 252 93; fax (071) 373 6676.
49 apartments. Studio £275–300 per week, one-bedroom £440–700, two-bedroom £850–950. A noisy, but convenient, situation. Some apartments have laundry facilities.

161

What an exciting place London can be for children! There are wonderful museums, parks and gardens, theatres and other fascinating places to visit, as well as toyshops, bookshops and restaurants designed with children in mind. A day out in London with the family can include a visit to one of the city's historic buildings, such as the Tower of London or Hampton Court; a trip on the river to view the Houses of Parliament and Westminster Abbey; a walk around an attractive shopping precinct such as Covent Garden, with its covered arcade of Victorian shops and its wide selection of restaurants. Finding things to do is not a problem; choosing between them may be. Listed below are some of the best ideas for keeping children happy in London.

THEATRE AND ENTERTAINMENT

London offers a wide variety of theatrical entertainment for children, including pantomimes (after Christmas), puppet shows, plays and musicals. Many theatres also provide workshops for budding actors and musicians. Programmes change every week, however, so it's worth a telephone call to avoid disappointment.

BARBICAN CENTRE   **17** S11   ⊖ Moorgate or Barbican
Silk Street, EC2; tel. (071) 638 4141. Open Monday to Saturday 9 a.m.–11 p.m.; Sunday/public holidays noon–11 p.m.
A year-round programme of plays, musical events, puppet shows and films. The Children's Cinema Club on Saturdays (11 a.m. and 2.30 p.m.) screens films for 6–12-year-olds. Also workshops in drama, model-making, puppetry and music-making, as well as storytelling sessions. (See also pp. 132 and 142.)

ICA CHILDREN'S CINEMA   **23** M8   ⊖ Charing Cross
The Mall, SW1; tel. enquiries (071) 930 0493; box office (071) 930 3647. Films start at 3 p.m.
The first of its kind—presenting a regular programme of films and special events designed to introduce children to all aspects of cinema. **163** Matinées in school holidays and a children's cinema club. All seats bookable. (See also pp. 139 and 140.)

Children on the brink of amazement meet London Zoo penguins.

NATIONAL FILM THEATRE   **24** O8   ⊖ Waterloo

South Bank, Waterloo, SE1; tel. enquiries (071) 928 3535 ext. 415; box office (071) 928 3232; recorded information (071) 633 0274. Box office open daily 11.30 a.m.–8.30 p.m.

An excellent programme of high-quality children's films, which changes every week. (See also p. 139.)

LITTLE ANGEL MARIONETTE THEATRE   ⊖ Highbury & Islington

14 Dagmar Passage, Cross Street, N1; tel. (071) 226 1787. Shows Saturdays 11 a.m. and Sundays 11 a.m. and 3 p.m.

Enchanting puppet shows every weekend throughout the year and during the week in school holidays—3–6-year-olds on Saturday at 11 a.m and 6 years and over every Saturday and Sunday at 3 p.m.

POLKA CHILDREN'S THEATRE   ⊖ Wimbledon

240 The Broadway, Wimbledon, SW19; tel. (081) 543 4888/0363. Open every day except Sunday and Monday.

A programme of children's drama and puppet shows throughout the year. Workshops specialize in puppet-making, music and drama. Also a children's café and play area.

PUPPET THEATRE BARGE   ⊖ Warwick Avenue

Little Venice, Blomfield Road, W9; tel. box office (0836) 202 745; enquiries (071) 249 6876.

A floating marionette theatre moored in Little Venice, which also does a tour on the Thames in summer. Hand-carved marionettes, shadow puppets, lighting and original music combine to present shows full of magic and fantasy. All in a converted, enclosed Thames barge, with sloping seating for 50.

SOUTH BANK ARTS CENTRE   **24** O8   ⊖ Waterloo
                                              or Embankment

South Bank, SE1; tel. box office (071) 928 8800; general information (071) 928 3002; recorded information (071) 633 0932.

164   Special events for children include readings by well-known children's authors, plays and Saturday workshops in music and drama. (See also p. 133.)

UNICORN THEATRE FOR CHILDREN   **14** M9   ⊖ Leicester
                                              Square

Great Newport Street, WC2; tel. enquiries (071) 379 3280; box office (071) 836 3334. Performances Saturday and Sunday, school holidays and half-terms 2.30 p.m. Also special school performances in term time.

The oldest theatre for children and the only professional theatre in the West End solely for youngsters. At least four plays every season for children between the ages of 4 and 13, each aimed at a particular age group, usually 5–7s, 7–9s and 9–13s. Also a children's club and workshop.

YOUNG VIC 25 P7 ⊖ Waterloo
66 The Cut, SE1; tel. box office (071) 928 6363.
Intimate atmosphere and high-quality works by first-class directors and actors. Special events include plays and musicals aimed at young people. Also a studio theatre.

MUSEUMS

Below is a selection of museums which are of particular interest to children of all ages. In addition, some of the establishments listed under Museums and Art Galleries (see pp. 33–53 and 55–61) may be suitable for older children and often run a programme of special activities during school holidays.

BETHNAL GREEN MUSEUM OF CHILDHOOD ⊖ Bethnal Green
Cambridge Heath Road, E2; tel. (081) 980 3204. Open Monday to Thursday, Saturday 10 a.m.–5.50 p.m.; Sunday 2.30–5.50 p.m.
A Father Christmas's grotto of toys in this department of the Victoria & Albert Museum. Includes a fine set of doll's houses (many of them perfect replicas of 18th- and 19th-century models), a large collection of dolls from all over the world, toys and games, magic lanterns, model railways and ships. Also a display of children's clothes, from Elizabethan times to the present. Arts workshops held on Saturdays (11 a.m.–1 p.m. and 2–4 p.m.).
Admission free.

BRITISH MUSEUM 14 N10 ⊖ Holborn or Tottenham Court Road **165**
Great Russell Street, WC1; tel. (071) 636 1555; recorded information (071) 580 1788. Open Monday to Saturday 10 a.m.–5 p.m.; Sunday 2.30–6 p.m.
Packed with fascinating treasures from different historical periods and cultures. Of particular interest to children are the Egyptian mummies, artefacts from Roman and Celtic Britain and treasure from the Sutton Hoo Ship Burial. There is a regular programme of special events for children, including storytelling and workshops. (See also pp. 34–5.)
Admission: free, but donation requested.

GEFFRYE MUSEUM AND GARDENS ⊖ Bethnal Green
Kingsland Road, E2; tel. (071) 739 9893; recorded information (071) 739 8543. Open Tuesday to Saturday 10 a.m.–5 p.m. (including all public holidays); Sunday 2–5 p.m.

See how people lived in the past at this interesting museum where each room is furnished as a typical middle-class English home of a particular historical period. One section is arranged as an 18th-century street, including a woodworker's shop and an open-hearth kitchen. Children's playground in the attractive garden. Free quiz sheets available on Saturdays and during school holidays and a regular programme of workshops on a variety of themes.

Admission free.

LONDON TOY AND MODEL MUSEUM 19 E9 ⊖ Queensway
21–23 Craven Hill, W2; tel. (071) 262 7905. Open Tuesday to Saturday 10 a.m.–5.30 p.m.; Sunday 11 a.m.–5.30 p.m.

Contains a large collection of toys, games and models attractively arranged in a maze of interconnecting rooms. Also has a working display of model trains in the garden, as well as a larger electric train to ride on. A 1920s hand-operated merry-go-round offers rides to the under-9s, and there is an old open-top London bus to climb on.

Admission: small charge.

LONDON TRANSPORT MUSEUM 14 N9 ⊖ Covent Garden
Covent Garden, WC2; tel. enquiries (071) 379 6344; recorded information (071) 836 8557. Open 10 a.m.–6 p.m.

Housed in the old Victorian flower market building, this fascinating museum presents an exhibition of London transport from the 17th century to the present day. Exhibits include horse-drawn omnibuses, trams, trolley-buses, motor-buses and tube trains. Lots of interactive displays, including a real bus or a tube train to "drive". Activity sheets, with cut-out models to assemble at home, and information packs for 8–12-year-olds, are available from the museum shop. (See also p. 46.)

Admission: charge, but family tickets available.

166

MUSEUM OF LONDON 16 R10 ⊖ Barbican or Moorgate
150 London Wall, EC2; tel. (071) 600 3699. Open Tuesday–Saturday 10 a.m.–6 p.m.; Sunday 2–6 p.m.

Devoted exclusively to London and its history from Neolithic times to the present day. Children will love the reconstructions of a Roman villa, an 18th-century drawing room and a Victorian pub, as well as the audio-visual display of the Great Fire of London, as narrated by Samuel Pepys. Special events during school holidays (see also p. 36).

Admission free.

MUSEUM OF MANKIND   22 L9   ⊖ Piccadilly Circus or Green Park
*6 Burlington Gardens, W1; tel. (071) 437 2224; recorded information
(071) 580 1788. Open Monday to Saturday 10 a.m.–5 p.m.; Sunday
2.30–6 p.m.*
A fascinating display of exhibits from around the world, illustrating the
different cultural traditions in Africa, Asia, North and South America,
Australia and Europe. The museum's Education Service provides
worksheets for children. (See also p. 37.)
Admission free, but donations requested.

MUSEUM OF THE MOVING IMAGE (MOMI)   24 O8   ⊖ Waterloo
or Embankment
*South Bank Arts Centre, SE1; tel. (071) 928 3535; recorded information
(071) 401 2636. Open Tuesday to Saturday 10 a.m.–8 p.m.; Sunday
and public holidays 10 a.m.–6 p.m.*
Recently opened to wide acclaim for its imaginative design, the
museum follows the development of film and TV from 19th-century
optical toys to 20th-century Hollywood. Children will enjoy the
interactive exhibits, such as the "real" movie set featuring a Wild West
saloon, or the "Superman" flying illusion. Actors, in character, are
employed as guides and there is also a permanent workshop where
children can learn to animate their own cartoons. (See also p. 41.)
Admission: charge, but family reduction.

NATIONAL MARITIME MUSEUM AND   ⇌ Greenwich or Maze Hill
OLD ROYAL OBSERVATORY   or by river bus to Greenwich
*Romney Road, Greenwich, SE10; tel. (081) 858 4422. Open Tuesday
to Saturday 10 a.m.–6 p.m.; Sunday 2 –5.30 p.m. (5 p.m. November to
February).*
Combine a trip on the river with a visit to this historical site, so important
for its role in world navigation. Spread over several buildings, the
exhibition includes a full-size 19th-century steamboat, a fine collection
of sailing boats from all over the world and some superb ship's
figureheads. Special exhibitions are imaginatively thought out to allow
scope for younger visitors. (See also p. 37.)
Admission: small charge.

167

NATURAL HISTORY MUSEUM   29 E5   ⊖ South Kensington
*Cromwell Road, SW7; tel. (071) 938 9123. Open Monday to Saturday
10 a.m.–6 p.m., Sunday 11 a.m.–6 p.m.*
Apart from the perennial appeal of dinosaurs, the museum presents a
wide range of exciting exhibits aimed at young visitors, including the
audio-visual and interactive displays in the Blue Whale Hall and the
Human Biology section, and the new "Creepy-Crawlies" exhibition on

the role of insects in the eco-system. The Discovery Centre invites children to join in a variety of activities focusing on the natural world; also storytelling sessions, and scientific lectures aimed at children. Activity sheets for children aged 6–18 are available. (See also p. 38.) Admission: small charge.

POLLOCK'S TOY MUSEUM   13 L11   ⊖ Goodge Street
1 Scala Street, W1; tel. (071) 636 3452. Open Monday to Saturday 10 a.m.–5 p.m.
A private organization run by an educational trust and housed in two adjacent old buildings, this delightful museum displays a fine collection of toy theatres, doll's houses, teddy bears and optical toys. Toy theatre performances are given from time to time during school holidays. Admission: small charge.

SCIENCE MUSEUM   29 E5   ⊖ South Kensington
Exhibition Road, South Kensington, SW7; tel. (071) 938 8000. Open Monday to Saturday 10 a.m.–6 p.m., Sunday 11 a.m.–6 p.m.
One of the most popular museums with children of all ages, presenting permanent displays of steam trains, spacecraft and automobiles, as well as "hands-on" exhibits demonstrating different scientific principles. Its newest and most enthralling exhibition is the "Launch Pad", where children can try out a whole range of activities involving light, sound, magnetism and electricity. (See also pp. 38–9.) Admission: charge.

THEATRE MUSEUM   14 N9   ⊖ Covent Garden
Russell Street, WC2; tel. (071) 836 7891; recorded information (071) 836 7624. Open Tuesday to Saturday 11 a.m.–7 p.m.
Any child with an interest in ballet or the theatre will find this a rewarding place to visit. Exhibitions on a variety of subjects, from the circus to the Chinese Opera, are regularly changed. Worksheets and quizzes are available. (See also p. 43.)

Admission: small charge.

VICTORIA & ALBERT MUSEUM   29 F5   ⊖ South Kensington
Cromwell Road, SW7; tel. (071) 938 8500. Open Monday to Saturday 10 a.m.–5.30 p.m., Sunday 2–5.50 p.m.
Older children will enjoy the excellent exhibitions of costumes through the ages, as well as the museum's other beautiful artefacts, but in general this is not a museum for young children. Events for children are, however, organized during school holidays. (See also p. 39.) Admission: free, but donation suggested.

INTERESTING THINGS TO SEE AND DO

BEKONSCOT MODEL VILLAGE
⇌ Beaconsfield

Warwick Road, Beaconsfield, Buckinghamshire; tel. (0494) 672 919. Open daily 10 a.m.–5 p.m. (March–October).

Children—frankly, not only children—are fascinated by this village in miniature, complete with lavish model railway wending its way past a Lilliputian village hall, shops, houses, windmill and church, and with horse racing and games of football into the bargain. More than 60 years old, the "oldest model village in the world" is all of two feet (60 cm.) high.

Admission: small charge.

CHANGING OF THE GUARD, 22/23 BUCKINGHAM PALACE
⊖ St. James's Park or Victoria

The Mall, SW1; tel. London Tourist Board (071) 730 3488. Every day 11.30 a.m. (every other day in winter).

Children enjoy the spectacle of the Guards, in their red tunics and distinctive bearskin helmets, marching from Wellington or Chelsea Barracks to the forecourt of the Palace. It's worth arriving in good time to get the best view.

CUTTY SARK
⇌ to Greenwich or Maze Hill or by river bus to Greenwich

King William Walk, SE10; tel. (081) 858 2698. Open Monday to Saturday 10 a.m.–5 p.m.; Sunday noon–5 p.m. (earlier in winter).

The last of the great 19th-century tea clippers, this historic sailing ship is a fascinating place for most children. Visitors can go up on deck to admire the intricate rigging, or down below to see the ship's living quarters, now converted into a museum and including a fine collection of ship's figureheads. (See also p. 44.)

Admission: small charge.

169

GUINNESS WORLD OF RECORDS 23 M9
⊖ Piccadilly Circus or Leicester Square

Trocadero, Piccadilly Circus, W1; tel. (071) 439 7331. Open every day 10 a.m.–10 p.m.

Thousands of facts and figures brought to life by audio-visual computer technology. Six interactive "worlds" to explore—Human, Animal, Sports, Our Planet Earth, Structures and Machines, and Entertainment.

Admission: charge.

CHANGING OF THE GUARD

Centuries of tradition lie behind these colourful and moving ceremonies, originally intended to ensure the monarch's safety. Except in very wet weather, they take place daily from the beginning of April to the end of July, and on alternate days for the rest of the year. You may need to get there early for a good view. For full details, ring the London Tourist Board on (071) 730 3488.

Buckingham Palace. At 11.30 a.m., lasting approximately half an hour. The Guard leaves Wellington Barracks at 11.27 a.m., marching via Birdcage Walk to the Palace.

Horse Guards, Whitehall. The Guard of the Household Cavalry is changed at 11 a.m. Monday to Saturday and at 10 a.m. on Sunday. The Guard leaves Hyde Park Barracks and rides via Hyde Park Corner and The Mall.

St James's Palace. The St. James's detachment of the Queen's Guard marches to Buckingham Palace and back at 11.15 a.m.

Tower of London. The Guard is changed at 11.15 a.m. in summer and 11.30 a.m. in winter.

GUARD MOUNTING

As practice for the Queen's Birthday Parade and the Trooping the Colour, the ceremony of Guard Mounting is performed on various days during May on Horse Guards Parade.

CEREMONY OF THE KEYS

For 700 years the ceremonial locking of the main gate of the Tower of London has been carried out by the Chief Yeoman Warder and his escort of Guards each evening at 9.50 p.m. Passes are essential and can be obtained free upon written application to: The Resident Governor, Queen's House, HM The Tower of London, EC3 4AB.

GUN SALUTES

Gun salutes take place annually on the following dates: February 6 (Accession Day), April 21 (Queen's Birthday), June 2 (Coronation Day), June 10 (Prince Philip's Birthday) and August 4 (Queen Mother's Birthday). **Note** that no Salute is ever fired on a Sunday but is held over to the next day.

Hyde Park. At noon in Hyde Park (except on April 21 when it takes place in Green Park). The 41-gun salute is fired by the King's Troop, Royal Horse Artillery. The soldiers gallop their horses down through the park pulling the massive gun carriages.

Tower of London. A 62-gun salute is also fired at the Tower at 1 p.m. by the Honourable Artillery Company.

HAMPTON COURT PALACE ⇌ or river to Hampton Court
East Molesey, Surrey; tel. (081) 977 8441. Open daily 9.30 a.m.–6 p.m. (4.30 p.m. in winter); gardens open until dusk.
Children particularly enjoy the famous Maze, but the palace itself (one of the most historic and handsome in Greater London) and its beautiful gardens offer other delights for the young visitor. Special activities for children during school holidays. (See also pp. 192–3.)
Admission: gardens free of charge; palace & maze or maze only: small charge.

HORSE GUARDS 23 N7 ⊖ Charing Cross or Westminster
Whitehall, SW1; Monday to Saturday the guard changes at 11 a.m.; Sunday at 10 a.m.
The permanent guard, mounted on beautiful black horses and clad in the distinctive silver breastplates and "horse's tail" helmets, is provided by the Household Cavalry. Also parades in the courtyard in summer.

KENSINGTON PALACE 19 D7 ⊖ Queensway, Notting Hill Gate or High Street Kensington
Kensington Gardens, W8; tel. (071) 937 9561. Open Monday to Saturday 9 a.m.–5 p.m., Sunday 1–5 p.m. Last admission 4.15 p.m.
Open to the public are the historic State Apartments which contain the unique collection of ladies' and gentlemen's court dress from 1750 to 1940 and may be of interest to older children. Special activities are organized during school and public holidays. (See also p. 24.)
Admission: charge.

LASERIUM 5 H11 ⊖ Baker Street
Marylebone Road, NW1; tel. box office (071) 379 4444; recorded information (071) 486 2242. Tuesday/Wednesday to Sunday, laser light concerts in the evenings.
Based in the Planetarium, the Laserium usually offers three evening shows, all popular with older children, which change at regular intervals. Film, lasers and loud music are the main attractions.
Admission: charge.

171

LONDON DUNGEON 27 T8 ⊖ London Bridge
28/34 Tooley Street, SE1; tel. (071) 403 0606. Open daily 10 a.m.–5.30 p.m. (4.30 p.m. in winter).
A rather gruesome exhibition depicting the darker side of British history, including Trials by Ordeal, Capital Punishment and Torture. An audio-visual presentation of the Great Fire of London is another attraction. Not for the very young or imaginative child.
Admission: charge.

SPECIAL ACTIVITIES

The **Historic Royal Palaces Agency** runs special activities for school children during term time and for families on public holidays and during school vacations and covers the following places of interest: Banqueting House, Whitehall; Hampton Court Palace; Kensington Palace; Kew Gardens and the Tower of London. For full details ring their Education Department on (081) 977 7222, extension 132. Or simply enquire at the entrance when you arrive.

LONDON PLANETARIUM 5 H11 ⊖ Baker Street
Marylebone Road, NW1; tel. (071) 486 1121. Open daily. Shows throughout the day, starting at 12.20 p.m. on weekdays and 10.20 a.m. on Saturday and Sunday.
A fascinating journey around the universe, including space travel, the life and death of stars and genesis of planets, which will enthral most children. Visitors can buy a combined ticket for the Planetarium and Madame Tussaud's, which is next door.
Admission: charge.

MADAME TUSSAUD'S 5 J11 ⊖ Baker Street
Marylebone Road, NW1; tel. (071) 935 6861. Open daily 10 a.m.– 5.30 p.m.
Popular with young and not so young alike, the famous wax museum now includes lifelike models of pop stars, entertainers, the Royal Family and many others. The new "Superstars" section is another big attraction. Special sound and light effects add to the thrills.
Admission: charge, also combined ticket with the London Planetarium.

ROYAL BRITAIN 16 R11 ⊖ Barbican
Aldersgate Street, EC2; tel. (071) 588 0588. Open daily from 10 a.m.– 5.30 p.m.
Interactive exhibits which attempt to bring to life the history of the British monarchy from the Dark Ages to the present day.
Admission: charge.

ROYAL MEWS 32 K6 ⊖ St. James's Park or Victoria
Buckingham Palace Road, SW1. Open Wednesday and Thursday throughout the year 2–4 p.m.
See the fairy-tale coaches which include the Gold State Coach, used for Coronations, and the Glass State Carriage. Horses are stabled here and there is a also a fine display of State harness and other regalia.
Admission: small charge.

172

SCHOONER KATHLEEN AND MAY   **26** S8   ⊖ London Bridge
St. Mary Overy Dock, Cathedral Street, SE1; tel. (071) 403 3965. Open daily 10 a.m.–5 p.m.
The last remaining three-masted, wooden topsail schooner has been restored and refitted by the Maritime Trust and offers a fascinating insight into cramped conditions on board a coastal trading craft.
Admission: small charge.

ST. PAUL'S CATHEDRAL   **16** R10   ⊖ St. Paul's or Mansion House
Ludgate Hill, EC4; tel. (071) 236 4128. Open Monday to Friday 7.30 a.m.–6 p.m.; Saturday and Sunday 8 a.m.–6 p.m. Galleries, crypt and ambulatory Monday to Saturday 10 a.m.–4.15 p.m.
A historic landmark, of educational interest to older children. Amongst its attractions are the famous Whispering Gallery around the inside of the Dome, and the tomb of Lord Nelson. (See also p. 17.)
Admission: small charge for the ambulatory, crypt and guided tours.

TOWER BRIDGE   **27** U8   ⊖ Tower Hill
SE1; tel. (071) 407 0922. Open daily 10 a.m.–6.30 p.m. (April to October); 10 a.m.–4.45 p.m. (November to March).
Children enjoy the panoramic views from the enclosed walkway over the river, as well as the exhibitions on the history of the bridge. (See also p. 30.)
Admission: small charge.

TOWER OF LONDON   **27** U8/9   ⊖ Tower Hill
Tower Hill, London EC3; tel. (071) 709 0765. Open (October to March) Monday to Saturday 9.30 a.m.–5 p.m., Sunday 2–5 p.m. (March to October); Monday to Saturday 9.30 a.m.–4.30 p.m.
Built by William the Conqueror in 1078, this historic building served as a fortress and state prison. Children will enjoy exploring the grounds, with the picturesque ravens and "Beefeaters", as well as the exhibitions of armour, weapons and the Crown Jewels in the Tower itself. *The Family Trail*, on sale in the White Tower, is an introduction to the exhibits, designed with younger visitors in mind. (See also pp. 30–1.)
Admission: charge.

173

WESTMINSTER ABBEY   **33** N6   ⊖ Westminster
Parliament Square, SW1; tel. (071) 222 5152. Open: nave only, Monday, Tuesday, Thursday to Saturday 8 a.m.–6 p.m., Wednesday 8 a.m.–7.30 p.m., and Sunday between services; Royal Chapels, Monday to Friday 9 a.m.–4.45 p.m., Saturday 9 a.m.–2.45 p.m. and 3.45–5.45 p.m.
This ancient and beautiful landmark contains many historic and interesting sights, including the Coronation Stone, Poets' Corner,

where memorials to famous writers such as Geoffrey Chaucer and Charles Dickens can be found, and the tombs of many British kings and queens. (See also p. 18.)
Admission: small charge for entrance to the Royal Chapels.

WINDSOR CASTLE ⇌ Windsor & Eton

Windsor, Berks.; tel. (0753) 868 286. Castle precincts open daily from 10 a.m. to between 4.15 and 7.15 p.m., depending on the time of year. State Rooms and Queen Mary's Doll's House, Monday to Saturday 10.30 a.m.–5 p.m., Sunday 1.30–5 p.m. (May–October); Monday to Saturday 10.30 a.m.–3 p.m. (November–April). Closed when the Royal Family is in residence.

A fascinating glimpse inside a "real-life" castle is irresistible to most children, as is the chance to see what must surely be the world's most beautiful doll's house, made by Sir Edwin Lutyens for Queen Mary in 1921. There are also 16 State rooms, packed with treasures—armour, splendid tapestries, painting and furniture. It's advisable to check before visiting, as the Castle is closed to the public for state occasions. (See also Windsor Safari Park p. 176.)
Admission: precincts, free; State Rooms, small charge.

WIDE OPEN SPACES

CHESSINGTON WORLD OF ADVENTURES ⇌ Chessington South

Leatherhead Road, Chessington, Surrey; tel. (0372) 727 227. Open daily (April to October) 10 a.m.–5 p.m. (November to March: zoo only).
The closest thing to Disneyland to be found in Britain, Chessington World of Adventures, about 12 miles (20 km.) south-west of London, appeals to all ages. There's more than enough to do: heart-stopping train rides, a monorail for panoramic views, a Wild West town complete with shooting gallery, and a large zoo. And a Circus Academy reveals Big Top skills, with several performances daily.
Admission: charge.

174

GREENWICH PARK ⇌ Maze Hill or Greenwich
or by river to Greenwich Pier

SE10; tel. (081) 858 2608. Open 7 a.m.–dusk.
A former royal hunting ground, Greenwich Park offers many features which appeal to children, including broad sloping lawns, a playground, a lake with wildfowl and an enclosed deer park. Combine a visit with a boat trip down the Thames. Other attractions are the hollow oak, reputedly visited by Elizabeth I, and the panoramic view over London.

HOLLAND PARK   18 B6/7
⊖ Holland Park
or High Street Kensington

W8.
Provides the largest stretch of natural woodland in central London. Of the Jacobean mansion which gave the park its name, only the orangery, the ballroom and the east wing remain. Children are irresistibly drawn to the rabbits, chickens, ducks and peacocks on the Yucca Lawn. (See also p. 185.)

HYDE PARK   20/21
⊖ Hyde Park Corner

W1. Open 6 a.m.–midnight.
Originally Henry VIII's hunting ground, Hyde Park is a welcome oasis of green in London, providing ample space for playing and walking. It is bisected by the Serpentine, an artificial lake which provides facilities for fishing, boating, bathing and canoeing. (See also p. 185.)

KENSINGTON GARDENS   19/20   ⊖ Queensway, Notting Hill Gate
or High Street Kensington

W8. Open 7 a.m.–dusk.
Adjoining Hyde Park, this relatively small but very pretty park boasts attractive flower gardens, a playground and the famous Round Pond, where children can sail model boats. (See also p. 185.)

KEW GARDENS
✈ Kew Bridge or by river to Kew Pier

Kew Green, Surrey; tel. (081) 940 1171. Open Monday to Saturday 9.30 a.m.–dusk/8 p.m.
Alongside the Thames, the Royal Botanic Gardens are delightful natural gardens and woods which contain many rare and beautiful plants, shrubs and trees. Also an attractive lake. Dogs are not allowed. (See also p. 186.)
Admission: small charge.

REGENT'S PARK   4/5   ⊖ Baker Street or Regent's Park
NW1; tel. (071) 486 7905. Open dawn–dusk.
Another former royal hunting ground, Regent's Park is the largest of the central London parks. Children will make a beeline for the boating pool, where boats can be hired between 10 a.m. and 7 p.m. every day. The proximity of London Zoo is another reason for coming here. (See also p. 186.)

175

ST. JAMES'S PARK & GREEN PARK   22/23   ⊖ St. James's Park
SW1. Open dawn–midnight.
A breathing space close to St. James's Palace and Buckingham Palace, where children love the lake with its many varieties of wildfowl, as well as the playground. (See also p. 186.)

ZOOS & SO ON

LONDON ZOO   **5** J13   ⊖ Baker Street then 74 bus
Regent's Park, NW1; tel. (071) 722 3333. Open daily April–September 9 a.m.–6 p.m. October–March 10 a.m.–4 p.m.
Lions, tigers, elephants, giraffes and all the usual attractions—as well as some unusual ones—are here in London's famous zoological gardens. A well-stocked children's zoo within the main enclosure features rabbits, sheep, and goats, as well as more exotic fauna. Feeding times can be checked on arrival. Also underwater marvels at the Aquarium.
Admission: charge.

LONDON BUTTERFLY HOUSE   ⊖ Gunnersbury then 237 bus
Syon Park, Brentford, Middlesex; tel. (081) 560 7272. Open daily 10 a.m.–5 p.m. (3.30 p.m. in winter).
A large, purpose-built greenhouse structure, displaying the hundreds of colourful, tropical butterflies that are bred here.
Admission: small charge.

WHIPSNADE WILD ANIMAL PARK   ⇌ Luton
Whipsnade, Dunstable, Bedfordshire; tel. (0582) 872 171. Open Monday to Saturday 10 a.m.–6 p.m., Sunday and public holidays 10 a.m.–7 p.m. (sunset in winter).
Although it's more fun than a standard zoo, Whipsnade is no mere showplace for lovable animals. It's renowned for its breeding programmes, under which members of endangered species have been recycled back into the wild. Most of the 2,000 or so animals roam uncaged in large enclosures which resemble their natural habitat. You can drive through or take the steam train (with commentary) that tours the park in summer and at weekends in winter. Additional attractions—a children's zoo, a sea-lion show and a Discovery Centre that will widen the eyes and horizons of any youngster.
Admission: charge.

176

WINDSOR SAFARI PARK   ⇌ Windsor
Winkfield Road, Windsor, Berks.; tel. enquiries (0753) 830 886; recorded information (0753) 869 841. Open daily 10 a.m.–4.30/7 p.m.
Children of any age adore a visit to a safari park where they can spot herds of wild animals roaming the wide open spaces in relative freedom. Well equipped and well laid out, the park also has regular shows (dolphins, parrots), a play centre and a tropical house. For those depending on public transport, a land train tours the property.
Admission: the all-inclusive ticket covers shows and everything.

SHOPPING

For children, London can be a shoppers' paradise selling everything from kites to doll's kitchens, from casual rags to top-class clothing. Clearly the big department stores (see pp. 65–6) lead the way in standard items and have a wonderful atmosphere before Christmas, with Santa Claus often in residence. Visits to trendy shopping areas such as Carnaby Street and the King's Road can provide those cute earrings or that witty, original tee-shirt, as well as an enjoyable outing just savouring the London scene. The suggestions given below are for something a little bit special or out of the ordinary.

TOYS ETC.

ERIC SNOOK   14 N9   ⊖ Covent Garden
32 The Market, Covent Garden, WC2; tel. (071) 379 7681. Open every day 10 a.m.–6 p.m.
A popular general toyshop, selling soft toys, games and wooden toys, as well as novelties and "fun" items.

FROG HOLLOW   28 D6   ⊖ Gloucester Road
15 Victoria Grove, W8; tel. (071) 581 5493. Open Monday to Saturday 9.30 a.m.–5.30 p.m.; Sunday 11 a.m.–5.30 p.m.
A wonderful selection of soft toys, novelty and party goods and, of course, frogs in all shapes and sizes. Also a branch (Frog Frolics) in Ifield Road, off the Fulham Road—tel. (071) 370 4358.

HAMLEYS   13 L9   ⊖ Oxford Circus
188–196 Regent Street, W1; tel. (071) 734 3161. Open Monday to Saturday 9.30 a.m.–6 p.m. (Friday until 8 p.m.).
Simply London's largest toyshop, with six floors of soft toys, dolls, cars, games and books—in short, just about every plaything possible.

177

THE KITE STORE   14 N9/10   ⊖ Covent Garden
48 Neal Street, Covent Garden, WC2; tel. (071) 836 1666. Open Monday to Friday 10 a.m.–6 p.m.; Saturday 10.30 a.m.–5 p.m.
A specialist shop, selling a huge range of kites.

THE SINGING TREE   ⊖ Fulham Broadway
69 New King's Road, SW6; tel. (071) 736 4527. Open Monday to Saturday 10 a.m.–5.30 p.m.
Specializes in doll's houses, doll's furniture and miniatures.

TIGER, TIGER   **36** G3   ⊖ Sloane Square

219 King's Road, SW3; tel. (071) 352 8080. Open Monday to Saturday 10 a.m.–6 p.m.

A good general toyshop, selling soft toys, doll's houses, games and wooden toys, as well as party paraphernalia and fancy dress.

CLOTHES

BAMBINO   **12**K9   ⊖ Bond Street

77 New Bond Street, W1; tel. (071) 491 8077. Open Monday to Saturday 10 a.m.–6 p.m. (until 7 p.m. Thursday).

Stylish clothes for babies and children up to the early teens.

BANANAS   ⊖ Holland Park

7 Clarendon Cross, W11; tel. (071) 727 1011. Open Monday to Saturday 9.30 a.m.–5.30 p.m.

A bright shop stocking British and Continental children's clothes, both traditional and more flamboyant. All ages up to 12 years catered for.

012 BENETTON   **12** J/K9   ⊖ Bond Street

22 South Molton Street, W1; tel. (071) 409 1599. Open Monday to Saturday 10 a.m.–6 p.m. (Thursday until 8 p.m.).

Mid-priced casual wear, for 0–12-year-olds. Branches of this fashionable and popular Italian chain in other districts of London, including Kensington High Street, tel. (071) 937 2960.

CLOTHKITS   **14** N9/10   ⊖ Covent Garden

39 Neal Street, Covent Garden, WC2; tel. (071) 240 7826. Open Monday to Saturday 9.30 a.m.–6 p.m.

178 Reasonably priced, colourful children's clothes for ages 0–13 come ready-made or in cut-out kit form.

LAURA ASHLEY   **13** K10   ⊖ Oxford Circus

256–258 Regent Street, Wl. tel. (071) 437 9760. Open Monday to Friday 9.30 a.m.–6 p.m. (Thursday until 8 p.m.); Saturday 9 a.m.–6 p.m.

Pretty, mostly floral print dresses, sailor suits and other traditional clothes for children 0–12 years. Also furnishings. Another shop at 47/9 Brompton Road, Knightsbridge, tel. (071) 823 9700, and branches in many districts of London.

LITTLE PERISHERS   ◯ Angel or Highbury & Islington
139 Upper Street, N1; tel. (071) 226 3344. Open Monday to Saturday 10 a.m.–6 p.m.
Kit out your youngsters (0–16) here in trendy garments and shoes by leading designers.

MAGITTY   **18** C7   ◯ High Street Kensington
39 Kensington Church Street, W8; tel. (071) 938 2371. Open Monday to Saturday 10 a.m.–6 p.m.
Mainly French- and Italian-designed clothes for babies, girls up to 12, and boys up to 8. Traditional and modern, including shoes.

MOTHERCARE   **12** J9   ◯ Marble Arch or Bond Street
461 Oxford Street, W.1; tel. (071) 629 6621. Open Monday to Saturday 10 a.m.–6 p.m. (until 7.30 p.m. Thursday).
This well-known store supplies everything for babies and children up to 10 years old. One of two shops in Oxford Street, the chain also has branches in other parts of London.

PEEK-A-BOO   **11** H11   ◯ Baker Street
42 Chiltern Street, W1; tel. (071) 486 2800. Open Monday to Friday 10 a.m.–5.30 p.m.; Saturday 10 a.m.–1 p.m.
Lovely babies' and very young children's clothes by leading designers, from traditional layettes to fun clothes for toddlers.

PLEASE MUM   **12** J9/10   ◯ Bond Street or Marble Arch
15a Orchard Street, W1; tel. (071) 486 1380. Open Monday to Saturday 10 a.m.–6 p.m. (until 8 p.m. Thursday).
Exclusive designer clothes for young children, from birth to 16. Another large branch at 69 New Bond Street, W1, tel. (071) 493 5880, and a smaller one in Golders Green Road.

SHRIMPS   **8** O11   ◯ Russell Square or High Holborn
89 Lamb's Conduit Street, WC1; tel. (071) 242 4855. Open Monday to Friday 10 a.m.–5 p.m.; Saturday 10 a.m.–1 p.m.

179

Fashionable casuals for young children (up to eight years) and traditional babywear.

YOUNGSTERS   ◯ Ladbroke Grove
230 Portobello Road, W10; tel. (071) 221 2910. Open Saturday 10 a.m.–6 p.m.
Fashion-conscious children (0–10 years) will love the range of clothes sold here, many of which are reasonably priced.

BOOKWORMS

THE PUFFIN BOOKSHOP   **14** N9   ⊖ Covent Garden
1 The Market, Covent Garden, WC2; tel. (071) 379 6465. Open Monday to Saturday 10 a.m.–6 p.m.
One of the best children's bookshops in London, offering a wide range of fiction and non-fiction for all, including children's classics, new titles, make-and-do, science, history and music books. Attractively laid out, with a children's reading corner. Also toys, games and stationery.

WATERSTONES   **13** M10   ⊖ Tottenham Court Road
121–125 Charing Cross Road, WC2; tel. (071) 434 4291. Open Monday to Friday 9.30 a.m.–7.30 p.m.; Saturday 10.30 a.m.–7 p.m.
A good general bookshop, offering a wide range of children's titles, including classics and new fiction. Other large branches throughout London.

RESTAURANTS

Although many London restaurants welcome children, those given below are particularly popular with the next generation.

BENIHANA   ⊖ Swiss Cottage
100 Avenue Road, NW3; tel. (071) 586 7118. Open Tuesday to Friday 12.30–3 p.m.; Saturday and Sunday 1–3 p.m.; Monday to Saturday 6.30p.m.–midnight; Sunday 6.30–11 p.m.; closed Monday lunch.
Popularized *teppan-yaki* restaurant particularly welcoming to children, providing their own menu at lunchtime on Saturday and Sunday. Children can watch the theatrical Japanese chefs at work and enjoy the tasty, sizzling results. Set lunches from £6, otherwise from £12.

CHUEN CHENG KU   **23** M9   ⊖ Piccadilly Circus
17 Wardour Street, W1; tel. (071) 437 1398. Open Monday to Saturday 11 a.m.–midnight; Sunday 11 a.m.–11.15 p.m.
Huge and famous Chinatown Cantonese restaurant popular for its *dim-sum* served from trolleys. Children love the totem pole outside and most find the food interesting and tasty. From £5 a head.

180

HAAGEN-DAZS ON THE SQUARE   **23** M9   ⊖ Leicester Square
14 Leicester Square, London WC2; tel. (071) 287 9577. Open daily 10 a.m.–midnight; Friday and Saturday until 1 a.m.
Bright modern ice cream parlour serving the entire range of delicious American ice creams. Expensive but worth it.

HARD ROCK CAFE   **22** J7   ⊖ Green Park or Hyde Park Corner
150 Old Park Lane; tel. (071) 629 0382. Open daily 11.30–12.30 a.m.
London's most famous and ever-popular American diner/café where
people queue every day for a table. Great burgers, great atmosphere
and great music! From £10 a head.

L. S. GRUNTS CHICAGO   **24** N9   ⊖ Covent Garden
PIZZA COMPANY   or Charing Cross
*12 Maiden Lane, WC2; tel. (071) 379 7722. Open Monday to Saturday
noon–11.30 p.m.; Sunday noon–9 p.m.*
Highly rated by adults and kids as one of the best places in town for
maxi or mini American-style pizzas. Non-alcoholic cocktails and
enticing desserts also a speciality.

ROCK ISLAND DINER   **23** M9   ⊖ Piccadilly Circus
*London Pavilion, 1 Piccadilly, W1; tel. (071) 240 3961. Open daily 11
a.m.–11.30 p.m. (until 10 p.m. Sunday).*
Jiving waitresses, 50s decor and American diner food, including
Haagen-Dazs ice cream. Children of all ages love it. From £8 a head.

SMOLLENSKY'S ON THE STRAND   **24** O9   ⊖ Charing Cross
*105 Strand, WC2; tel. (071) 497 2101. Open Monday to Saturday noon–
midnight; Sunday noon–10.30 p.m.*
A restaurant which positively welcomes children, offering entertainment, videos, a supervised play area and a special children's menu,
including a selection of children's "cocktails". The adult menu is good,
too. Also Smollensky's Balloon, 1 Dover Street, W1, tel. (071) 491 1199.

TALL ORDERS   ⊖ Parson's Green
*676 Fulham Road, SW6; tel. (071) 371 9673. Open daily noon–
midnight.*
The name of this large, bustling, busy restaurant refers to the fact that
the food is served in Chinese wicker steaming baskets that arrive piled
on top of each other. Portions are between appetizer and main-course
size and most people settle for 4–6 of each. Food is Mediterranean-
style, tasty and interesting. From £12 a head, less for children
depending on what is ordered.

181

TEXAS LONE STAR SALOON   **29** E4   ⊖ Gloucester Road
*154 Gloucester Road, SW7; tel. (071) 370 5625. Open Monday to
Thursday noon–11.15 p.m.; Friday and Saturday noon–12.15 a.m.*
Tex-mex food served in an appropriately saloon-style setting. Great
ribs too. Especially popular with younger children at the weekend.

Whether you choose London for sightseeing or art, shopping or entertainment, there will come a time when you want to escape the hustle and bustle and the crowds in favour of some fresh air—a bit of exercise or simply a rest on a park bench—to recharge your batteries. That's the time to visit one of the magnificent parks with which London is outstandingly endowed.

Alternatively, you may choose to see the sights from the comfort of a coach. A clever way to get an overall view of London (and get your bearings for further exploration on your own) is to take one of the double-decker bus tours that cover the main attractions. Or enjoy a half- or full-day visit to some of the major historic buildings.

For a different view of the city, by day or night, try a boat trip. Among other possibilities, river buses ply the Thames both up- and downstream and you can take advantage of the outing to visit one of the riverside sights, such as Greenwich, the Docklands or Hampton Court Palace.

If you're feeling energetic, join one of the guided walks that take you off the beaten track, for a journey back to Roman times, an architectural adventure—or a pub crawl.

LEAFY RETREATS

The map of London is spattered with green, the colour of the envy other cities feel about London's profusion of parks. No matter how crowded the capital becomes, a breath of really fresh air is never far away. The city's parks—including former royal gardens and hunting grounds—were long ago acquired on behalf of the public for their pleasure and leisure. Most of London's parks are enclosed; their gates are locked at night. Any sports and other facilities have their own operating hours, rules and regulations. Otherwise, make free use of the wide open spaces, and enjoy all the peace and fresh air you need.

On a sunny day in London, the big charms of Little Venice beckon.

BATTERSEA PARK   36/7   ⇌ Battersea Park

Queenstown Road or Albert Bridge Road, SW11. Open every day dawn to dusk.

On the south bank of the Thames, stretching from Chelsea to Albert Bridge and just a short walk from the centre of Chelsea itself, Battersea is one of London's youngest parks, opened in 1858. Designed more for recreation than contemplation, it possesses over 30 tennis courts, several football and hockey pitches and an athletics track, as well as boating lakes and children's playgrounds. The rather showy Festival Gardens are a surprising formal contrast, and the latest, most visible, addition is the London Peace Pagoda, built by Japanese Buddhist monks and nuns in 1985.

GREENWICH PARK   ⇌ Greenwich or Maze Hill
                                         or by river to Greenwich Pier

SE10. Open daily dawn to dusk (summer); 7 a.m.–6 p.m./dusk (winter).

Ideal for long rambles and energetic walks, Greenwich Park is a haven of woods and lawns by the Thames, a short train or boat ride from Central London. Once a royal park, with good hunting grounds stocked then, as now, with deer, it was laid out in more or less its present form in the 17th century to a design by Le Nôtre, landscape architect responsible for the château gardens at Versailles. The focal point is Inigo Jones' Queen's House (see p. 28), flanked on either side by Sir Christopher Wren's Royal Naval Hospital (see p. 29), giving wonderful views of, and from, the river. The Old Royal Observatory (see p. 27) on top of the hill completes this harmonious group of buildings and spacious grounds.

HAMPSTEAD HEATH   ⊖ Hampstead or Belsize Park

NW3. Open 24 hours a day.

The very existence of Hampstead Heath, 800 acres (324 ha.) of unspoiled countryside just a few miles from the West End, is an extraordinary tribute to early conservationists who battled against Victorian builders for its survival. Its rolling acres fluctuate from carefully tended, formal parkland to untamed woods and open fields. A favourite spot for jogging, walking, fishing or flying kites, it's not lacking in sports facilities. A number of ponds for swimming and great views over London from the top of Parliament Hill complete the attractions of this charming corner of the capital. Kenwood House, on the north-western edge of the heath (see p. 57), is open to the public, and if you are in need of refreshment, the famous nearby pubs—Spaniards Inn or Jack Straw's Castle—await you.

HOLLAND PARK   18 B6/7

⊖ Holland Park
or High Street Kensington

W8. Open daily 8 a.m.–dusk.
Once a private park graced by an early 17th-century Jacobean house, Holland Park stretches northwards from Kensington High Street to Holland Park Avenue in Notting Hill. Its formal flower gardens command attention, but most of the park consists of unspoiled woods containing a surprising contingent of wildlife—from noisy woodpeckers to the colourful peacocks that strut proudly on the yucca lawn. Part of Holland House, restored after heavy bombing during World War II, is now a youth hostel and its front terrace has been turned into a theatre.

HYDE PARK   20/1

⊖ Hyde Park Corner, Knightsbridge, Marble Arch or Lancaster Gate

W2. Open daily 6 a.m.–midnight.
With 340 acres (nearly 138 ha.) of lakes, gardens, open fields and sports facilities, Hyde Park is by far London's biggest park (Hampstead Heath, nearly three times bigger, is not officially a park). All year round, Hyde Park offers something for everyone. Summer sees sunbathers on the grass and swimmers at the Lido, while a fine day brings out strollers and joggers and tempts people to row a boat on the Serpentine, an artificial lake created on the orders of Queen Caroline around 1730. Horse riders exercise their mounts in Rotten Row, the bridle path whose name was derived from the *Route de Roi* of King William III. He had the path lit in a forlorn attempt to deter highwaymen.

Freedom of speech is the watchword at Speaker's Corner, the world capital of soap-box oratory, at the north-east angle of the park near Marble Arch. Nearby, Wellington Gate, the neoclassical entrance designed by Decimus Burton, has stood, unmoved by all the eloquence, since 1828.

KENSINGTON GARDENS   19

⊖ Lancaster Gate
or High Street Kensington

W8. Open daily 7 a.m.–dusk.
Another welcome oasis of greenery and tree-lined walks in central London is Kensington Gardens, divided by road from the western border of Hyde Park. From the Italian Gardens in the north, the Serpentine curves down towards Hyde Park. Sir George Frampton's well-known Peter Pan statue is still a favourite of small children. A converted tea house, the Serpentine Gallery (see p. 59) is reputed for innovative art shows. Close by, proudly stands the elaborately pinnacled Albert Memorial (with Prince Albert perusing the catalogue of the 1851 Great Exhibition), erected in 1872 in honour of Queen Victoria's consort.

185

LONDON'S CANALS

The coming of the railways in the early 19th century marked the decline of London's canal network, which formed the major link in the chain between the industrial Midlands and the port of London. In recent years, the canals have undergone something of a revival, and there are several companies operating boat trips. British Waterways, Greycaine Road, Watford, Hertfordshire, tel. (0923) 226 422, can provide a map and other information on request.

London's man-made waterways extend from the Willesden area to Limehouse, going round Regent's Park and through Camden Town. The best-known and most popular stretch is Regent's Canal, from Little Venice through Regent's Park to London Zoo and Camden Lock. For details of the narrowboats (barges) that ply the water regularly, contact:

Jason's Trip, 60 Blomfield Road, W9; tel. (071) 286 3428
Jenny Wren, 250 Camden High Street, NW1; tel. (071) 485 4433

But you don't have to be waterborne to enjoy the peace and quiet the canals have to offer. Their 55 miles (nearly 90 km.) of tow paths (open roughly from 9 a.m. to dusk) provide pleasant walks away from the noise and fumes of London traffic. You can also cycle on the tow paths, but only with a permit from British Waterways (see above).

ST. JAMES'S PARK AND GREEN PARK   22/3   ⊖ Green Park
or St. James's Park

The Mall, SW1. Open daily dawn to dusk.
Only a stone's throw from Buckingham Palace, these two adjacent small parks are absolute gems. Stretching between the Mall and Birdcage Walk is St. James's Park with its picturesque lake, towering trees and friendly flocks of birds, while Green Park, lying to the north of the Queen's London residence, takes in Constitution Hill on its way west to meet up with Hyde Park.

REGENT'S PARK   4/5   ⊖ Regent's Park or Baker Street
NW1. Open daily 5 a.m.–dusk.
Laid out in the early years of the 19th century as part of the extravagant plans of the then Prince Regent, the park was to be the apex of a grand thoroughfare leading to Buckingham Palace. Fellow-conspirator and architect John Nash was responsible for the elegant, white terraces that form a theatrical backdrop to the southern and eastern boundaries. Besides Queen Mary's Rose Garden, amenities include tennis courts, a large boating lake, an open-air theatre and, last but not least, London Zoo. Regent's Canal, with its narrow boats and tow path, provides a pleasant way to reach the park from Little Venice.

BUS TOURS

Here's a list, in alphabetical order, of some of the reputable companies that run tours inside and outside the capital. Except for the regular, half-hourly services, it's wise to reserve in advance. Taped multi-lingual commentaries are common, but some of the more popular tours have live explanations in various languages.

CAN-BE-DONE

7-11 Kensington High Street, W8; tel. (081) 907 2400.
This company can tailor a tour to suit your needs. Outings for the disabled are a speciality.

CITYRAMA

Silverthorne Road, Battersea, SW8; tel. enquiries (071) 720 6663 (24 hours a day); reservations (071) 627 8512.
A very basic trip, with recorded commentaries in several languages. Buses leave every half hour in the season from various points.

ENSIGN BUS COMPANY

Arterial Road, Purfleet, Essex; tel. (0708) 865 656.
One of the least expensive in London. Departures from the Strand and Charing Cross Station, every 30 minutes in summer and every hour in winter. Taped commentaries, in 12 languages.

EVAN EVANS

26 Cockspur Street (Trafalgar Square), SW1; tel. (071) 930 2377.
Offers a wide selection of half- or full-day trips in addition to the usual short tour. Destinations include the Tower, the Royal Albert Hall and a combined river/road excursion to Greenwich. Air-conditioned coaches and live commentaries by qualified guides; over 30 pick-up points.

FRAMES RICKARDS

11 Herbrand Street, WC1; tel. (071) 837 3111 and (071) 936 9344 (night service).
Half- and full-day excursions accompanied by recognized guides and a short panoramic tour with taped multi-lingual commentaries. Six pick-up points and hotel courtesy service. Booking is essential.

LONDON COACHES

187

Jews Row, Wandsworth, SW18; tel. (071) 227 3456.
Every 30 minutes, red double-decker buses leave Victoria Street, the Haymarket and Marble Arch for an inexpensive tour to an informative live commentary. Other buses from Baker Street have taped commentaries in eight different languages. Other excursions around and outside the city.

GUIDED WALKS

CITY WALKS
9/11 Kensington High Street, W8; tel. (071) 937 4281.
An unbelievable choice of walks, just about every day of the year, public holidays excepted, covering virtually every aspect of London you could wish for.

LONDON WALKS
P.O. Box 1708, NW6; tel. (071) 435 6413.
Ghosts, the plague, the Great Fire, the Blitz and historic pubs are some of the themes of London Walks, scheduled two or three times a day.

LONDONER PUB WALKS
3 Springfield Avenue, N10; tel. (081) 883 2656.
Meet outside the Temple Underground station at 7.30 p.m. on any Friday to explore some of the best London pubs. Peter Westbrook tailors each outing to suit the participants. Parties should ring first; individuals just turn up—with a thirst.

BOAT TOURS
The river Thames, a historically vital waterway, is relatively little-used these days. Once an important thoroughfare until modern roads and railways eclipsed river traffic, it has seen something of a revival in recent years. Today, the accent is on the pleasure of the voyage as much as the destination: round trips, supper or disco cruises or simply a pleasant alternative to bus or tube.

From central London (Westminster Pier or Charing Cross Pier), you can go upstream to Richmond, Hampton Court or Kew, or downriver past the Docklands to Greenwich and the Thames Flood Barrier. From Westminster Pier, the trip upstream to Hampton Court takes 3–4 hours; to Richmond 2 hours; and to Kew 90 minutes. Seawards, the journey to Tower Pier takes 20 minutes; to Greenwich Pier 45 minutes; and to Barrier Pier 75 minutes. Services downriver are in the region of every half hour in summer; upriver several times a day.

The Riverboat Information Service of the London Tourist Board, tel. (071) 730 4812, can supply up-to-date information on all day and evening trips, and the Westminster Passenger Services Association, (071) 930 2062/4721, will give details of all upriver sailings.

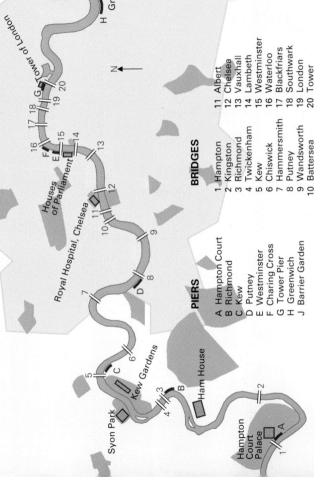

THE THAMES

BRIDGES

1 Hampton	11 Albert
2 Kingston	12 Chelsea
3 Richmond	13 Vauxhall
4 Twickenham	14 Lambeth
5 Kew	15 Westminster
6 Chiswick	16 Waterloo
7 Hammersmith	17 Blackfriars
8 Putney	18 Southwark
9 Wandsworth	19 London
10 Battersea	20 Tower

PIERS

A Hampton Court
B Richmond
C Kew
D Putney
E Westminster
F Charing Cross
G Tower Pier
H Greenwich
J Barrier Garden

Thames Barrier

Greenwich

Tower of London

Houses of Parliament

Royal Hospital, Chelsea

Kew Gardens

Ham House

Syon Park

Hampton Court Palace

N

The lion's share of England's sights may seem to be concentrated in the centre of London, but a whopping bonus of equally worthy attractions awaits you beyond the city walls. Day trips—even half-day excursions—take you to stately homes, university cities, ancient monuments and bracing seaside towns. These outings, a welcome break from tramping around the capital, also provide added insight into Britain's heritage.

Here we've divided the destinations into two categories: first, the ones on the outskirts of London, followed by those further afield. Some of the sights are included in tours run by the coach companies (listed on p. 187 under WALKS AND TOURS). Otherwise you can get there under your own steam, by car, bus, train or even Underground.

For details of railway timetables and fares, call in at one of British Rail's information offices, or ring their recorded message services:

Euston (071) 387 7070, for the West Midlands, North Wales, North-West England and Scotland.

Paddington (071) 262 6767, for South Wales, the West Country, Avon and South Midlands.

Liverpool Street (071) 928 5100, for East Anglia and Essex.

King's Cross (071) 278 2477, for Yorkshire, North-East England and Scotland.

St. Pancras (071) 387 7070, for East Midlands and South Yorkshire.

If you have a yearning to break away from London completely and explore to the far corners of the British Isles, you can get all the information you require from the British Travel Centre, 4–12 Lower Regent Street, SW1, tel. (071) 730 3400.

191

Hampton Court Palace: Henry VIII honeymooned here—repeatedly.

THE OUTSKIRTS

EPPING FOREST

⊖ Loughton or Epping
⇌ or Chingford

Epping Forest, Essex.
Deer still roam parts of Epping Forest, on the north-eastern edge of London, as they did when it was a royal hunting ground. In response to public outcry, an Act of Parliament back in 1878 saved these 6,000 acres (more than 2,400 ha.) of common land from enclosure. With woodland, heath, marsh and ponds stretching from Chingford to Epping, the forest is home to 144 species of birds and 300 kinds of flowering plants—not to mention more than a thousand different kinds of beetle!

Londoners, with or without binoculars to aim at birds or beetles, come here for walks and picnics. Adventurous explorers may stumble on two ancient Briton camps (Loughton and Ambersbury), or even meet Dick Turpin's ghost on a dark, moonless night.

HAM HOUSE

⊖ Richmond
then 71 bus to Fox and Duck

Ham Street, Ham, Richmond, Surrey; tel. (081) 940 1950. Open Tuesday to Sunday 11 a.m.–5 p.m.
This superb 17th-century house near the Thames has been carefully renovated to exploit the lavish Restoration interior, sumptuously furnished—down to the cavernous kitchens. Among the paintings hanging in the Great Hall are a Reynolds portrait of Horace Walpole's niece (once the mistress of the house) and a rare Hilliard of the mighty Elizabeth I. The gardens, laid out in the style of the period, are open every day.
Admission: small charge.

HAMPTON COURT

⇌ Hampton Court

Hampton Court, Surrey; tel. (081) 977 8441. Open: palace April to October, daily 9.30 a.m.–6 p.m.; October to March, Monday to Saturday 9.30 a.m.–4.30 p.m.; grounds daily dawn to dusk.
The most romantic way to approach Hampton Court is as Henry VIII used to do, by river (see p. 188). Built in 1515 for the upwardly mobile Cardinal Wolsey, this very desirable residence was appropriated by an envious Henry 15 years later, after Wolsey's fall from favour (they didn't see eye to eye over Henry's proposed divorce of Catherine of Aragon). Characteristically, the king enlarged and embellished the already large and magnificent red-brick Tudor house which he had so high-handedly

192

acquired. He added courtyards, the great hall, towers, gardens, summerhouses and a "real" (royal) tennis court, still in use. One and a. half centuries later, on the orders of William III and Mary, Sir Christopher Wren designed extensive additions and restored much of the original Tudor building.

Beyond the extravagant architecture, the furnishings and paintings, Hampton Court is worth visiting for the grounds, too. With the Elizabethan knot garden to explore, the 17th-century maze to get lost in and many formal and informal gardens for stretching your legs or simply admiring the scenery, there's plenty outdoors to enjoy. Admission: gardens free of charge; palace & maze or maze only: small charge.

KEW GARDENS ⊖ Kew Gardens or ⇌ Kew Bridge

Kew Green, Surrey; tel. (081) 940 1171. Open Monday to Saturday 9.30 a.m.–dusk/8 p.m. Sunday 9.30 a.m.–8 p.m. in summer.

Officially called the "Royal Botanic Gardens", Kew was founded in the 18th century as a centre for scientific research. Although it's a top tourist attraction today, research remains its major function. The buildings and grounds, originally laid out by Sir William Chambers in the second half of the 18th century, cover nearly 300 acres (about 120 ha.).

The landmark glass-and-iron Palm House, designed by Decimus Burton in 1844, has recently re-opened after restoration; its warmth shelters every known species of palm in the world. The Orangery now houses a restaurant rather than citrus specimens, and in the Marianne North Gallery there are over 800 botanical paintings by this prolific Victorian amateur artist.

Outdoor highlights include the bohemian bluebell wood, aquatic garden, 17th-century herb plot and lakes—all conducive to enjoyable, fragrant strolls for the whole family. Admission: small charge.

OSTERLEY PARK HOUSE ⊖ Osterley

Osterley, Isleworth, Middlesex; tel. (081) 560 3918. Open Tuesday to Sunday 11 a.m.–5 p.m.

Originally an Elizabethan mansion, Osterley Park was remodelled by Robert Adam in the 1760s; Horace Walpole described it as a palace that must cause its rich and powerful neighbours many pangs of jealousy. Restored to its full 18th-century glory, it's now an outpost of the Victoria & Albert Museum. Don't miss the Etruscan Room and the tapestry room with its excellent display of Gobelins. Admission: charge.

193

RICHMOND PARK

⊖ Richmond

Richmond, Surrey ; tel. (081) 948 3209. Open March to September 7 a.m. daily; October to February 7.30 a.m. Closes half an hour before dusk.

Richmond Park meanders along the banks of the Thames, skirting the pretty, sleepy town of Richmond, which has become virtually a London suburb. An idyllic place for long rambling walks through woods of beech and sweet chestnut trees, the park has been colonized by red and fallow deer. There are great patches of rhododendrons, magnolias, azaleas and camellias, which make glorious splashes of colour when in bloom. The park can be reached by river to Richmond Pier or by Underground.

SYON HOUSE

⊖ Gunnersbury or ⇶ Syon Lane

Syon Park, Brentford, Middlesex; tel. (081) 560 0881. Open March to September: house Thursday to Sunday noon to 5 p.m.; gardens daily 10 a.m.–dusk.

This fine house dates from the 15th century, but the interior is a masterpiece of 1760s restoration by Robert Adam. The rooms, strongly coloured, feature the ornamental plasterwork characteristic of the architect. Most notable are the Great Hall, the dining room, the red drawing room and the long gallery. Lancelot "Capability" Brown landscaped the grounds, where two other attractions have been built: the London Butterfly House (see p. 176) and the Heritage Motor Museum.

FURTHER AFIELD

BATH

⇶ from Paddington

Tourist Information Centre, The Colonnades (ground floor), Bath Street, Bath, Avon; tel. (0225) 462831 (Monday to Saturday during normal office hours and Sunday in summer).

The name couldn't be more blunt: Bath is a spa. In the time of the Roman empire, it was a steaming rest-and-recreation centre for tired governors and soldiers. In the 18th century the English, rediscovering the hot springs, engineered a miracle of urban planning and turned the city into a honey-coloured dream in stone.

194   Immortalized by Jane Austen in *Northanger Abbey*, Bath is situated on the edge of the Cotswolds, a little over a hundred miles west of London (a journey of about an hour and a quarter by train). The key to the elegance of the city is a medley of crescents, the best being Royal Crescent, where a townhouse at No. 1 has been turned into a museum.

The Georgians gave Bath its social cachet: the Pump Room (Stall Street), ostensibly the therapy centre for those taking the waters, was in fact the fashionable meeting place; more "society" marriages were contracted there than anywhere else outside London. The Pump Room is now open as a genteel restaurant also offering afternoon tea. Opposite is Bath Abbey, built in the 15th century on the site of the Saxon abbey where Edgar, the first king of all England, was crowned in 973.

The Bath Museum of Costume, in the Assembly Rooms, Bennett Street, has an interesting display of historical dress. The Holburne of Menstrie Museum, Great Pulteney Street, includes silver, porcelain and a good collection of 18th- and 19th-century British paintings. About three miles (5 km.) south-east of Bath, the American Museum in Britain at Claverton Manor, has one of the most comprehensive collections of Americana outside the United States.

BEAULIEU   ⇌ from Waterloo to Brockenhurst, then taxi (7 miles) or Southampton, then bus

Lyndhurst, Hampshire; tel. (0590) 612345. Open daily Easter to September 10 a.m.–6 p.m ; October to Easter 10 a.m.–5 p.m.

The family of Lord Montagu has been collecting cars for decades, and the resulting National Motor Museum contains one of the most impressive arrays of vintage cars anywhere. The great house itself is full of history, with medieval components and Victorian additions. In the grounds, too, are the ruins of a Cistercian abbey founded by King John of *Magna Carta* fame. Incidentally, the English pronounce Beaulieu "Bewlee"—seriously.

Admission: charge, with family ticket available.

BLENHEIM PALACE   ⇌ Oxford, then 20 bus or by bus from Victoria

Woodstock, Oxfordshire; tel. (0993) 811325. Open daily (mid-March to end October) 10.30 a.m.–4.45 p.m.

The name comes from a small Danube village that was the scene of the first Duke of Marlborough's famous victory over the French and Bavarians, in 1704. Queen Anne built Blenheim Palace out of gratitude to her successful general. It was an extravagant gift, a house taking up a large chunk of a 2,500-acre (over 1,000 ha.) park. The palace was designed by Sir John Vanbrugh, the English master of Baroque architecture who also led a double life as a playwright. Its solidity is relieved by courtyards and arcades and a roofline bristling with trophies of war and chimneys. The magnificent gardens were laid out by Lancelot "Capability" Brown, the 18th-century's poet of landscaping. Winston Churchill was born in the palace (more than 60 miles—

195

nearly 100 km.—north-west of London), and some of the rooms contain mementoes of the wartime prime minister plus a rich collection of paintings, furniture and furnishings.
Admission: charge.

BRIGHTON
⇌ from Paddington

Tourist Information Centre, Marlborough House, 54 Old Steine, Brighton, East Sussex; tel. (0273) 23755 or 29801. Open Monday to Saturday during normal office hours, with a reduced service on Sunday.

The fantastic centrepiece of Brighton, some 50 miles (80 km.) south of London, is a 19th-century, brilliantly white oriental folly, complete with turrets and domes and interiors of lime-green, rich golds and reds. The Royal Pavilion, completed in 1820, was the very eccentric idea of the Prince Regent, aided and abetted by John Nash, an architect better known for sober Palladian designs.

Thanks to the Prince Regent (the future King George IV), the town turned into a fashionable playground for the rich during the Regency period. This was followed by almost a century of prominence as Britain's favourite seaside resort. In spite of a wave of gentle decay, Brighton retains a sort of antiquated charm. The long, straight shoreline is still occupied by hotels and the once sparkling Brighton Pier now offers a standard funfair diet of one-arm bandits, souvenir shops and hot-dog stands.

More popular is The Lanes, an enclave of narrow streets lined with antique shops, clothing stores, tea shops, restaurants, pubs and wine bars. The Brighton Art Gallery and Museum, Church Street, is notable for its collection of paintings and decorative art.

CAMBRIDGE
⇌ from Liverpool Street or King's Cross

Tourist Information Centre, Wheeler Street, Cambridge; tel. (0223) 322640 (open during normal office hours Monday to Saturday noon, plus weekends in summer).

Tradition, erudition and charm reign in Cambridge, the university city 55 miles (about 90 km.) north of London. Originally settled by the Romans, the town developed its educational bent in medieval times, when the monasteries influenced both teaching and architecture. The first college, **Peterhouse**, was founded in 1284 by the Bishop of Ely. The 25th college, **Robinson**, dates from 1979. In between, hallowed buildings represent most of Britain's characteristic architectural styles.

196 Much of the character of Cambridge comes from the river Cam, which meanders silently behind the medieval colleges, between green lawns overhung with willows. You can take a punt or a leisurely stroll along "The Backs" that pass the peaceful college gardens, away from the traffic.

Close to the great university colleges, the **Fitzwilliam Museum**, Trumpington Street, has a notable Egyptian collection and important paintings by the likes of Breughel, Canaletto, Turner and Constable. The **Cambridge and County Folk Museum**, Castle Street, displays everyday artefacts from the Middle Ages. The **Kettle's Yard Art Gallery**, Castle Street, deals in paintings and sculpture from the 20th century.

Your view of the colleges may be limited to the grounds unless you are lucky with your timing. The Cambridge Information Centre (see above), which runs guided tours, can give you information on days and times when the main college buildings are open to visitors.

DOVER CASTLE
Dover Priory or bus from Victoria
Dover, Kent; tel. (0304) 201628. Open (Easter to end September) daily 10 a.m.–6 p.m.); (October to Easter) daily 10 a.m.–4 p.m.

This was a site just waiting for a lookout post, and there's been one here atop the white cliffs of Dover since prehistoric times. The oldest one still around is a Roman lighthouse, adjacent to the Saxon church of St. Mary. Some 70 miles (115 km.) south-east of London, Dover Castle first saw the light of day as a 12th-century Norman keep, added to and improved over the centuries, including Georgian and Victorian earthworks and underground passages. It still keeps an eye on the comings and going in the English Channel; on a clear day the coast of France is visible, just 22 miles (35 km.) away.

The old buildings bear many memories, if not scars, of battles glorious, and will share them with you: a guided tour through cliff tunnels reveals the secret command headquarters from World War II; special effects enhance a re-creation of the history of the Queen's Regiment; and thousands of lead soldiers are deployed in a 19th-century model of the Battle of Waterloo.
Admission: charge.

FISHBOURNE ROMAN PALACE
from Victoria (via Chichester)
Salthill Road, Fishbourne, Chichester, West Sussex; tel. (0243) 785859. Open daily 10 a.m.–6 p.m. (May to September); 10 a.m.–5 p.m. (March, April, October); 10 a.m.–4 p.m. (November); Sunday 10 a.m.–4 p.m. (December to February).

The most extensive Roman residence ever uncovered in England, Fishbourne was probably the home of Cogidubnus, a Celtic prince governing the region on behalf of the Roman empire, and clearly sharing his superiors' grandiose ideas about property. The palace was **197** burned down in the 2nd century A.D.; the ruins lay undisturbed until the 1960s. The four wings of the palace surround a formal garden, now reconstructed. The restored north wing houses a museum of Roman

Britain, its showpiece a superb mosaic floor depicting a winged figure on a dolphin. The palace is about 60 miles (close to 100 km.) south of London.

Admission: small charge.

HATFIELD HOUSE ⇥ Hatfield

Hatfield, Hertfordshire; tel. (0707) 262823. Open (25 March to mid-October) house Tuesday to Saturday noon–4.15 p.m.; Sunday 1.30–5 p.m. Park daily 10.30 a.m.–8 p.m.

The empire-building queen Elizabeth I provides more than a footnote to this historic corner of England. She spent her childhood in the Old Palace, only a section of which survives. Today it's exploited for mock medieval banquets: ring (0707) 262 055 for information. The present Hatfield, 21 miles (33 km.) north of London, is a Jacobean house begun in 1607 by Robert Cecil, 1st Earl of Salisbury and prime minister to James I. It's still the home of the Cecil family, but they'll let you in to admire the wood-panelled Great Hall, grand Renaissance staircase and separate state apartments for any visiting king and queen. Mementoes of Elizabeth I range from two famous portraits to her gardening hat and silk stockings.

Admission: charge.

LEEDS CASTLE ⇥ from Victoria to Bearstead or coach

Maidstone, Kent ; tel. (0622) 765400. Open daily 11 a.m.–5 p.m. (April to October); Saturday and Sunday 11 a.m.–4 p.m. (November to March).

Straddling two islands in the middle of a mirror-like lake, Leeds Castle—some 35 miles (56 km.) south-east of London—is everyone's idea of a Norman castle. Dating back to the 9th century, it was home to many a king and queen from Edward I onwards. Henry VIII transformed it from a spartan fortress into a comfortable and spacious royal palace. The lavishly landscaped park contains an aviary, maze and grotto, woodland walks and a fragrant flower garden. Inside you can admire 14th- and 15th-century tapestries, medieval furnishings, paintings of the Impressionist school and, even more unexpectedly, a museum of dog collars. Sorry, no dogs allowed.

Admission: charge.

OXFORD ⇥ from Paddington, or by bus from Victoria

Tourist Information Centre, St. Aldgates, Oxford; tel. (0865) 726871. Open Monday to Saturday during normal office hours and Sunday afternoon in summer.

The "dreaming spires" of Oxford, some 60 miles (95 km.) north-west of London, go back a long way in time. The world's oldest English-speaking university was launched here in 1167, the year English students were forbidden to study at the University of Paris. Nowadays Oxford has 35 colleges and more than 12,000 students and the surrounding town is big enough to have factories and traffic jams.

Since college life was originally religious, the hallowed Oxford atmosphere reflects monastic style: a campus of chapels, refectories, cloisters and "quads" or quadrangles. The list of architectural masterpieces starts with what may be the oldest college, Merton, dating from 1264. Gardened Magdalen (pronounced maudlin) College, founded in 1458, is considered the most beautiful, with a serene Gothic cloister and Perpendicular style bell tower. Most colleges are open to visitors, if only for a limited period; check with the tourist information office (see above). For an overview of the city, get your bearings by climbing the Carfax Tower, the only surviving part of St. Martin's Church, sited at the very hub of the city.

A great centre of learning needs a great library, and the Bodleian, in the centre of Oxford, fits the bill with a superb collection of rare books and manuscripts. Additional literary treasures can be seen in the adjoining Perpendicular Gothic building known as the Divinity School. Serving as an offshoot reading room, the Radcliffe Camera (Chamber) is a handsome Baroque design. Finally, Oxford offers several world-class museums, the finest being the 300-year-old Ashmolean Museum, Beaumont Street, which almost bulges with a magnificent display of Renaissance art, Egyptian artefacts, European silverware, musical instruments and important archaeological finds.

SALISBURY & STONEHENGE
✈ from Waterloo or by coach
Tourist Information Centre, Fish Row, Salisbury, Wiltshire; tel. (0722) 334956.
The quaint old market town of Salisbury, some 90 miles (nearly 150 km.) west of London, is dominated by its great Gothic cathedral. Built in the 13th century, it's considered the purest and most harmonious example of the Early English style of architecture. The landmark spire, immortalized in the paintings of John Constable, was added later, in 1334. A drastic restoration programme late in the 18th century fortunately spared some wonderful medieval stained glass and choir-roof painting.

An essential side trip from Salisbury takes in the massive and mysterious stone circle of Stonehenge. Britain's moodiest monument evolved in three distinct phases over a period of more than a thousand years. In 2800 B.C., it's reckoned, a Neolithic people laid claim to the site. Seven hundred years later the Beaker people put up concentric rings of bluestones. The more or less final version came a century later,

199

the work of Bronze Age folk. The Druids, with whom the site is so closely associated, came much later, in the 3rd century B.C.

One way or another, Stonehenge is a source of wonder: how 6-ton pillars got there from more than 135 miles (215 km.) away, how they were erected and, of course, what the point of it all was. One thing is clear; the Stone Age planners knew enough astronomy to align the axis of the stones with the sunrise on the first day of summer, June 21st. Today, modern "Druids" attempt to reclaim the site at solstice time, bringing great disruption to this peaceful part of the world and causing the monument to be closed to the public.

Opening hours are from 9.30 a.m. to 6 p.m. in summer and 4 p.m. in winter, every day. If you go by train, take the no. 3 bus from the Endless Street bus station.

STRATFORD-UPON-AVON

⇌ from Paddington, or Euston to Coventry, then bus, or bus from Victoria

Tourist Information Centre, Judith Shakespeare's House, 1 High Street; tel. (0789) 293127. Open Monday to Saturday during normal office hours, and Sunday afternoons in summer.

The spirit of Shakespeare pervades Stratford, an appealing town on the banks of the River Avon, less than 100 miles (160 km.) north-west of London. Even the tourist office is housed in a venerable building with Shakespearean connections. From the Henley Street house in which he was born (in 1564) to his tomb (1616) at Holy Trinity Church, this typical English town is awash with memories of England's greatest playwright. For instance, Hall's Croft, in the street named Old Town, a pretty house where his daughter Susanna lived. And Nash House, on Chapel Street, which belonged to Shakespeare's granddaughter. It's a 15-minute stroll along the canal to Anne Hathaway's Cottage at Shottery, the country's most photographed thatched farmhouse.

As might be expected in the home of the Bard, Stratford maintains a serious theatrical reputation. Its three theatres, all run by the Royal Shakespeare Company, are usually heavily booked. For details of what's on at the Royal Shakespeare Theatre and the two smaller venues, the Swan and the Other Place, telephone the company's recording service on (0789) 69191 or (0789) 295623 for reservations by credit card.

WINDSOR

⇌ from Paddington, or by bus from Victoria

Tourist Information Centre, Windsor and Eton Central Station, Windsor, Berkshire; tel. (0753) 852010.

200

Sorry, but you can't tour the whole castle when the Queen's at home. Even so, Windsor's a thoroughly worthwhile outing, and it's only about 25 miles (40 km.) west of London.

The original castle, dating back to William the Conqueror, was a fortified lookout. Atop a bluff beside the Thames, it makes a wonderful viewpoint, although its original purpose was military rather than scenic—much less touristic. As additions were made piecemeal over the centuries, it grew into the world's largest occupied castle. Among the highlights: **St. George's Chapel** (1478–1511), a triumphant example of the Perpendicular style, and the luxurious **State Apartments**, begun by Charles II, featuring Gobelins tapestries and paintings by Rubens and van Dyck. Don't miss **Queen Mary's Doll's House**—anything but a plaything; a charming period piece, it was designed by the outstanding architect of the day, Sir Edwin Lutyens. (See p. 174 for full details of the castle opening times.)

The town at the castle's feet has succumbed to the tourist imperative; prices are generally steep. You can visit the local branch of **Madame Tussaud's**, in what used to be the Windsor and Eton Central Railway Station, as well as "**Royalty and Empire**", an exhibition commemorating Queen Victoria's Diamond Jubilee. The Guildhall, built by Sir Christopher Wren in the late seventeenth century, has a fine collection of paintings. A couple of miles north of Windsor is **Eton College**, the oldest of England's "public" schools. Its 15th-century buildings, still in use, are open to visitors in the afternoons. Some pre-Reformation wall paintings have been restored in the chapel. Out of the town, Windsor Safari Park is an effortless introduction to the world of free-ranging big game wildlife. (See p.176.)

WOBURN ABBEY   bus from Victoria

Woburn, Bedfordshire; tel. (0525) 290666. Open (Easter to October) Monday to Saturday 11 a.m.–5 p.m.; Sunday 11 a.m.–5.30 p.m; (January to Easter) Saturday and Sunday 11 a.m.–4 p.m.

Designed by Henry Holland, the 18th-century seat of the Duke of Bedford occupies the site of a Cistercian monastery. Three wings surround a central courtyard, echoing the layout of the old cloisters. A fourth wing of the building was lost to dry rot in 1950, an event which precipitated the Duke of Bedford's entry into the stately home business. The abbey's treasures include one of the world's finest private collections of paintings (van Dyck, Gainsborough and Reynolds), wonderful tapestries, porcelain, silverware and furniture. But for many, especially the young, the main attraction of Woburn Abbey, just over **201** 40 miles (65 km.) north of London, is its Wild Animal Kingdom and Leisure Park, laid out in the spacious gardens.

Admission: charge.

AIRPORTS

London is served by two major airports: Heathrow (principally for scheduled flights) and Gatwick (scheduled and charter). Two smaller and more distant airports, Stansted and Luton, specialize in charter traffic.

Heathrow is located 15 miles (24 km.) west of London and has four terminals. Terminal 1 serves mainly British and Irish airlines; Terminal 2, European airlines; Terminal 3, intercontinental flights and Terminal 4, mainly British intercontinental flights. Free buses run continuously between the terminals.

The "Airbus" A1 and A2 express service, operated by London Transport, connects the four terminals with the centre of London—A1 to Victoria, calling at Cromwell Road and Hyde Park Corner, A2 to Euston, calling at Holland Park Avenue, Notting Hill Gate, three points in the Bayswater Road, Marble Arch, Bloomsbury and Russell Square. The journey takes about an hour. Green Line "Flightline" 767 buses run direct from the airport to Victoria Coach Station in about 40 minutes.

The Piccadilly Underground line to Heathrow provides the fastest connection with all parts of London.

Gatwick is in West Sussex, 27 miles (35 km.) south of Central London. There are two terminals(linked by train), the North Terminal (for British Airways and many British Caledonian flights) and the South Terminal (for other companies).

Travel into London is fast and convenient. Air-conditioned, non-stop "Gatwick Express" trains leave the main terminal building for Victoria Station every 15 minutes during the day and take 30 minutes. There is also an hourly direct train service to London Bridge which takes about 35 minutes. In addition, "Flightline" 777 coaches run direct from Gatwick to Victoria in about 70 minutes.

CAMPING

It's "No Camping Allowed" in London's parks, which are locked every night after being checked by police. Unfortunately but understandably, legitimate campsites are a long way from the city centre. For full details, ask the London Tourist Board (see p. 208) for their leaflet *Camping Sites in and around London,* or contact the Camping and Caravanning Club Ltd, 11 Lower Grosvenor Place, SW1; tel. (071) 828 1012.

COMMUNICATIONS

Post office hours. Larger post offices are open from 9 a.m. to 5.30 or 6 p.m., Monday to Friday, and from 9 a.m. to 12.30 p.m. on Saturdays. Smaller district post offices have shorter hours. The post office near Trafalgar Square is open from 8 a.m. to 8 p.m. on weekdays and from 10 a.m. to 5 p.m. on Sundays. Address: 24/28 William IV Street, WC2; tel. (071) 930 9580.

Poste restante (general delivery). If you don't know where you'll be staying, you can have mail sent to you c/o poste restante. The most convenient way would be to specify the Trafalgar Square office (see above). Take your passport or identity card when picking up mail.

Stamps are sold at post office counters and from vending machines outside post offices. They are now also sold in a variety of other shops with a red sign "stamps".

Telegrams/telemessages/faxes. Telemessages have replaced inland (domestic) telegrams. Overseas telegrams and telemessages may be sent from any telephone. Dial 190 or 193. Telefaxes may be sent from most post offices.

Telephone

Directories. There are three telephone directories for London, two for residential numbers (A–K and L–Z), and one for business and services. There are also Yellow Pages, listing commercial companies under headings, and divided into geographical regions.

London dialling codes. London phone numbers are prefixed by either 071 or 081, the former being a central London number, the latter, Greater London. To call a central London number from outer London, the prefix should be added, and vice versa.

Charges. With the exception of some operator services, all telephone calls are charged at rates which vary according to the time of day, the cheapest time being between 6 p.m. and 8 a.m. and all day Saturday and Sunday. For international calls, it's cheaper to dial the number directly than to go through the operator. If possible, avoid making calls from hotels, where you may be charged much more than the basic cost. Or, if you are dialling home, reverse the charges.

Call boxes. Both long-distance and international calls can be made from call boxes. Those with the green Phonecard symbol take pre-paid cards (available at post offices and some newsagents), priced at 10p a unit and issued in blocks of between 10 and 200 units. Other call boxes accept coins—2p, 10p and 50p in some cases and 2p, 5p, 10p, 20p, 50p and £1 in others. Unfortunately, many do not have telephone directories; to obtain a number, dial 142 for London addresses, 192 for those outside the capital and 153 for international ones.

CONSULATES

Contact the embassy, consulate or high commission of your home country if things go seriously wrong—for example, if you lose your passport, get into trouble with the police or have an accident. Staff there can issue emergency passports, give advice on obtaining money from home and provide a list of lawyers, interpreters and doctors. They cannot pay your bills, lend you money or obtain a work permit for you. They are open during normal office hours, Monday to Friday.

Australia	Australia House, Strand, WC2; tel. (071) 379 4334
Canada	Canada House, Trafalgar Square, SW1; tel. (071) 629 9492
Eire	17 Grosvenor Place, SW1; tel. (071) 235 2171
New Zealand	New Zealand House, Haymarket, SW1; tel. (071) 930 8422
South Africa	South Africa House, Trafalgar Square, WC2; tel. (071) 930 4488
U.S.A.	24 Grosvenor Square, W1; tel. (071) 499 9000

EMERGENCIES

For police, fire brigade or ambulance, dial 999 from any telephone (no coin required), telling the operator which service you need. Otherwise contact Capital Help Line, tel. (071) 388 7575. If you need legal help, phone the nearest Citizens Advice Bureau (listed in telephone directory) or dial (071) 251 2000 for information; open Monday to Friday 9.30 a.m.–5 p.m.

For medical emergencies, go to one of the 24-hour hospital casualty departments:

Charing Cross Hospital	St. Dunstan's Road, W6; tel. (081) 846 1234
London Hospital	Whitechapel Road, E1; tel. (071) 377 7000
St. Mary's Hospital	Praed Street, W2; tel. (071) 725 6330
St. Thomas's Hospital	Lambeth Palace Road, SE1; tel. (071) 928 9292
University College Hospital	Gower Street, WC1; tel. (071) 387 9300
Westminster Hospital	Dean Ryle Street, Horseferry Road, SW1; tel. (081) 828 9811; adults only.

For dental emergencies, phone the Dental Emergency Care Service; tel. (081) 677 6363/8383.

Late-opening chemist: Bliss Chemist, 5 Marble Arch, W1; tel. (071) 723 6116; open daily 9 a.m.–midnight.

LOCAL TRANSPORT

The Underground system and buses come under the umbrella of London Regional Transport, which has **Travel Information Centres** located at the following Underground stations: Euston; Heathrow Airport (terminals 1, 2, 3 & 4); King's Cross; Oxford Circus; Piccadilly Circus; St. James's Park and Victoria (opposite Platform 8), as well as at West Croydon bus station. You can get free maps, night-bus timetables, etc. For London travel enquiries phone (071) 222 1234, or (071) 222 1200 (recorded information).

Fares. Bus and Underground fares are based on a zone system. The cheapest way to travel around London is with a daily, weekly or monthly *Travelcard*, which allows unlimited use on buses and the Underground (the daily card has some time restrictions). They are available from underground stations, some newsagents and some British Rail stations; you need a passport-sized photograph for the weekly and monthly cards.

Children refers to those under 16 years of age. Under-5s travel free. Under-16s pay a child's fare until 10 p.m., and 14- and 15-year-olds must carry a *Child Rate Photocard* and *Child Bus Pass* (free, available at Underground stations, Travel Information Centres and post offices).

Buses. Red double-decker buses with conductors are used on some central routes only. Elsewhere they have been replaced by driver-only buses. When there's a conductor, he or she will come round and collect fares or check your pass; otherwise, pay the driver as you enter. Keep your ticket until you get off.

Bus stops bear the LRT symbol of a red circle with a red horizontal line on a white background; signs where the colours are inverted indicate a request stop (where you must wave at the driver) and blue-and-yellow signs with route numbers are for the night buses which run from Central London via Trafalgar Square (about 11 p.m. to 6 a.m.).

Underground. Called the "Tube" by the locals, it is the fastest way of getting around the city. Trains run daily, except on Christmas Day, starting at around 5.30 a.m. Monday to Saturday, 7 a.m. on Sunday. Last train times vary according to routes and journeys but are usually between 11.30 p.m. and 1 a.m. on week nights, and 11.30 p.m. on Sundays. Details are given at stations and on timetables issued free at Travel Information Centres.

NO SMOKING

Smoking is illegal anywhere on the Underground, including ticket halls, stairs, escalators and platforms, as well as aboard the trains.

Docklands Light Railway (DLR). Part of the Underground system, the DLR runs from Tower Gateway, near the Tower of London, to the Isle of Dogs, with access to Greenwich via a pedestrian tunnel, Monday to Friday 5.40 a.m. to 9.30 p.m. The nearest Underground stations at each end of the line are Tower Hill and Stratford.

Green Line, single-decker buses run between Central London and the suburbs and towns within a 40-mile (64 km.) radius. The main departure point is Eccleston Bridge, SW1 (near Victoria Station). Information (081) 668 7261.

Taxis. Driven by knowledgeable drivers who have had to pass a stringent test, the traditional distinctive London cab should have a "For Hire" sign on the top and a white plate at the back. The Fare Table behind the driver's seat gives details of standard charges. Unless you are going out of the London Metropolitan Police area, you can only be charged the amount shown on the meter, set to start at £1, the minimum charge. For journeys outside this area—for example, to Heathrow Airport—negotiate the fare before you start. Tips are usually between 10 and 15%.

If the yellow sign on top of the cab is lit, the taxi is available for hire and the driver who stops is obliged to take you wherever you wish to go, provided it is a journey of no more than 6 miles (9.6 km.). Any complaints should be made to the Public Carriage Office, (071) 278 1744; quote cab number, date, time and journey.

You can order a black cab by phoning 24 hours a day on (071) 286 0286, (071) 272 0272, (071) 272 3030 or (071) 253 5000. If you leave anything in a black cab, contact the Metropolitan Police Lost Property Office, at 15 Penton Street, N1, open Monday to Friday 9 a.m.– 4 p.m.

Minicabs, normally lacking any distinguishing signs, may be ordered by phone. They are useful for late-night or exceptionally long trips.

Boats. A high-speed riverbus service went into operation in 1988. Passenger catamarans call at major piers up- and downriver. For full details, see p. 188.

LOST & FOUND PROPERTY

Finding a lost object depends on where you lost it. If it was in a bus or on the underground, go to the London Transport Lost Property Office at: 200 Baker Street, NW1 (no telephone enquiries).

For belongings left on a train, contact the railway terminal where you arrived in London; in a taxi, the Public Carriage Office (see above).

International Travellers' Aid helps foreign visitors who have lost their money, passport, luggage, etc., and will also try to settle other problems. The office (open every afternoon and evening except on Christmas Day) is located at:

Victoria Station, platform 10; tel. (071) 834 3925.

MONEY MATTERS

The British pound (£) is divided into 100 pence. Coins: 1p, 2p, 5p, 10p, 20p, 50p, £1, £2. Banknotes: £5, £10, £20, £50.

You can change foreign currency at virtually any bank, and branches are to be found in shopping streets throughout London and in the suburbs. Opening hours are Monday to Friday 9.30 a.m. to 3.30 p.m., with some doing business on Saturdays from 9.30 a.m.–noon as well. Currency exchange offices *(bureaux de change)* generally keep longer hours (some are open 24 hours a day), but you might get a less favourable rate as they often charge a hefty commission. If you're stuck, your hotel might come to the rescue, although you'll pay for the privilege. The same applies to foreign currency or traveller's cheques cashed in shops or restaurants. Always take your identity card or passport along when you change money or cash traveller's cheques.

Credit cards are accepted in most hotels, restaurants and department stores. Report lost or stolen credit cards immediately to the police, to your bank and to the following 24-hour services:

Access	(0702) 352 255
American Express	(0273) 696 933
Barclaycard/Visa	(0604) 230 230
Diners Club	(0252) 516 261; (0252) 513 500
Mastercard/Eurocard	(0702) 362 525.

Value added tax. With Britain a member of the Common Market, practically all merchandise and services are subject to a form of sales tax (VAT) which is currently 15%.

Tax refunds for tourists. Most large stores, quality and specialist shops participate in a scheme whereby visitors from countries outside the Common Market are refunded the VAT paid on merchandise, usually above a stipulated amount (£50 or £100) and less a small service charge. To qualify for a refund, you must leave the country within three months of purchase. Ask the shop to issue you with the appropriate form to be presented with the goods for validation to the customs officer on duty at the airport or other point of departure. The tax will be refunded by cheque, or the amount transferred to your credit card, according to your instructions.

Visitors from EEC countries will be refunded the difference between the VAT rate applicable in Great Britain and that in their own country on articles valued at £163 or more (less for residents of Greece and Ireland).

The tax is deducted immediately on purchases forwarded from a shop to a passenger ship. A customs form must accompany the goods.

For further information on VAT refunds contact the Shopping Advisory Service in the British Travel Centre, 12 Regent Street, tel. (071) 730 3400.

PUBLIC HOLIDAYS

British public holidays are known as "bank" holidays. Banks and many shops are closed, and public transport is run on Sunday timetables. There are eight public holidays throughout the year: New Year's Day, Good Friday, Easter Monday, May Day (first Monday in May), Spring Bank Holiday (last Monday in May), Summer Bank Holiday (last Monday in August), December 25 (Christmas Day) and December 26 (Boxing Day). (If one of these last two falls on a Saturday or Sunday, the usual practice is for the following Monday to be a public holiday.)

TOURIST INFORMATION OFFICES

The British Tourist Authority can provide you with information before you leave home:

Australia :
and New Zealand
171 Clarence St., Sydney NSW 200; tel. 29 8627

Canada:
Suite 600, 94 Cumberland St., Toronto, Ont. M5R 3N3; tel. (416) 925 6326

U.S.A.:
Suite 3320, John Hancock Center, 875 N. Michigan Ave., Chicago, IL 60611; tel. (312) 787 0490
Cedar Maple Plaza, 2305 Cedar Springs Road, Dallas, TX 75201; tel. (214) 720 4040
World Trade Center, Suite 450, 350 Figueroast, Los Angeles, CA 90017; tel. (213) 623 8196
40 West 57th St., Suite 320, New York, NY 10019; tel. (212) 581 4700.

The London Tourist Board and Convention Bureau is concerned with tourist activities in and around London. Write for information to: 26 Grosvenor Gardens, SW1W ODU.

 See p. 153 for other Tourist Information Centres around London.

MAP SECTION

Key

Scale 1 : 9 000

	English / French	German / Dutch
	Built-up area / Agglomération	Bebaute Fläche / Bebouwde Oppervlakte
	Park or Sports ground / Parc ou Terrain de sport	Park oder Sportplatz / Park of Sportveld
	Motorway / Autoroute	Autobahn / Autosnelweg
	Main Road / Route principale	Hauptstraße / Doorgangsroute
	Railway with Station / Chemin de Fer avec Gare	Eisenbahn mit Bahnhof / Spoorweg met Station
	Underground with Station / Métro avec station	U-Bahn mit Bahnhof / Metro met Station
SOHO	District / Arrondissement	Stadtteil / Stadsgedeelte
	Public Building / Bâtiment Public	Öffentliches Gebäude / Openbaar Gebouw
	Church / Eglise	Kirche / Kerk
	Theatre, Cinema etc. / Théâtre, Cinéma etc.	Theater, Kino usw. / Schouwburg, Bioscoop enz.
PARK HOTEL	Hotel / Hôtel	Hotel / Hotel
	One Way Street / Sens Unique	Einbahnstr. / Eénrichtingverkeer
	Post office / Bureau de Poste	Postamt / Postkantoor
	Police / Police	Polizei / Politiebureau

Overall map p. 2: numbers in blue refer to map pages

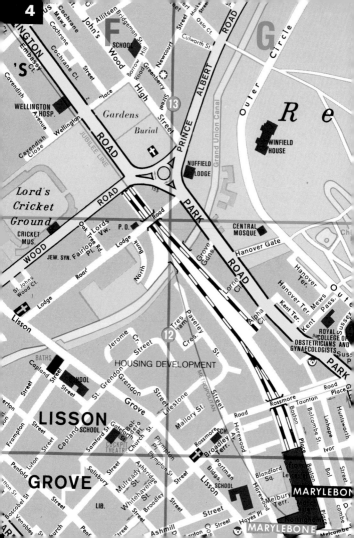

4

F
G

WELLINGTON
Embassy
Cochrane Mews
Cochrane
Cochrane
Allitsen
Bridgeman
John's
NGTON
Cavendish
'S
Cochrane
Court
St.
John's Wood
Newcourt
Oslo Ct.
Culworth St.
ROAD
G
SCHOOL
Borrow Hill
Wood
Greenberry
High
Place
Wellington
Street
Street
Street

WELLINGTON HOSP.
Avenue
Wellington
JUBILEE LINE
Cavendish
Close
ROAD
Gardens
Burial
PRINCE
13
ALBERT
ROAD
Grand Union Canal
Outer
Circle
R e
WINFIELD
HOUSE

Lord's
Cricket
Ground
ROAD
155
NUFFIELD
LODGE
CRICKET
MUS.
WOOD
Oak Tree
Lords
VW.
P.O.
Road
PARK
Grove
Gdns
CENTRAL
MOSQUE
Hanover Gate
Chi
JEW. SYN.
Fairlop
Lodge
Pl.
Bank
ROAD
Lorne
Ct.
Hanover
Ter.
Outer
St. Johns
Wood Ct.
Road
North
Paveley
Tresham
Hanover Ter. Mews
Kent Ter.
Hanover
Pass.
Sussex
Lisson
Lodge
Jerome
Cr.
Street
St.
Cres.
12
St.
Alpha
Ct.
Kent
Mews
ROYAL
COLLEGE OF
OBSTETRICIANS AND
GYNAECOLOGISTS
PARK
Sus
BATHS
Copland
St.
Street
HOUSING DEVELOPMENT
METROPOLITAN
Road
Place
St. Grendon
Grendon
SCHOOL
Lilestone
Street
LISSON
Grove
Street
Mallory
St.
Rossmore
Taunton
Boston
Balcombe St.
Linhope
Huntsworth
Ivor
Frampton
Luton
Salisbury
Capland
SCHOOL
Gateforth St.
Samford St.
Bolton
Plympton
Street
Pympton
Road
Harewood
ROSSMORE SCH.
BROADLEY
Terr.
Portman
Bldgs.
Blandford
Sq.
Place
Boston
Penfold
COCKPIT
THEATRE
St.
Ashbridge
Mulready
St.
Whitehaven
St.
Lisson
SCHOOL
Melbury
Terr.
Melcombe
LISSON
GROVE
Boscobel
St.
Venables
St.
Pent
Broadley
Street
Hayes Pl
Ashmill
Street
LIB.
MARYLEBONE
MARYLEBONE

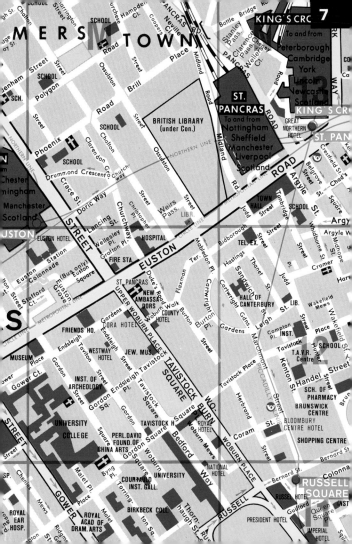

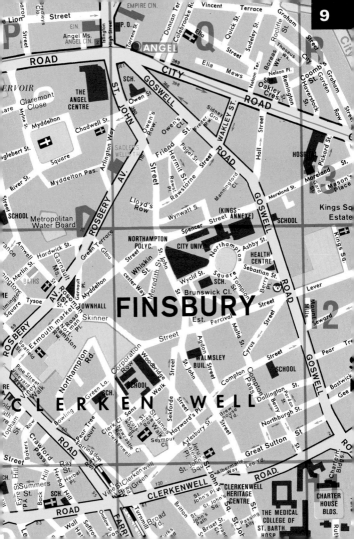

E

F

SCH.

Cromer

Hall

Boscobel Row

Street

Whitehaven St.

LIB.

Broadley

Ashmi

Ashland

Park Place
Villas

Park Place
Gardens

Cuthbert

Adpar St.

EDGWARE

Venables St.

Church

Carlisle
Mews

Penfold

Street

Howley

John Aird
Court

Place

St. Mary's
Mans.

Recreation

TECHN.
COLL.

Phillips Pl.

STREET

Place

Broadley

Miles Place

Penfold Place

SCHOOL

Porteus Road

Hogan
Mews

Fleming
Court

Paddington

Terrace

Church

St. Albans St.

Green

Corlett

Bell

BAKERLOO LINE

Grounds

St. Mary's
Sq.

TOWN
HALL

Newcastle Pl.

KENSINGTON

(Westway) Motorway

Flyover

EDGWARE Rd

CHAPE

28B

CLASSIC CIN

GOODS
DEPOT

BISHOPS BRIDGE ROAD

UNION CANAL

POL.
ST.

Dudley
St.

North

ELEC.STA.

SCHOOL

Hermitage
St.

Wharf

Road

Harbet

Road

ST.

Sale Place

Street

Street

2073

EASTBOURNE

WATERLOO LINE

METROPOLITAN LINE

Paddington

Basin

South

Wharf

Road

CLINIC

MEDICAL
SCH.

Praed

Junction

Michael's

Bouverie St.

Sale Place

Southwick

Rainsford St.

Junction Ms.

SCH.

PADDINGTON

To and from
Windsor Oxford
Birmingham
Bristol Devon
Cornwall
South Wales
etc.

ASHTONS
HOTEL

St.

London

Winsland

ST.MARY'S
HOSP.

St.

London

Praed

Norfolk Place

Southwick St.

GARDENS

Somers
Mews

Norfolk
Cres.

10

Eastbourne Ms.

TERRACE

Chilworth

GREAT
WESTERN HOTEL

Winsland M.

Street

St.

Talbot

PADDINGTON

NEW
NORFOLK
HOTEL

Conduit

Road

Norfolk
Square

London
Street

Norfolk
Sq. News

Norfolk

Square

PADDINGT

Mews

Radnor
Cres.

Somers
Cres.

Radnor Place

ST.
JOHN AND
ST. MICHAE

Hyde Park P.

Chilworth

Gloucester Ms.

brook

Mews

Craven

Terrace

Smallbrook
Ms.

SUSSEX

Conduit
Pass.

Spring

Conduit
Square

Street

Talbot

SUSSEX

Bathurst Mews

Sussex

Clifton Pl.

Place

Sussex
Ms.

Gloucester

Square

Radnor

Mews

Southwick St.

Hyde P.
Sq. Ms.

PADDINGT

Hyde Par

shire Ter.

Mews

Brook

Craven

Terrace

Westbourne
Cres.

West

Cres.

North

**SUSSEX
GDNS.**

Corney
Ms.

Bathurst St.

Sussex

Ms. West

Stanhope
Terrace

Clifton
Place

Hyde Park Gardens Mews

Strathearn Pl.

Square

Clarendon Ms.

Clarendon Cl.

SCH.

Brook Mews

Craven

Terrace

BARRIE
ESTATE

Elms Mews

Marlb

LANCASTER

**LANCASTER
GATE**

WESTBOURNE

Sussex

Ms. West

Stanhope
Gdns.

Hyde Park
Square

Hyde Park Gardens

Brook

CENTRAL LINE

Clarendon
Place

Hyde

Clarendon
Gate

11

ST. MARYLEBONE

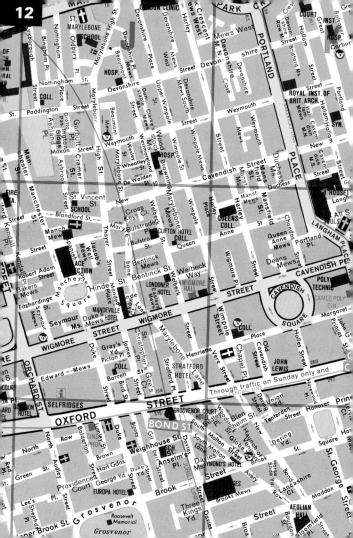

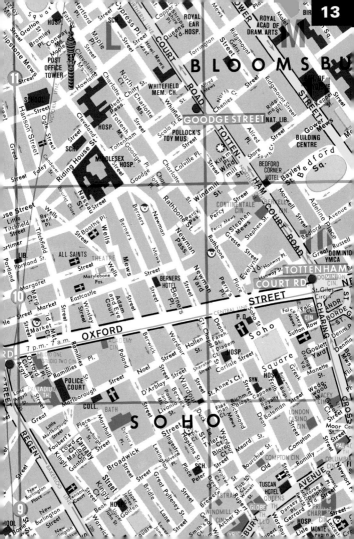

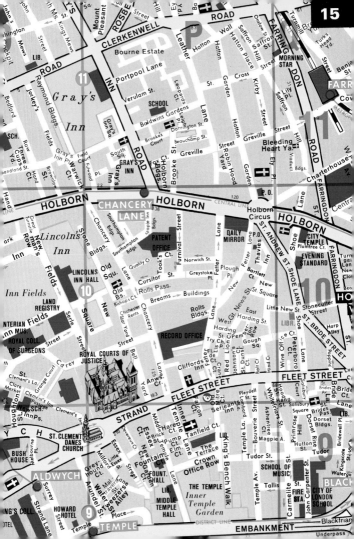

Mount Pleasant
Mount St.
LIB.
ROSBE
ROAD
CLERKENWELL
ington
Street
St.
Wall
Turnmill
Turks
Head
FARRINGDON
MORNING
STAR
FARR
Cou
METROPO
Mews
ton
Mrs.
King's
St.
St.
Bartt
Street
Eyre
Onslow St.
Saffron Hill
Ba
Saffron
Bedford
Row
Ray
Raymond Bldgs.
Jockey's
Ct.
Three
Cups
Yd.
SCH.
Fox
St.
Leather
Hatton
Place
Saffron
Cross
Street
Hatton
Lily
Benja
Bldgs.
ROAD
Bourne Estate
Portpool Lane
Verulam St.
SCHOOL
Baldwins Gardens
Dorrington St.
St.
Garden
Kirby
Hatton
Street
Greville
Greville
Bleeding
Heart Ya
Ely
Viaduct
Charterhouse
11
Gray's
Inn
11
Gray's
Inn
Fields
South
Court
Fox Ct.
Greville
Robin Hood
Yard
Garden
Ely
W.
FARRINGDON
P.O.
RD.
Central
11
Gray's Field
Bronn
St.
andland St.
Warwick
Ct.
Gray's Inn Pl.
St.
GRAY'S
INN
Brooke
St.
Brooke
St.
St.
120
CENTRAL
LINE
HOLBORN
HOLBORN
CHANCERY
LANE
Holborn
Circus
HOLBORN
Hand
LINE
Fulwood Pl.
INN
ROAD
Stone
Bldgs.
Southampton
Bldgs.
DAILY
MIRROR
ST. ANDREW ST.
CITY
TEMPLE
Plumtree Ct.
FARRINGDON
Lincolns Inn
New
Sq.
Row
Chancery
Lane
Southampton
Bldgs.
PATENT
OFFICE
Furnival
Street
Norwich St.
Ct.
Plough
Pl.
Fetter
Thavies
Bartlett
Lane
New
St. Square
EVENING
STANDARD
10
HO
ark
Greville
Street
LINCOLNS
INN HALL
Old
Sq.
Quality Ct.
Cursitor St.
Rolls Pass.
Greystoke
Pl.
New
Little New St.
Stonecutter
Street
10
Inn
10
Inn Fields
Old
Bs.
Bishop's Ct.
Chichester
Rents
Star Yard
Chancery
Breams
Bldgs.
Rolls
Bldgs.
East
Harding St.
West
St. Pet.
Harp
Alley
ST. BRIDE STREET
LIBR.
NTERIAN
nn MUS.
LAND
REGISTRY
Serle
Street
Street
RECORD OFFICE
Harding
Gt. New St.
St.
St. Dunstan's
Gough St.
St. Peter's
Red Lion
New St.
Peterboro
Ct.
Pemb
Fleet
Poppin
Ct.
ROYAL COLL.
OF SURGEONS
Carey
Bell
Yard
ROYAL COURTS OF
JUSTICE
Try Ch Ct.
Inn
Fetter
Cr.
St.
Ct.
Hood
Whitefriars
St.
FLEET STREET
Cliffords
Ct.
Court
Sea
FLEET STREET
St. Clement's La.
Clement's
Inn
125
193
Serjeants
Inn
Salisbury
Square
Bride
Lane
Bride
La.
LIB.
Clare
Market
Grange Court
Clement's
Inn
Pass.
New
Inn
Pass.
STRAND
Pleydell
Court
Hood
Bouverie
Salisbury
Ct.
Dorset
Bldgs.
NEW
SCH.
InnPs.
Ct.
Clement's
Inn
Middle
Temple
La.
Essex
Brick
Ct.
Harpe
Ct.
St.
Pump
Ct.
Tanfield Ct.
Magpie A.
The
Terrace
Ashentree
Ct.
Hutton St.
Bride
Court
Dorset Rise
Bridewell
Pl.
LIB.
Kincaste
BUSH
HOUSE
ST. CLEMENT
DANES
CHURCH
Grey
hound
Ct.
Milford
Little
Essex
St.
Fountain
Ct.
Elm Ct.
King's Bench Walk
Tudor St.
Tudor
Melbourne
Houghton
Essex
Street
Arundel
Street
Strand Lane
Surrey
St.
Maltravers
St.
Milford
Lane
Water
St.
FOUNT.
HALL
Crown
Office Row
SCHOOL OF
MUSIC
Carmelite
St.
John Carpenter St.
CITY OF
LONDON
SCHOOL
BLACK
ALDWYCH
Temple Av.
Tallis
Watergate
HOWARD
HOTEL
9
Inner
Temple
Garden
DISTRICT LINE
EMBANKMENT
Blackfriar
Underpass
ING'S COLL.
TEL
TEMPLE
Temple
Place
THE TEMPLE
MIDDLE
TEMPLE
HALL
FIRE
STA.
9

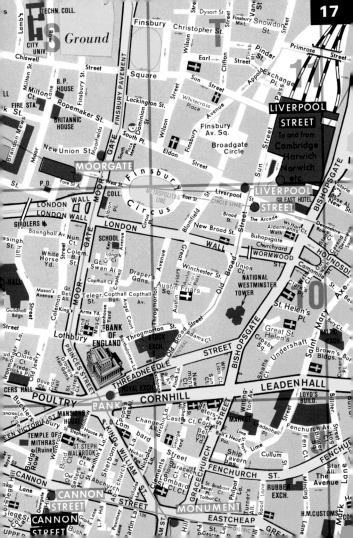

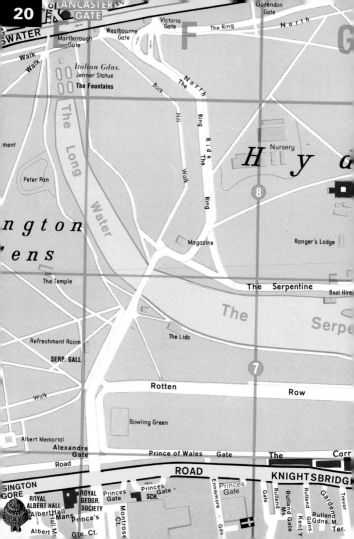

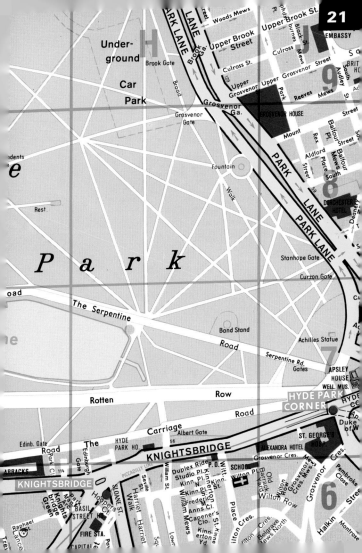

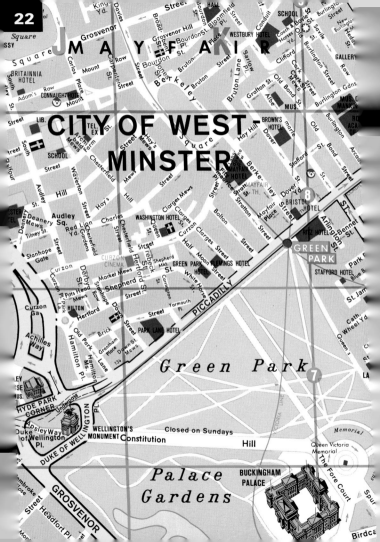

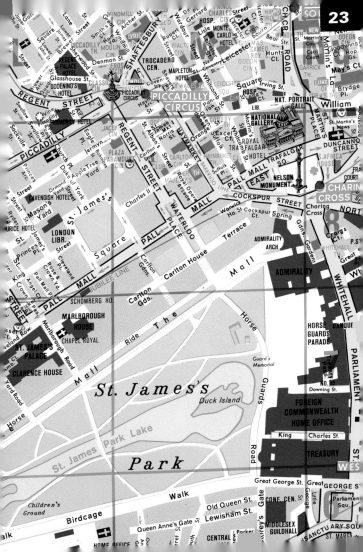

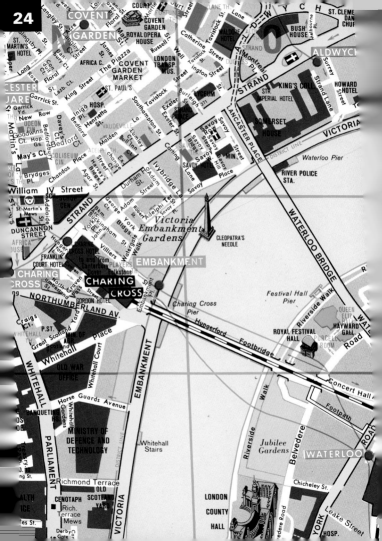

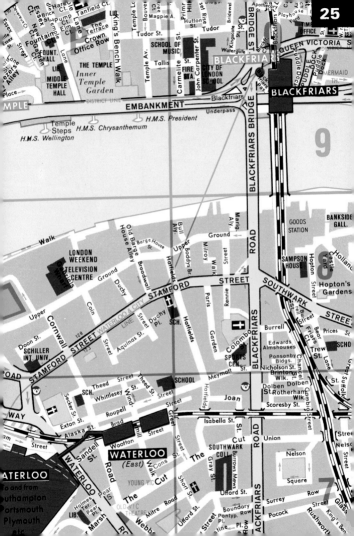

Essex St.
Essex Ct.
Pump Ct.
Tanfield Ct.
Temple La.
Bouverie St.
Primr. Hill
Magpie A.
Hutton St.
Bridewel
Apothcary
Playhouse
TIME OFFICE

The Terrace
Crown Office Row
Tudor St.
Tudor St.
Temple Av.
SCHOOL OF MUSIC
Tallis
Carmelite St.
FIRE BR'A. St.
John Carpenter St.
Watergate
BLACKFRIARS
QUEEN VICTORIA S

FOUNT. HALL
THE TEMPLE
MIDDLE TEMPLE HALL
King's Bench Walk
Inner Temple Garden
CITY OF LONDON SCHOOL
Puddle Dock
BLACKFRIARS
MERMAID TH.

MPLE
EMBANKMENT
Blackfriars Underpass
BLACKFRIARS BRIDGE

DISTRICT LINE

Temple Steps
H.M.S. President
H.M.S. Chrysanthemum
H.M.S. Wellington

9

Walk
Old Barge House Alley
Bull Aly.
Barge House St.
Upper Boddy's Br.
Ground
Ground
Maid
Road
GOODS STATION
BANKSIDE GALL.

LONDON WEEKEND TELEVISION CENTRE
Gardens
Ground
Duchy
Broadwall
Upper
Hatfields
Milroy Walk
Paris
Walk Street
Rennie
Street
SAMPSON HOUSE
SOUTHWARK
Hopton
Castle Yard
Holla
Hopton's Gardens

8

Upper
Cornwall
STAMFORD
Coin
STREET
Street
Duchy Pl.
STAMFORD
Street
Paris Garden
STREET
STREET
Bear La.
Pris. St.
SCHO

WATERLOO & CITY LINE
128
125
SCH.
SCHILLER INT. UNIV.
Doon St.
Street
Aquinas St.
Hatfields
Colombo SPORTS CEN.
Burrell
BLACKFRIARS
Zoar St.
Edwards Almshouses
Trew St.

ROAD
Secker St.
STAMFORD
Theed Street
SCHOOL
Whittlesey St.
Wind.
Theed St.
Meymott
Hatfields
Ponsonby Bldgs.
Nicholson St.
Brintons Wlk.
St.
SCHO

Street
Roupell
Street
Street
Joan
Dolben Dolben
St. Rotherham Wlk.
Scoresby St.
Street

WAY
Exton St.
Alaska St.
Brad
Street
Isabella St.
Union
Nelson
Street

ATERLOO
To and from
outhampton
Portsmouth
Plymouth
etc
Sandell St.
WATERLOO Road
WATERLOO (East)
Cons
Wootton St.
The Cut
Gray St.
SOUTHWARK COLL.
Burrow Mews
Nelson Square
Row
Nelso
Street

Holmes
Pear Pl.
LIB.
YOUNG VIC
Marsh
The
OLD VIC THEATRE
Webber
Short St.
Ufford St.
Ufford St.
Boundary Row
Pontyp. Row
Mitre Road
Pl.
Line
Surrey Row
Pocock
ACKFRIARS ROAD
Rushwort
King's Cha.
Glass
Street
Street

7

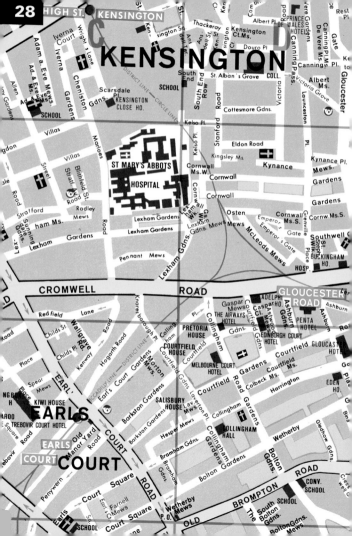

BEL-GRAVIA

Belgrave Square

Chester Place
Chester Close
Chester Mews

Wilton
Wilton Ter.
Halkin St.
Halkin Pl.
Chesham Mews

Belgrave Mews N.
Belgrave Square

Chapel Groom Pl.
Upper
Wilton Mews

Chester
Little Chester Ms.
Lower Chester Street
Dorset Ms.

PLACE

ROYAL MEWS

LOWER GROSVENOR PL.
GORING HOTEL
Goring Pl.
Beeston Pl.
Victoria
Square
Eaton Lane

BUCKINGHAM

ST. PETER'S

HOBART
GROSVENOR PLACE

GROSVENOR GARDENS

VICT

Belgrave
Belgrave
Belgrave
Place
Belgrave
Mews West
South

Chesham Cl.
Lyall Mews
East
Roberts
Lowndes
Close
Lowndes
Pl.
North

Eccleston Mews
Eaton Square
Eaton Row
Lower Belgrave
Grosvenor Gdns. Ms. N.
Gdns. Ms. S.

Grosvenor
Sta. Ms. E.
Gipsy Gdns.
Chester
Sta. Ms. W.
SCH. St.

VICTORIA
Term.

Chesham
INS
JTEL
EL. EX.

Lyall
St.
Place
King's
ROAD

Square

Eccleston

South
Square
Square

EBURY COURT
SCH.

VICTO
GROSVENOR
HOTEL
To and f

Lyall
Ms. W.
Lyall
Ms. E.

Eaton
Mews
North

King's
ROAD

Mews
South
Square

Chester Ms.
Ebury Ms.
East
Phipp's Pl.
COLL.

5
Chatham Car
Brighton New
Dover and the C

West
Eaton
Eaton Ms. W.

Eaton
Place
King's

Eaton
Square

Eaton
Boscobel
Pl.
Chester

Ebury
Eccleston

Eccleston
St.
BATHS
CIRCLE LINE
Eccleston
Street

Eccleston Br.

D'Oyley St.

Eaton
Terr. Ms.
Eaton
Place
KING'S

Elizabeth
Street
West

ST. MICHAEL'S

Chester
Mews

Ebury

ROAD

Bel
10
ECCLE
Hugh
Mews

Grosvenor
Cotts.
ROYAL
CT. HO.

Eaton
Gate
EATON
GATE
PL.

South
Eaton
Minera Ms.
Row
Eaton Ms. W.
Lwr Chester Row

Gerald Rd.
Gerald
Mews

Ebury
Street

DISTRICT LINE
PLACE

SCH.
LIB.

Eccleston

St. George's
ECCLE

ANE
UARE

Eaton
Close

Caroline Ter.
Eaton

Bourne St.
Chester
Terrace
Terrace

Burton
Place
Mews

Semley
Place

Elizabeth
Br.

Cambridge

ROYAL COURT TH.

Graham Ter.
Palace Ms.

VICT.
COACH STA.

Hugh

St. Alderney

Holbein Place

Whittaker
St.

SCHOOL

SCHOOL

Bourne St.
Graham Ter.
Orange
Square
Brandt

Avery
Mondesse
Bunhouse
PIMLICO

Cundy
St.

Cundy
St.

St. E.
SCHOOL

BUCKINGHAM

AIR
TERM.

Warwick
Manor
Estate

Cumberland
Winchester

Sloane
Gardens

Bloomfield
Terrace

ROAD
SCH.

Grove
Ranelagh

Road

Suth
Row

Sutherland

4
P

Holbein Mews

Dove
Walk

Barnabas
St.

Ebury
Bridge
Estate

Ebury Br.
Bridge

Ebury Bridge

STREET

Road

CHELS

CHELSEA BARRA

SCH.

Sutherland
SCH.

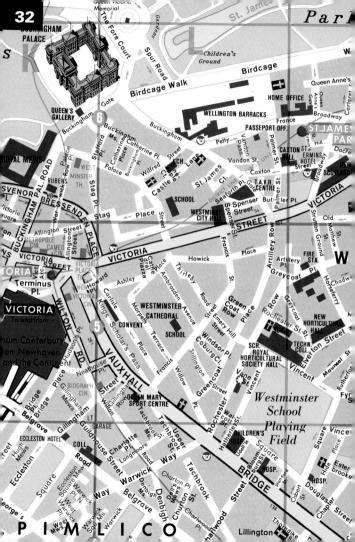

Road
TREASURY
ST.

Westminster
Pier
N

Great George St. Great
Queen St.
isham St.
CONF. CEN.
GEORGE ST.
BRIDGE STREET
WESTMINSTER BRIDGE

Queen St.
Gate
Storey's
Parliament
Squ.
New
Palace Yard

Parker Street
MIDDLESEX
GUILDHALL
BIG BEN

RAL
HALL
Matthew
The
Sanctuary
SANCTUARY SQU.
ST. MARG.
WESTMINSTER
HALL

NIOC
HOUSE
STREET
Broad
WESTMINSTER
ABBEY
Poets'
C.
Old
Palace
Yard
HOUSES OF
PARLIAMENT

Great
Smith
Dean's
Yard
WESTMINSTER
SCHOOL
JEWEL
TOWER
MARGARET ST.
Embankment
ST. THOMAS
HOSPITA

CHURCH
HO.

St.
Ann's
Street
SCH.
LIB.
BATH
CHURCH
HOUSE
College
St.
Great
College
St.
Victoria
MEDICAL
SCHOOL

reat
Peter
Street
Cowley
St.
St. Peter
Street
Tower
Albert
PALACE

MINSTER
Gayfere
St.
CROWN
AGETS F.
OVERSEAS
GOV.
MILLBANK
Gardens
LAMBETH
MUS.
GARDEN
HIST.

Monck
Street
Street
DEP.
OF THE
ENVIRONMENT
Bennetts
Yd.
Lord North
Dean
Trench
St.
Smith
Square
Dean
Stanley St.
Lambeth
Pier
ST.
MARY

seferry
Romney
Road
Romney
Dean
Bradley
St.
Horseferry
Road
LAMBETH
BRIDGE
LAMB

rosvenor
Estate
Marsham
WEST-
MINSTER
HOSP.
Dean
Ryle St.
Thorney
Road
Street
EMBANKMENT
LAM

Street
Street
Page
St. MINISTRY
OF POWER
Street
FIRE BDE.
H.Q.
SCHOOL

Street
Islip
MILLBANK
Whitgift
LOST
PROPERTY
OFF.

SCH.
Herrick
St.
John
QUEEN ALEXANDRA'S
HOSP.
Black
Salamanc

SCH.
St.
Oswulf
St.
Bulinga
St.
Bulinga
St.
VICKERS
BUILDING
Sala
Salamanca
Rd.
Manca
Rd.
Granby's

au ston
Erasmus
Street
Herrick
St.
Atterbury
Atterb
TATE
GALLERY &
CLORE
GALL
Randall
Randall Row

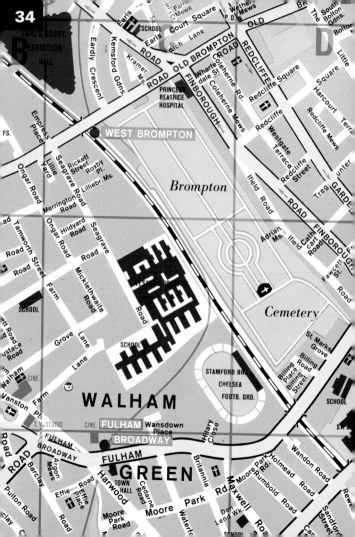

CHELSEA BARRACKS

Ebury Bridge
Estate

Gatliff

Franklin's Row
Road
CHELSEA BRIDGE ROAD

Burtons

ROYAL HOSP.
CHAPEL

ROYAL HOSPITAL

Ranelagh

Gdns.

Public Gardens

Ebury Bridge

Road

Wellington
Bldgs.

LISTER INST.

Grosvenor
Canal

Dock

GROSVENOR

ROYAL
HOSP.

East
Road

Embankment Gdns.

CHELSEA EMBANKMENT

Title
Street

CHELSEA
COURT

Grosv. Coll. Stairs

CHELSEA BRIDGE QUEENSTOWN

Battersea W

Drive

MES

CAR-
PARK

North

Drive

Tennis Court

East

RUNNING TRACK

Row

2
DEPOT

Terrace Walk

Drive

Rotten

Pleasure Gardens

Drive

Drive

Central

Drive

Fountain
Lake

ttersea

ROAD

1

Lake

ark

QUEENS
CIR.

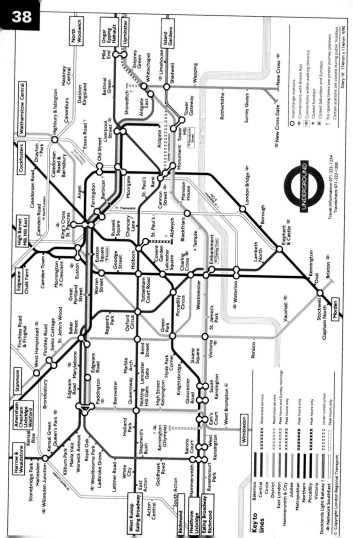

247

248

249

251

253

029/112 RP